Evaluating Empowerment

INTRAC NGO Management and Policy Series

1. *Institutional Development and NGOs in Africa: Policy Perspectives for European Development Agencies* Alan Fowler with Piers Campbell and Brian Pratt

2. *Governance, Democracy and Conditionality: What Role for NGOs?* Edited by Andrew Clayton

3. *Measuring the Process: Guidelines for Evaluating Social Development* David Marsden, Peter Oakley and Brian Pratt

4. *Strengthening the Capacity of NGOs: Cases of Small Enterprise Development Agencies in Africa* Caroline Sahley

5. *NGOs, Civil Society and the State: Building Democracy in Transitional Countries* Edited by Andrew Clayton

6. *Outcomes and Impact: Evaluating Change in Social Development* Peter Oakley, Brian Pratt and Andrew Clayton

7. *Demystifying Organisation Development: Practical Capacity-Building Experiences of African NGOs* Rick James

8. *Direct Funding from a Southern Perspective: Strengthening Civil Society?* INTRAC

9. *Partners in Urban Poverty Alleviation: Urban NGOs in the South* INTRAC

10. *Financial Management for Development: Accounting and Finance for the Non-specialist in Development Organisations* John Cammack

11. *NGOs Engaging with Business: A World of Difference and a Difference to the World* Simon Heap

12. *Power and Partnership? Experiences of NGO Capacity-Building* Edited by Rick James

13. *Evaluating Empowerment: Reviewing the Concept and Practice* Edited by Peter Oakley

14. *Knowledge, Power and Development Agendas: NGOs North and South* Emma Mawdsley, Janet Townsend, Gina Porter and Peter Oakley

Evaluating Empowerment

Reviewing the Concept and Practice

Edited by Peter Oakley

INTRAC NGO Management and Policy Series No. 13

An INTRAC Publication

INTRAC:
The International Non-governmental Organisation Training and Research Centre

A Summary Description
INTRAC was set up in 1991 to provide specially designed management, training and research services for NGOs involved in relief and development in the South and dedicated to improving organisational effectiveness and programme performance of Northern NGOs and Southern partners where appropriate. Our goal is to serve NGOs in (i) the exploration of the management, policy and human resource issues affecting their own organisational development, and (ii) the evolution of more effective programmes of institutional development and cooperation.

INTRAC offers the complementary services of:
Training;
Consultancy; and
Research

First published in 2001 in the UK by
INTRAC
PO Box 563
Oxford
OX2 6RZ
United Kingdom

Tel: +44 (0)1865 201851
Fax: +44 (0)1865 201852
e-mail: intrac@gn.apc.org

Copyright © INTRAC 2001

ISBN 1-897748-62-0

Designed and produced by
Davies Burman Associates
Tel: 01865 343131

Printed in Great Britain by
Antony Rowe Ltd., Chippenham, Wiltshire

Sadly, Peter Oakley died soon after this book was completed: INTRAC, Oxfam, Save the Children and the universities of Reading and Swansea are saddened by such a tragic turn of events.

All our warm thoughts are with him and his family.

This book offers insights into Peter's lively mind, and will be a lasting tribute to a noted career.

Acknowledgements

This book is based upon the deliberations of and contributions to the Fourth International Workshop on the Evaluation of Social Development. This is part of a series of workshops that was begun in 1989 at the University of Swansea by David Marsden and Peter Oakley, at that time from the Universities of Swansea and Reading respectively. Since that date, subsequent workshops have been held under the name of INTRAC – The International NGO Training and Research Centre – which has been responsible for their organisation and for publishing the ensuing books.

For this Fourth International Workshop INTRAC was supported by a Steering Group whose members were Tamsyn Barton (ITDG), Gweneth Berg (Norwegian Church Aid), Howard Dalzell (Concern Worldwide), Ros David (ActionAid), Colin Kirk (DFID), Ronald Lucardie (Cordaid) and Jo Rowlands (VSO). We are most grateful for these colleagues for contributing both their time and their energy to helping INTRAC to develop and prepare for the Fourth Workshop. Furthermore we would like to add a very special vote of thanks to those development agencies that generously gave INTRAC financial support for the Workshop: ActionAid, Christian Aid, Cordaid, DanChurchAid, Department for International Development, Norwegian Church Aid, Netherlands Organisation for International Development, Swedish International Development Agency, SNV and Voluntary Service Overseas.

Finally an enormous vote of thanks to Nancy Eimhjellen for work on the initial structuring of the contents of this book; to Debora Kleyn for doing much of the work of getting a massive volume of written material ready for editing; and to Jon Taylor, Laura Jarvie, Lorraine Collett and Simon Heap for finally preparing it for publishing.

Peter Oakley
August 2001

Contents

Acronyms 1
Notes on Contributors 3
Introduction *Brian Pratt* 7

CHAPTER 1 **Empowerment in Development**

1.1 Understanding Empowerment *Peter Oakley* 11
1.2 Globalisation and people's Empowerment *M. Anisur Rahman* 24
1.3 Empowerment and Women *Musimbil Kanyoro* 32
1.4 Concluding Comment *Peter Oakley* 36

CHAPTER 2 **Empowerment and its Evaluation**

2.1 Introduction 38
2.2 The M&E of Empowerment: Current practice and Operational
 Dilemmas *Peter Oakley* 39
2.3 Empowerment and its Evaluation: A Framework of Analysis and
 Application *Frits Wils* 55

CHAPTER 3 **Institutional Approaches to Evaluating Empowerment**

3.1 SIDA: Sweden *Ylva Lindstrom* 76
3.2 Monitoring Empowerment Within ActionAid: A Partial View
 Rosalind David and Charles Owusu 79
3.3 Empowerment and DFID *Colin Kirk* 87

Chapter 4 **Regional Reviews of the Evaluation of Empowerment**

4.1 African Regional Workshop: Arusha, Tanzania
 Grace Mukasa and Sering Falu Njie 95
4.2 Asian Regional Workshop: Rajendrapur, Bangladesh
 Subrata Chakrabarty and Amjad Nazeer 100

4.3 Latin American Regional Workshop: Managua, Nicaragua
   Brenda Bucheli and Mirtha Ditren 105
4.4 Middle Eastern Regional Workshop, Amman, Jordan
   Munif Abu-Rish 109
4.5 Synthesising the Findings of The Four Regional Workshops 112

CHAPTER 5 **Perpectives on the Evaluation of Empowerment**

5.1 So Now They Are Going to Measure Empowerment *James Taylor* 116
5.2 Does Empowerment Start At Home? And If So Will We Recognise It?
   Rick Davies 128
5.3 Grasping the Monitoring and Evaluation Framework as a Tool for
   Empowerment *Mark Waddington* 137
5.4 Participatory Programme Learning for Women's Empowerment in
   Micro-finance Programmes: Negotiating Complexity, Conflict and
   Change *Linda Mayoux* 152

CHAPTER 6 **Concluding Discussion** *Peter Oakley* 168

List of Conference Participants 182
Bibliography 186

Acronyms

ALPS	Accountability Learning and Planning System
APRS	ActionAid's Planning and Reporting System
APSO	Agency for Personal Service Overseas
BMFI	Balay Mndanaw Foundation Incorporated
CARP	Comprehensive Agrarian Reform Programme
CB	Capacity Building
CBO	Community-Based Organisation
CDRA	Community Development Resource Association
CRIES	Coordinadora Regional de Investigationes, Economicas y Sociales
DAC	Development Assistance Committee
DANIDA	Danish Agency for Development Assistance
DCA	DanChurchAid
DFID	Department for International Development, UK
DIP	Development In Practice
DLRO	District Land Reform Office
FGD	Focus Group Discussion
IDT	International Development Targets
IEGA	Income and Employment Generating Activities
IIED	International Institute for Environment and Development
ILO	International Labour Organisation
IMF	International Monetary Fund
INGO	International Non-Governmental Organisation
ITDG	Intermediate Technology Development Group
JOHUD	Jordanian Hashemite Fund for Human Development
KSCS	Kebkabiya Smallholders' Charitable Society
LFA	Log Frame Analysis
M&E	Monitoring and Evaluation
MIS	Management Information Systems
MSJ	Mohi Jagarn Samiti
MST	Movimento dos Trabalhadores Rurais sem Terra
NCA	Norwegian Church Aid
NGDO	Non-Governmental Development Organisation

NGO	Non-Governmental Organisation
NNGO	Northern Non-Governmental Organisation
OD	Organisational Development
OU	Open University
PALS	Participatory Appraisal Learning Study
PAR	Participatory Action Research
PIP	Participatory Implementation Plan
PLA	Participatory Learning and Action
PME	Participatory Monitoring and Evaluation
PRA	Participatory Rural Appraisal
PRADAN	Professional Assistant for Development Action
PRCA	Participatory Rural Communications Appraisal
PVSM	Participatory Voluntary Self-Monitoring
RELMA	Regional Land Management Unit
SEWA	Self-Employed Women's Association
SHIA	Solidarity, Humanity, International Aid
SIDA	Swedish International Development Agency
SMART	Specific Measurable Achievable Relevant and Timed
SSA	Soft Systems Analysis
STD	Sexually Transmitted Disease
TG	Target Group
TOR	Terms of Reference
UN	United Nations
UNAC	United Nations Association in Canada
UNDP	United Nations Development Programme
UNIFEM	United Nations Development Fund for Women
VCC	Village Centre Committee
VDC	Village Development Committee
VSO	Voluntary Services Overseas
WID	Women in Development
YWCA	Young Women's Christian Association

Notes on Contributors

Munif Abu-Rish is the Director of Social Development for the Queen Alia Fund in Amman, Jordan.

Therese Borrman has been for the past five years Desk Officer at the NGO Division of SIDA (Swedish International Development Agency), Stockholm, Sweden. She previously worked for the Swedish Association of Local Authorities.

Brenda Bucheli has more than 10 years of extensive and intensive experience in development projects in different sectors, and in overall project management. In the last years, she has specialised in project design, monitoring and evaluation (DME). She was DME Co-ordinator in CARE Peru; she is the current Executive Director of Pact Peru.

Subrata Chakrabarty is currently Assistant Project Co-ordinator of the Agriculture and Natural Resource department of CARE in Bangladesh. With more than ten years experience in monitoring, evaluation, impact assessment andpolicy research, she has previously worked in Bangldesh for Save the Children (USA), ActionAid UK and PROSHIKA.

Rosalind David has been Head of Impact Assessment at ActionAid for the last three years. Prior to that she worked for Oxfam and SOS Sahel.

Rick Davies is a social Development Consultant, specialising in monitoring and evaluation. His interest is in participative and qualitative approaches, both at the field level of development activities through to the analysis of performance according regional and global strategic objectives. He manages Monitoring and Evaluation NEWS (www.mande.co.uk), a website funded by six UK NGOs. He is a Research Fellow at the Centre for Development Studies, University of Wales – Swansea, and is an adviser to CIIR, Christian Aid and the Memorial Fund.

Mirtha Ditren Perdomo is a former M&E coordinator of World Vision Dominican Republic. She has previously worked for several private firms and NGOs, and in projects with international cooperation agencies like UNICEF, IDB, UNDP and GTZ.

Sering Falu Njie of ActionAid in Gambia, is the author of 'Monitoring and Evaluation of Capacity Building for Environmental Management Projects in the Gambia'. He is also the joint author of 'Employment-based Family Planning Services'.

Dr. Musimbi R. A. Kanyoro has 25 years of experience working in international and cross-cultural contexts. She has a strong background in social and cultural analysis. As a writer, trainer, and communicator, Dr. Kanyoro has contributed to the leadership development of women and girls. Since February 1998, Dr. Kanyoro has been General Secretary of the World YWCA.

Dr Colin Kirk is an anthropologist by training. He worked on the Water Programme in India for the Natural Resources Institute (NRI), then for DFID since 1992. Colin has conducted major evaluations during this time, and is currently Head of the Evaluation Department at DFID.

Ylva Lindstrom works as Programme Officer and Deputy Head of the NGO Division for SIDA, Stockholm, Sweden. During her thirty years work at SIDA, she has regularly served in posts abroad, the most recent assignments being with the Swedish Embassies in India and Namibia.

Linda Mayoux is currently a freelance consultant working on gender, enterprise development and impact assessment. She has done extensive research in South Asia, Africa and Central America. Her recent work includes a series of consultancies on empowerment, gender mainstreaming and microfinance for DFID, UNIFEM, ILO and a number of NGOs. She is currently working more generally on participatory and qualitative methodologies of impact assessment for enterprise interventions for DFID, including ethical development and microfinance.

Grace Mukasa is a Ugandan with a Masters in Gender and Development from the Institute of Development Studies (IDS), University of Sussex, where she wrote her thesis on the link between Participation, Gender and Empowerment. Presently she is Executive Director of Action for Development (ACFODE), whose programmes focus on policy advocacy from a gender perspective. She worked previously with Plan International as the Programme Unit Manager for its Urban Programme and with Save the Children Norway for seven years as Child Advocacy Officer, Regional Coordinator, Coordinator Partnership Development and Programme Manager with focus on Child Rights Advocacy, Basic Education and Psycho-social Rehabilitation of Children in Emergencies.

Amjad Nazeer is currently a Cheevening Scholar, studying Governance and Development at the University of Birmingham. He was previously Programme Officer for Social Development for four years at South Asia Partnership in Lahore, Pakistan.

Dr Peter Oakley was Research Director of INTRAC. After an academic training, he was successively OXFAM Field Director in Brazil and Northern Ethiopia from the late 1960s to mid-1970s. Between 1976 and 1991, he was Senior Lecturer at Agricultural Extension and Rural Development Department (AERDD), University of Reading. He returned to Latin America between 1991–96 as Head of Save the Children's Regional Office for Latin America and the Caribbean, based in Bogota. After being Senior Research Fellow, Centre for Development Studies, University of Swansea, he joined INTRAC in 1998. He conducted several major consultancies for a wide range of development agencies including those of the United Nations (ILO, WHO, World Bank) as well as European bilateral organisation (DFID, DANIDA,

SIDA, NORAD) and a range of both large and small NGOs. He died in August 2001.

Charles Owusu is the Facilitator of ActionAid's Impact Assessment Network. He has been working for ActionAid for ten years and on Impact Assessment for the last four years. Prior to that, he managed ActionAid's Programme in Bawku, Upper East Region, Ghana.

Dr Brian Pratt has worked in development since 1973, initially at the University of Cambridge and then in Peru on the political economy of Peru. He was also a Field Director for OXFAM in the Andean Countries, before returning to the UK to develop OXFAM programmes of Research, Evaluation, Development Policy and Information systems. He has worked in many countries as a consultant and researcher for NGOs, multi-lateral and bi-lateral agencies. Brian is one of the founding members of INTRAC and has been its Executive Director since its beginning in 1991. His publications and consultancy work tend to focus on strategic policy issues for NGOs and Monitoring and Evaluation.

James Taylor is a consultant and director of the Community Development Resource Association (CDRA) in South Africa. CDRA is an NGO advancing learning about development processes and the art of intervention. CDRA aims to bring about and support development practice amongst organisations working towards those forms of social transformation that most benefit the poor and marginalised.

Muhammad Anisur Rahman was Professor of Economics at Islamabad University and the University of Dhaka and a member of the first Bangladesh Planning Commission. From 1977 to 1990 he co-ordinated the ILOs programme on Participatory Organisations of the Rural Poor, from Geneva. Upon retirement from the ILO, he returned to Bangladesh and is currently President of the Bangladesh Economic Association.

Mark Waddington is a graduate of Leeds University, with a geography degree drawing on extensive practical experience in land resource planning and appraisal in Malawi and Zaire, who went on to obtain an M.Sc with distinction for Rotary Club-funded community development work in Tanzania. In 1995 he joined a UK-based NGO, Village Aid, working in West Africa. In six years as Africa Programme co-ordinator he has helped move the organisation from a grassroots project focus to an integrated rights-based approach targeting the most marginalised amongst rural communities.

Frits Wils is an Associate Professor at the Institute of Social Studies, The Hague. He works in various fields including NGOs and development, urban poverty reduction, decentralisation of Civil Society and inclusion of the poor. His regional focus is on South Asia, South-east Asia and Latin America.

Introduction
Brian Pratt

The last two decades of the twentieth century witnessed a major resurgence in the concept and practice of **social development** as a counterbalance to the dominant economic and quantitative approaches to *development* that have influenced much of the post-war period. The explanations of this resurgence are many, and largely to be found in structural, as opposed to physical, explanations of *underdevelopment*. While social development was not an entirely new concept – social welfare and the provision of basic social services have long been the basic components of social development – its interpretation in a more structural sense profoundly influenced development practice in the 1980s and 1990s. In those two decades social development became the basic driving force of many development agencies and was the platform from which such dynamic concepts as 'participation', 'sustainability' and 'empowerment' emerged. By the end of the twentieth century development thinking and practice had taken on fundamentally different perspectives from those of the 1960s and 1970s. While some saw the apotheosis of social development in the UN World Summit in 1995, others saw this as an act of hijacking by established interests and were confident that the practice would be sustained by the emerging range of civil society structures. The literature that has accompanied this emergence of social development as both a relevant analytical tool and a form of development intervention has been enormous and vital in sustaining its dynamic. Works such as Long (1977), Oakley and Winder (1981), Chambers (1983), Richards (1985), Rahman (1993), Carmen (1996), Midgley (1995) and Booth (1996) reflect the growing influence of social development, particularly with respect to its operationalisation at the development intervention level.

By the 1990s social development had become a major *goal* of both non-governmental organisations (NGOs) and bilateral development agencies. It became apparent, therefore, that there would be a need to re-visit the existing dominant paradigm of the Monitoring and Evaluation of development interventions and to develop approaches and methods that were more suited to capturing and explaining the processes inherent in social development. The first substantial exercise in this respect was the First International Workshop on the Evaluation of Social Development. This workshop, held at the University of Swansea in 1989, brought together some eighty people from both the South and the North and from both development practice and academia. This First Workshop sought to lay out the terrain and to examine broadly both contemporary understandings of social development and also the key elements in its evaluation. Essentially the workshop drew the distinction between a *technocratic* as opposed to an *interpretative* approach to evaluation and used this distinction to explore four major areas of programme and project evaluation: (a) qualitative indicators, (b) methodology, (c) the role of the evaluator and (d) partnership in evaluation. The workshop also explored issues related to the role of evaluation as a learning exercise, the importance of a critical understanding of the cultural context in which the evaluation process takes place and, finally, issues such as the style of an evaluation, the use of external consultants, their qualifications and the problems of pre-determined evaluation design. The proceedings of this First Workshop were published by Oxfam with the title, *Evaluating Social Development Projects* (Marsden and Oakley 1990).

Such was the positive response to the First Workshop that the Second International Workshop on the Evaluation of Social Development was convened at Amersfoot in the Netherlands in 1992. At this workshop the emphasis was placed on the **methodology** of the evaluation of social development. By design this was a smaller workshop in terms of the number of participants. The workshop was based on a number of detailed case studies of development agencies in different parts of the world that had sought to evaluate social development programmes or projects. Essentially the case studies used a common framework of analysis and explained the process and their approach to the evaluation within the following framework:

- Preparation
- Execution
- Analysis
- Reflection

Key issues that arose during the Second Workshop included: (a) the problems of time and cost in relation to process evaluation, (b) the balance between quantitative and qualitative approaches, (c) the difficulties of letting the process follow its natural course before linking it to more formal procedures and (d) the current gap between theoretical commitment and the operational practice. The key papers and proceedings of this Second Workshop were published by INTRAC as *Measuring the Process: Guidelines for Evaluating Social Development* (Marsden, Oakley and Pratt 1994).

By the mid-1990s there was a noticeable concern among development agencies to understand the **impact** of development interventions. This had given rise to a number of *Impact Studies* that sought to assess what development interventions had not only done but, more importantly, *achieved*. In the light of this concern the Third International Workshop on the Evaluation of Social Development was convened near Leiden in the Netherlands in 1996 on the theme of the **outcomes** and **impact** of social development programmes and projects. The workshop was attended by almost 100 people and approximately forty case studies were presented that explored the boundaries between the strong rhetoric about impact assessment and the rather weaker reality of the practice. Issues raised at the workshop included the need for client-based methods of evaluation, the importance of recognising a plurality of views and experiences both in assessing impact and in ways of analysing qualitative data. One key conclusion was that, while quantitative methods and data were relevant, only qualitative data would ensure a full and authentic understanding of impact. As with other workshops, the contributions and proceedings were published by INTRAC as a book entitled *Outcomes & Impact: Evaluating Change in Social Development* (Oakley, Pratt and Clayton 1998).

Since the Third Workshop (1996) there has been a series of studies exploring the concept of *impact* in relation to development interventions. For example, both ActionAid and Oxfam have completed studies of impact, the former more directly related to its own field operations while the latter has greatly advanced our knowledge of impact as a process over time (Roche 1999). Furthermore, INTRAC completed a study of the impact of Danish NGOs (Oakley 1999) while a similar study is currently underway in relation to Dutch NGOs (Van Nieurkirk, forthcoming). Intriguingly, SIDA commissioned a study that assessed the impact of an earlier impact study (Riddell 2000). These and other studies have begun to identify a number of key issues in relation to the evaluation of **impact**:

- The rediscovery of the need for effective **monitoring** without which it is difficult to assess impact. There have been several systematic attempts at impact assessment but these have inevitably run into problems, in the absence of continuous monitoring, of identifying the **changes** that may have occurred during the life of a project. Such assessments have then to rely on the memories of those involved even if these are not always accurate. Sometimes it is impossible to piece together information in retrospect after the main actors have moved on and the development focus has been changed. Linked to this rediscovery is also a concern to re-evaluate the function of baseline data collection, not in a slavish mechanical way but in a way that recognises a moving baseline against which change can be assessed.

- The inherent tensions between the formal M&E systems, often introduced by donor agencies, which stress the M&E of outputs and activities as symbolised in the log frames which are now so common. M&E systems must move beyond simple outputs and grapple with the assessment of **change**. In this respect the evidence seems to show that this can only be done with a mix of both qualitative and quantitative methods. It also follows that if change is the focus of interest, it opens up the debate on whose definition of change we are using. Is it that of a distant donor, a programme director, an external academic evaluator or are we looking at changes as defined by key stakeholders?

- The move to **client-based M&E systems** is one of the most exciting innovations of recent years. It owes its development to a concurrence between those who stress the importance of participation and those who feel we should use free market analysis. Free market analysis stresses a *demand*-based system of development rather than a supply-led approach in which the poor receive whatever they are lucky enough to receive rather than having a voice in determining the types of development intervention most appropriate to their needs and rights.

In the context of the above it was decided to convene the Fourth International Workshop and to focus it on an emerging process that has come to characterise much recent development effort: **empowerment**. The previous workshops had concentrated on broad themes as their focus – interpretation, methodology, impact – but we agreed that the Fourth Workshop would focus on the M&E of this contemporary process. Furthermore, we decided to regionalise the Fourth Workshop and to hold workshops on the Indian sub-Continent and in sub-Saharan Africa, Central America and the Middle East. These **regional workshops** were held between November 1999 and March 2000 and were each attended by about 40 participants. Two representatives from each of the regional workshops were subsequently invited to present the outcomes of their meetings at the Fourth International Workshop in April 2000.

This book, therefore, presents the proceedings of the Fourth International Workshop. Its contents are based not only on a number of papers that were presented in plenary sessions, but also on the outcomes of sessions based both on the regional workshops and on presentations made by several development agency representatives on their approach to the M&E of empowerment. About one hundred participants attended the workshop, many of whom were practitioners or development agency staff engaged at the programme or project level. An even balance was achieved between participants from the South and the North and contributions were made on an equal basis. The Fourth Workshop combined plenary sessions, 'home group' discussions and also sessions based on a review of the practice to date. The commissioned plenary papers are presented in full, as are several individual contributions concerning current practice. The remainder of the book is based upon the reports and findings of the regional sessions, the presentations by four development agencies and the final group work that examined the current state of play in terms of the M&E of empowerment.

CHAPTER 1
Empowerment in Development

1.1 Understanding Empowerment
Peter Oakley

The rhetoric – if not entirely the practice – of planned social change has been transformed in the last two decades of the twentieth century. Any comparison of bodies of literature across the sectors between the 1970s and the late 1990s would reveal profound changes in the ways in which the concept of 'development' has been perceived. The genesis of the changes in thinking and practice can be traced to the debate and parallel explosion of accompanying literature that milled around the confrontation between the 'modernisation' and the 'dependency' schools of thought in the late 1960s and 1970s. Until, of course, the post-modernists arrived and poured scorn on all meta explanations. Great explanations were presented and analyses undertaken of different contexts, largely in the developing world, to show that existing structural 'inequalities and imbalances' and 'marginalisation' and 'oppression' were the basis of explanations for the poverty of the millions. Essentially a new form of analysis emerged that has largely shaped approaches to explaining and tackling poverty and underdevelopment over the past decade or so. At the core of these explanations and analyses lay the concept of power and the inevitable division of many societies into those with power and the powerless. Initially the term was rarely used so explicitly, although it remained a major influence as those involved in working with processes of development and change sought to adjust to the changing scenario. While we can say, therefore, that this adjustment has occurred across the sectors and similarly across a range of actors involved in these processes, it could also be argued that it has yet to be converted into significant initiatives to tackle these inequalities and imbalances.

We can trace back to the 1970s the early analytical work that ultimately influenced the emergence of 'power' as *the* central concept that defines all processes of development. The vigorous debate in the 1970s between the 'modernisation' and the 'dependency' schools of analysis on the root causes of underdevelopment focused attention on the relationship between 'power' and 'poverty' (Long 1977). Furthermore the powerful analysis of Freire (1974) convincingly argued that only access to real power could break what he termed the 'culture of silence' that was characterised by the dependence and marginality of the powerless. In the 1980s a major analytical thrust began to collect the evidence on which much of the contemporary 'empowerment' energy is based (Pearce and Stiefel 1979; Galjart 1982; Bhasin 1984; Rahman 1984). This thrust is often referred to as the 'alternative development' school in that it stands in sharp contrast to the essentially delivery-mode approach of the modernisation school. At the same time the concept of people's 'participation' in development began its long period of influence on development thinking and practice. Attempts to promote 'development' via massive programmes of physical or social improvement had by the 1980s clearly failed. Thus by the 1990s even the larger bilateral and multilateral development agencies had become convinced that only structural reform and the more equitable distribution of 'power' could offer any prospect of breaking the cycle of endemic poverty in much of the world.

Although the 'development community' stumbled upon and readily adopted the notion of **'power'** as central to the development and change that they were seeking to promote, it can hardly be argued that it is an entirely new concept in terms of social change. Power is both experienced and encountered in almost all activities of daily life and is the basis on which most interactions and relations are conducted. From the unit of the household and the personalised face-to-face relations of its different members, through the myriad administrative structures that manage most people's lives to the access to resources and opportunities for advancement, 'power' plays a dominant role in determining those who progress and those who fall by the side. Sociological studies similarly distinguish between three basic forms of power – **social, political and economic** – and show how access to these different sources can have a positive effect on an individual's, family's or group's ability to progress. Furthermore anthropologists have long argued that 'development' is nothing new, that societies are in a continual process of developing and that 'power' is central to the ability of different groups within society to promote their own development. Similarly anthropologists have stressed the distinction between 'power' and 'authority'. The latter is exercised with free public support and is based on consensus while the former often implies the threat of action without specific recourse to people's wishes. As early as 1974 Roberts declared that *'Development is the more equal distribution of power among people'*. He further argued that historically all efforts, both internal and external, to bring about 'change' have essentially hinged upon the nature of power and its distribution within the context in which the change is being sought.

The anthropological tradition of seeing 'change' as a constant societal process embedded in social, economic and political power and the refining of 'alternative' development paradigms of the 1980s and 1990s appear to have coalesced in the early 1990s around the notion of **empowerment**. Within a very short space of time the term became common currency and appeared to fit easily into the development perspectives and strategies of actors ranging from CBOs at the grassroots level to institutions such as the World Bank and the major multilateral and bilateral agencies. Empowerment suddenly became a 'sanitised buzz-word', divorced from a real understanding of power, and the literature followed suit. Across the sectors, themes, geographical regions and actors the literature on 'empowerment' exploded just as it did around the concept of 'participation' a decade earlier (Cheater 1999). In terms of the actions and processes associated with the promotion of development and change we currently live in the age of empowerment. It has become a word that slips easily from our tongues. And yet it is the most complex of terms; intangible, culturally specific and at the basis of all livelihoods. It is difficult not to conclude that, to a degree, we have trivialised this complex term and that many of those that now readily use it may not yet have stood back and reflected on the daunting task and the possible consequences of their proposed actions.

By the 1990s, therefore, **empowerment** had become a central concept in development discourse and practice. As a result, 'empowerment' as an operational objective is now widely evident in the policies and programmes of both national and international NGOs and is also beginning to have an increasing influence on bilateral and multilateral development agencies. This complex term is not easily defined and is thus open to a wide variety of interpretations. Any attempt to assess whether or not a particular development intervention has 'empowered' people must recognise this and, for this reason, an understanding of the concept in development terms is critical to its operationalisation as a development aim or objective. Inevitably the concept of empowerment is more easily espoused than put into practice and much of the literature that accompanies the practice lacks the rigour that is important if such a complex concept is to be used in operational terms. Power – formal, traditional or informal – lies at the heart of any process of change and is the fundamental dynamic that determines social and economic relations. To talk of 'empowerment' is to suggest that there are groups which are completely devoid of power and thus need support to be 'empowered'. This is too facile an assumption since *all* social groupings will possess some power in relation to their immediate environment. When, therefore, we talk of a process of 'empowerment' we are referring to relative positions of formal and informal power enjoyed by different socio-economic groups and the consequences of gross imbalances in the distribution of this power. A process of 'empowerment' seeks to intervene and re-dress these imbalances and to boost the power of those groups relatively 'powerless' in relation to those who enjoy and benefit from their access to and use of formal and informal power.

Since the early 1990s there has been an ever-expanding literature on empowerment. Van Eyken (1991), Friedmann (1992), Craig and Mayo (1995) and Rowlands (1997) have all examined the concept and focused on the notion of 'power', its use and its distribution as being central to any understanding of social transformation. However, the examination has not been uniform but has revealed contrasting views on the centrality of power in a development context:

- **Power** in the sense of bringing about **radical change** and the **confrontation** between the powerful and the powerless as the crucial dynamic of social change. This interpretation argues that it is only by a focus on change to existing patterns of power and its use that any meaningful change can be brought about.

- **Power** in the Freirian sense of increased awareness and the development of 'critical faculty' among the marginalised and oppressed. This is power '**to do**', '**to be able**' and of feeling more **capable** and in **control** of situations. It concerns recognising the capacities of such groups to take action and to play an active role in development initiatives. It also implies the breaking down of decades of passive acceptance and of strengthening the abilities of marginalised groups to engage as legitimate development actors.

These two explanations offer contrasting interpretations of the meaning of 'power' and hence attempts at 'empowerment' in a development context. Power is essentially the basis of wealth, while powerlessness is the basis of poverty, and both the 'powerful' and the 'powerless' are categories of actors fundamental to understanding the dynamics of any development process. Power can be seen as an asset owned by the state or a dominant class and exercised in order to maintain its control and to stamp its seal of authority and legitimacy. Power, furthermore, operates at many different levels and is manifest in the conflicting interests of different groups within any particular context; for example, local or regional patrons, the power that men often exercise over women and the power that institutions such as the church exercise over people. Power defines the basic pattern of social and economic relations within any context and, therefore, will have a fundamental influence on any intervention that could potentially threaten the existing distribution. Consequently, the lack of an analysis of the locus and distribution of power within a particular context *before* a planned development intervention can have a profound effect on access to the expected benefits.

In her study on the empowerment of poor women in Honduras, Rowlands (1997) distinguishes between '**power over**', '**power to**' and '**power within**'. She used these distinctions to great effect in examining both the context within which 'powerless' women seek to gain greater recognition and also the critical nature of developing the inner power that even poor women can have if they organise and challenge existing structures. In another important study, Craig and Mayo (1995) contrast the notions of power as a '**variable sum**' and as a '**zero sum**'. In the notion of power as a variable sum, the powerless can be empowered without altering the nature and the levels of power already held by existing powerful groups. Power as a '**zero sum**' implies that any gain in power by one group inevitably results in a reduction of the power exercised by others. These are clearly two irreconcilable views that could have unfortunate consequences if incorrectly applied. However, given the evidence of the reaction that can be caused by efforts to 'empower' previously powerless groups, there would appear to be more weight in the notion that the empowering of one group will have consequences for the power already held by other groups. Power is also related to **knowledge**, which is both a source of power and a means for its acquisition. In this respect it could be argued that all development work has to do with the control of knowledge and that, if the 'underprivileged' were able to control the sources of knowledge, the structures of existing power relations would be radically altered. Knowledge can confer legitimacy and authority and its construction and dissemination are powerful tools. Knowledge also helps us to interpret and to shape the context in which we live. Thus, without it, we lack this power (Ocampo 1996).

The recognition of power as central to efforts to promote effective social change has been operationalised in the concept of **empowerment** as the process that would seek both to redress gross power imbalances and also actively 'empower' the powerless. The essence of the process can be understood in the following statements:

> Alternative development involves a process of social and political empowerment whose long-term objective is to rebalance the structure of power within society by making state action more accountable, strengthening the powers of civil society in the management of their own affairs and making corporate business more socially responsible. (Friedmann 1992)

> Empowerment is about collective community, and ultimately class conscientization, to critically understand reality in order to use the power which even the powerless do possess, so as to challenge the powerful and ultimately to transform that reality through conscious political struggles. (Craig and Mayo 1995)

> While the empowerment approach acknowledges the importance for women of increasing their power, it seeks to identify power less in terms of domination over others and more in terms of the capacity of women to increase their self-reliance and internal strength. This is identified as the right to determine

choices in life and to influence the direction of change, through ability to gain control over crucial material and non-material sources. It places less emphasis than the equity approach on increasing women's status relative to men, but seeks to empower women through the redistribution of power within, as well as between, societies. (Moser 1991)

Empowerment is an intentional and ongoing dynamic process centred on the local community, involving mutual dignity, critical reflection, caring and group participation, through which people lacking a valid share of resources gain greater access to and control over those resources, through the exercise of an increased leverage on power. (Van Eyken 1991)

Empowerment became a major purpose of many social development interventions in the 1990s. Social development as **transformation** is predicated on a power analysis and on actions to empower groups that lack access to those resources and institutions that would enable them to compete more effectively in the struggle to sustain their livelihoods. As a development objective empowerment has been operationalised into practical project methodologies and, in terms of its effect and impact, it is beginning to be translated into **observable and measurable actions**. Concretely, people's empowerment can manifest itself in three broad areas:

- Power through greater confidence in one's ability to successfully undertake some form of **action**.
- Power in terms of increasing and effecting **relations** that powerless people establish with other organisations.
- Power as a result of increasing **access** to economic resources, such as credit and inputs.

Social development as empowerment does not see poor people as deficient and needing external support; more positively, it seeks to create an interactive and sharing approach to development in which people's skills and knowledge are recognised. Empowerment is not merely a therapy that makes the poor feel better about their poverty, nor simply the encouraging of 'local initiatives' or making people more politically 'aware'. Similarly it does not assume that people are entirely powerless and that there do not already exist networks of solidarity and resistance through which poor people confront the forces which threaten their livelihoods. On the contrary, empowerment has to do with 'positive change' in an individual, community and structural sense, with organisation and with negotiation. But, as Rowlands (1997) has commented, 'empowerment takes time' and it is not a process that necessarily achieves results in the short term.

As with other development concepts, such as civil society or participation, there is always a danger that the use of empowerment in the context of development interventions may be based on a superficial understanding of local relations of power. Empowerment may be limited to little more than greater participation in project decision-making and have little, if any, impact on wider structural change. This has led to some concern that the use of the concept in development tends to mask the true nature of power relations. A recent collection of papers by anthropologists reflects this growing scepticism about the increasing use of the concept of empowerment (Cheater 1999). James, for example, notes that:

> Notions of sharing power, of stakeholders, of participation and representation and so on seem to refer increasingly to the self-contained world of projects themselves: the external structures of land-holding and subsistence economy which have perhaps been disrupted, of political and military formations which have shaped and still shape the forms of social life in a region, tend to fade from view in the world of development-speak. (James 1999:13–14)

Much of the concern is that many development projects concerned with empowerment fail to understand and analyse the historical dynamics of local politics with its complex interplay between different local interest groups, state policy and the wider political economy (e.g. Werbner 1999; Chabal 1994). These criticisms of the current utilisation of the concept of empowerment are important to bear in mind. Yet, while James urges fellow anthropologists and other academics to distance themselves from the term, this is not a realistic option for development practitioners. Empowerment is a key objective of such a wide range of development interventions; the challenge for development practitioners is to deepen their understanding of the term, recognise its complexities, strengths and limitations, and explore how they may be able to assess whether or not 'empowerment' has taken place.

The starting-point of any analysis of empowerment in development interventions must consider the diverse range of meanings associated with it. Like participation and civil society, empowerment is a motivational concept that evokes a wide range of different responses among different groups. It is important, therefore, to understand how different organisations have used the term empowerment, and what type of empowerment they have sought to bring about. With this in mind we present below a number of short **examples** taken from the practice, which illustrate how a number of different development agencies have tried to promote empowerment within the context of a development project. Together the three examples provide a broad spectrum of interpretations of empowerment and help us to understand the very broad nature of its meaning.

Empowering Communities: The Kebkabiya Project in West Sudan

This case provides an example of a project-centred view of empowerment. The Kebkabiya project is essentially a food security project, but Oxfam has named it as part of a process of community empowerment. Hence the title of the book based on the project is *Empowering Communities*. As is shown in the brief statement below, the use of empowerment in this project is very much in terms of facilitating the participation of communities, and especially women, in project decision-making and by Oxfam itself being prepared to relinquish control of the KSCS.

> The Kebkabiya Project in West Sudan emerged out of the Oxfam relief programme in West Sudan following the 1984 famine. It represented a shift from relief to development and the main objective of the project was to increase food security in the communities around Kebkabiya. The project was initially managed directly by Oxfam, but later a local organisation, the Kebkabiya Smallholders' Charitable Society (KSCS) was created, and gradually took over the management of the project.
>
> The initial objective of the project was to establish twelve seedbanks and the first phase of the project enabled Oxfam staff to gain a clearer sense of other perceived problems in the communities in the area. The second phase of the project, begun in 1989, introduced additional components to address these problems, notably animal health, animal traction, pest control, soil and water conservation and community development. The key organisational change in the management was that while overall co-ordination of the project was handled by Oxfam staff, this was done in conjunction with a new democratic structure of community representation, the Village Centre Committees. Each village from a group of five to twelve villages elected one man and one woman to represent it on the Village Centre Committee. In turn, each Village Centre Committee elected one man and one woman to a Project Management Committee.
>
> In 1990 the PMC registered as an independent organisation and KSCS was created. It is a membership organisation drawn from the communities in which the project has been working. In 1992 KSCS held a constitutional workshop which set out the society's system of community accountability, and formalised the representational structure that had been introduced in the project; i.e. each village sending a male and female representative to the VCC, etc. During the 1990s Oxfam began a process to hand over direct control of the project to the KSCS.
>
> For Oxfam, the project represented a successful example of how an Oxfam-managed food security project was transformed into a project in which local communities have become increasingly involved. Whereas at the start of the project, local people, particularly women, had little if any say in project deci-

sion-making, the project is now under the management of KSCS. Democratic structures have been put in place, notably through the creation of the KSCS, which have improved the accountability of project management to the community. From the perspective of the Oxfam staff involved in the project, this has resulted in community empowerment.

Source: P. Strachan with C. Peters (1997), *Empowering Communities: A Casebook from West Sudan*, Oxfam.

Empowering the Landless: Movimento dos Trabalhadores Rurais sem Terra (MST), Brazil
This example is drawn from the experiences of Christian Aid (a British NGO) and its partners in working for a more just system of land distribution in Brazil and other countries. Empowerment is seen in terms of securing access to land for poor people and in providing them with the means to farm it productively and in a sustainable manner. The example outlined below shows how Christian Aid and its partners have worked with the poor in improving their access to productive land.

MST defines itself as a mass social movement of landless rural workers who seek access to land, and campaign for agrarian reform and broad political changes in Brazilian society. Between 1991 and 1997 MST helped 600,000 landless people gain land, build houses and start schools. It has done this through a strategy involving three stages: firstly, MST identifies land that is not being used for production and attempts to negotiate for the use of the land. If this fails a large number of people occupy the land and build a camp; secondly, usually the owners, police and judiciary attempt to evict them but MST either resists or requests to be transferred to other similar land. The support of churches, trade unions, urban movements and NGOs is important during this stage; thirdly, MST works with the land trying to make it more productive, building roads, schools, health facilities etc. In addition to this form of direct action MST, along with many other groups, is campaigning for agrarian reform in Brazil. In doing so it has recognised that this is not isolated from wider macro-economic challenges confronting the country. While Brazil has paid huge amounts on debt repayment over the last five years, rural development budgets have been cut and poverty in rural and urban areas has increased.

This example, and the others in the overall study, reflect the dynamic, even perilous, nature of empowerment in the context of land reform, which has been a continuous struggle for the landless. All attempts involved victories as well as

> setbacks, and in each of the countries studied, the farmers and NGOs concerned have been met by strong opposition from established elites. In each case, local level action has been supported by national level campaigning and lobbying on land reform and even the macro-economic policy. Empowerment clearly does not end with a change in the law or approval of access to land. These are only the beginnings of a process of achieving secure, productive and sustainable livelihoods for the poor.
>
> Source: M. Whiteside (1999), *Empowering the Landless: Case Studies in Land Distribution and Tenure Security for the Poor*. Christian Aid.

Empowering Health Promoters: Honduras

This example examines women's empowerment in the context of a health promoter's training programme in Honduras. This particular programme was set up in Urraco in 1985 with the support of an American NGO which provided a volunteer and funding for programme's activities. Although the programme was not set up initially with the specific aim of empowering women, both the American volunteer attached to the programme and some of the co-ordinating team have increasingly seen it as essentially concerned with women's empowerment.

> The programme provided a two-year course to train members of local communities in preventative healthcare and basic treatment. The course is organised around study circles in 26 communities, and involves weekly meetings for about two hours each and monthly sectoral meetings when all the groups meet together to discuss a common theme. Eighty women have been trained as health promoters over a three and a half year period. Other women have been actively involved in the programme through providing meals for malnourished children, craft work and goat projects. There is a co-ordinating team of five women who work full time on the programme, and who are each responsible for three to six of the study circles. In the programme, empowerment is understood at three levels:
>
> *Personal empowerment.* Women who joined the study circles have experienced an increase in self-confidence and self-esteem as a result of their participation. Furthermore, they also highlighted the importance of learning new skills through the programme, such as diagnosing common medical conditions and treating them and checking their children's nutritional status. A few had even managed to secure employment. The sense of personal empowerment was particularly

> marked among those women who were members of the co-ordinating team. In particular they had been given the opportunity to attend meetings and courses in other parts of Honduras and even abroad, which enabled them to look beyond their traditional position within the home.
>
> *Empowerment in relationships.* Some women who have been involved in the programme stated that their relationships with their husbands and families changed. They have noted such changes as more involvement in decision-making on money matters, greater freedom of movement around their communities, improved treatment by their husbands and they, in turn, have been more conscious of improving their relationships with their children.
>
> *Collective empowerment.* There was little evidence to suggest that the study circles themselves had led to any collective empowerment. Some activities were undertaken as a group but this did not result in the groups becoming more able to organise collectively in order to meet their needs or gain more access to economic, social or political power. However, there was some evidence of collective empowerment among the co-ordinating team. For example, they were now running the programme without the support of an American volunteer and they were also involved in networking with other organisations in the country.
>
> Source: J. Rowlands (1997), *Questioning Empowerment*, Oxfam.

The above three examples reflect very different notions of empowerment. In the case of the Kebkabiya project, community empowerment is seen very specifically in terms of increasing the role of the community in managing the project. This is a rather narrow view of empowerment that makes little reference to the wider social and economic context and how the 'empowered' communities engage with this. The example from Honduras looks beyond the immediate project and stresses the importance of women's empowerment in terms of building up their self-confidence and self-esteem. However, like the Kebkabiya project, the empowerment of women involved in the Uracco project has not extended to their broader political and economic rights. By contrast, the Christian Aid land reform studies do provide examples of broader processes of empowerment. Landless people have successfully struggled for access to productive land, in particular for new laws that would recognise the demands of peasant farmers. Furthermore, while the Christian Aid supported campaigns had a clear objective from the start of empowering the landless through campaigning for their land rights, in the case of the other two projects empowerment was not the initial objective but rather has emerged as the project process had developed. Both of these examples have been far less politically controversial because, unlike the land reform campaigns, they did not attempt to redistribute control over productive resources.

The fact that the concept of empowerment is open to such wide interpretation presents particular challenges for **evaluating** its **impact** as a development process. In particular, there is the issue of whether or not empowerment is assessed in relation to the specific project objectives, however limited these may be. For example, a starting-point could be to undertake the assessment within the project framework: what are the empowerment objectives of the project or other type of intervention, and to what extent have they been achieved. Yet an alternative starting-point is to undertake first an analysis of local power structures in order to highlight which factors have been most significant in creating conditions of powerlessness among poor and marginalised people. This would allow more critical and demanding questions to be asked of the empowerment process.

For example, while the Kebkabiya project appears to have made significant progress in achieving its objective of empowering communities through involving them in project management, the project report makes no reference to the engagement of these communities with wider political and economic structures in Sudan. While participation in project decision-making is an important development in itself, it is only so within the context of the project. As the quote from James (1999) above noted, many development agencies see empowerment only in terms of the 'self-contained world of projects', yet in doing so they underestimate or ignore much deeper power structures which have a much greater bearing on peoples' lives. In assessing empowerment resulting from development interventions, it is important to undertake both. In the first instance, the intervention can be **monitored** against its original objectives. But in order to understand whether or not the intervention has had any long-term impact, a much wider assessment of local power structures will be needed.

In conclusion we can summarise what appear to be the main **dimensions** of a process of empowerment that would form the basis of attempts both to understand and to **monitor** its progress. Breaking the overall concept down into one or more of these dimensions becomes the first step to understanding it as a dynamic process and to mounting an appropriate monitoring system. We summarise these main dimensions in Table 1 opposite.

There can be no doubting the widespread use of, and the commitment to, a process of empowerment in many development interventions. However, it could be argued that in the past five years or so this commitment has encountered difficulties. There is evidence that many development projects which placed 'empowerment' to the forefront of their objectives have become frustrated by their inability to monitor and explain the process and thus 'evaluate' its outcomes. In this respect the above dimensions offer a general framework that could form the basis of the evaluation of empowerment. It is because of this apparent impasse in coming to

Table 1: **The Dimensions of Empowerment**

Psychological	**Cultural**
Self-image and Identity	Redefining Gender Rules and Norms
Creating Space	Recreating Cultural Practices
Acquiring Knowledge	
Social	**Economic**
Leadership in Community Action	Attaining Income Security
Action for Rights	Ownership of Productive Assets
Social Inclusion	Entrepreneurial Skills
Literacy	
Organisational	**Political**
Collective Identity	Participation in Local Institutions
Establishing Representative Organisation	Negotiating Political Power
Organisational Leadership	Accessing Political Power

grips with the M&E of evaluation that the Fourth International Workshop was convened. In this respect we would argue that the crucial first step in the M&E of empowerment is to ensure that a power-focused **contextual analysis** is undertaken that would provide the basic analysis on the from which judgements concerning 'effect' or 'impact' could be made. This contextual analysis could build on the following four **questions**:

- What are the key **dimensions of power** – traditional, informal and formal – how it is exercised and by whom?
- What are the key **political, social and economic** differences between those with power and the powerless within the development context?
- What are the main **characteristics** of **powerlessness** that will have to be addressed if a development intervention is to 'empower' local people?
- How could we assess the historical and the current **distribution** of power between different socio-economic groups?

These, and other questions, constitute the initial **contextual analysis of power** that must be undertaken if we are to be able to assess to what extent a particular project has changed the locus, pattern and distribution of power. All too often development projects seek to assess to what extent they may, or may not, have influenced the power equilibrium in a particular context, but most are unable to do so for lack of an initial contextual understanding. Once this contextual analysis has been satisfactorily concluded, the key elements in an appropriate M&E system will need to be determined. We shall examine this task in other sections of this book.

1.2 Globalisation and People's Empowerment
M. Anisur Rahman

I felt that I had found my religion at last, the religion of Man, in which the infinite becomes defined in humanity and came close to me so as to need my love and co-operation (The Vision – Rabindranath Tagore).

Social Change and Development
Human civilisation has made impressive progress in many directions since it first appeared on this globe. But most of us may agree about one fundamental failing: the bulk of the world's population has been deprived of a fair share of this progress. For many the conditions of life have deteriorated as the rest of civilisation has progressed. Compassionate concern for this has been endless, but no decisive corrective action has yet been taken on a global scale.

Since the beginning of known human history, sages, prophets and philosophers have called for a more humane civilisation. They have called for a more just social order than has prevailed at any given time; an order no less caring for human values than for pursuit of material wealth. These calls have been in vain. Over the last couple of centuries a philosophy of revolutionary social change inspired social and political activists across the globe, frightening those who held to the status quo. It called for the liberation of the oppressed from domination, and for promotion of the communal spirit in social life. The process resulted in great convulsions in a number of societies around the globe. But changes inspired by this philosophy have nowhere yielded a social order that does justice to the inspiration. Edifices built upon major social upheavals for such change have collapsed, and the world is back to an unchallenged supremacy of an ideology of the competitive race for private gains. This ideology expresses itself today through a call for '**globalisation**', to remove barriers against capitalist pursuits in all countries irrespective of popular aspirations, culture or national differences and in any stage of development. In fact, today no alternative ideology with a credible operational content exists.

On the 'liberal' side the last half century has also seen the rise and fall of a faith in 'development' that has mobilised thinking and action on a world scale. The call for 'development' promised prosperity to 'developing' nations without radical social upheavals. The development discourses swept the social sciences and national and international establishments; foreign 'development assistance' flowed to 'developing' countries to hasten the promised prosperity; and state powers swelled to deliver the product. Definition of the product was monopolised by the discipline of economics, using aggregate economic growth as the supreme measure, with concerns for distribution permitted only as a debating point. However, to the masses of people in the 'developing' countries the trumpet and march have signified very little – if not alienation – from their indigenous search for life. As a whole, no significant improvement in their material condition has resulted, while economic and social inequalities have sharpened. Social corruption and crime have grown alarmingly, usurping both domestic and international resources in the name of development. This is a race in which the political elite and state organs have given impressive leadership. For a time the 'South Asian miracle' appeared like a breakthrough, only to nosedive to reveal the extreme vulnerability of such flights. Today there is little left of the faith in 'development', although national and international establishments and the mainstream of the economics profession continue to use the rhetoric, promising now that while state efforts have failed, the 'free market' is the best way for nations to 'develop'.

'Poverty Alleviation' and the 'Cheap Labour' Theory of Development

In the hands of protagonists of 'development' the definition of the product has now taken a rather curious turn. Economic growth remains the leading indicator. Concern for equity in its distribution has been virtually abandoned in reverence for competitive pursuit of private interest, acclaimed as the main stimulation for growth. In its place we find a concern for 'poverty alleviation'. Within this discourse poverty is assessed in terms of a lack of minimal needs, which are themselves a function of one's *relative material status* in society. Such a concern for poverty alleviation in a minimalist and static sense amounts in effect to a concern for barely *maintaining the productivity of labour of the ordinary people:* 'livestock' to be fed and sheltered to yield returns for the privileged in society.

From the point of view of rigorous accounting, this 'livestock' notion of poverty provides only for *maintenance* of 'human capital', and the real question of distribution of social income comes in fact *after* this provision. Universalisation of this notion of poverty and of a concern for 'poverty alleviation' in this sense signifies the final ideological triumph of capitalism on a global scale. The underprivileged themselves are being manipulated to internalise this ideology by being christened as 'poor', notwithstanding the human qualities that they possess.

One may see the import of such concerns for 'poverty alleviation' in a global strategy of development. The 'globalisation' implies the flow of international capital to exploit *cheap labour* in 'developing' countries which promises, on the one hand, greater employment to alleviate their 'poverty', and on the other, high returns of capital. This is the essence of the rationalisation of 'globalisation' for world development, for which client nation states are being purchased with so-called 'development assistance'. This assistance is now increasingly confined to the development of infrastructure in order to facilitate private entrepreneurship, with the condition that states open their capital and labour markets to international capital to exploit their cheap labour.

Mass poverty in this 'livestock' sense has persisted unabated with the shift toward privatisation. We have entered the new century with international and national establishments that have little idea as to its solution. Like the 'decades of development' one after another, 'poverty alleviation' even as a bare subsistence concept, has served more as a soundbite than as a seriously pursued task. Meanwhile, 'poverty' is selling rather well in the international market to keep bringing external resources to the 'poor'. But it further helps the elite in such countries in their bid to catch up with modern consumption standards, a chase that also suits the interest of international capital by creating markets for its ostentatious goods.

In all of this one sees a crisis of moral values which are fast losing their force in societies, leaving rising personal crimes and institutional abuse of power to be checked mainly by law-and-order machineries which are themselves declining rapidly in integrity. *Institutions of Ethical Power* (Heller 1998) are fast eroding. Electoral choices are being reduced to a choice between opposing political forces, each using money and sadistic muscle in its bids for power. Together, the economic deprivation of the bulk of the world's population and the shedding of moral values by guardians of societies are strengthening *religious fundamentalism*, to which the establishments are giving only a law-and-order response. Finally, *male domination* persists, so that women in the underprivileged classes are being doubly oppressed, in itself a sad commentary on our civilisation.

The Enlightenment

I present this scenario not as one of despair but as one of *enlightenment*. We know today that structural change alone does not prevent domination; there is a question of **values** to be promoted, which have on the whole been overlooked in radical discourses. As a corollary, there is no way to ensure, by reform or by revolution, that the state will be transformed into a perpetually benign institution. Nor are there known ways of transferring values that may inspire social change to succeeding generations who do not share the historical experience behind that inspiration.

The last century has been generous in revealing these insights, dispensing with some basic illusions that have inspired many committed actions toward radical social change. As for 'liberals', the efforts of the last half-century have also taught that societies cannot be 'developed' by channelling resources to 'middlemen' (such as functionaries of state or other development agencies) as agents of development. Finally, the instinct for male domination will not disappear without more social education and feminine struggle.

Throughout all this, one positive force has advanced and that is the ***awareness*** *of democracy and human rights.* Totalitarianism, where it still reigns, does so without any pretence of righteousness. Yet the 'voice of the people', when it expresses itself anywhere, has a legitimacy today that cannot be easily dismissed. Human rights movements (including women's rights) are more assertive than ever before. It is this ascendance of democratic and human rights awareness on which grassroots work toward people's **empowerment** may stand today to review and re-articulate its mission.

The Challenge of Social Activism Today

The credibility of political activism for social change is currently rather low. Committed political groups have the task of redefining their vision and promise in order to win critical social support. This has widened the space in general for **'civil' social activism**, since this also charges such activism with greater responsibility. The basic task of civil social activism today may be seen as a struggle to promote the **democratic participation** of the underprivileged (including women as a 'doubly oppressed' category therein) toward achieving greater **social justice** and **respect for human rights**. Its aim is also to enhance the intellectual (critical awareness) and ethical (or 'spiritual') content of this participation. Toward this, however, civil (non-party) activism may contribute only indirectly. But notwithstanding the character of macro-power, **people power** in the ultimate analysis is a *countervailing power*. This power includes an ability to assert, protest, resist and clear grounds to march forward, and the promotion of such power is what people's empowerment is about.

Not all NGOs have an agenda to promote people's empowerment. Many are doing 'poverty-alleviation' or 'development' work, with the focus more on economic betterment of the 'poor', rather than on their empowerment. One might argue that with economic betterment people have greater staying power and hence are empowered in their overall social and political struggle. However, in general such work is fostering an environment of **dependence** of the people upon the benefactor NGOs in which the people rarely have the freedom to assert themselves. People cannot be empowered to assert themselves by benefactors whose service creates a permanent benefactor-beneficiary relation that defines the boundaries of people's critical questioning and social action.

There are, however, many NGOs doing work with a real commitment to people's empowerment. Some of these are inspired by the Freirian ideology of '**conscientisation**' or '**liberating education**'; some belong to the paradigm of '**participatory action research**' (PAR) that also seeks to 'conscientise' or promote the intellectual self-awareness of the people through critical self-inquiry (Tilakaratna 1984). Other NGOs are working out of a spontaneous urge to promote popular initiatives with elements of conscientisation/PAR built into their work. This type of work aims to promote **autonomous collective inquiry** and action of the people to which external activists serve as 'animators' and 'facilitators'. In some cases such external activists have withdrawn from base groups whom they have thus helped, working elsewhere and leaving the initial groups to function independently.

Principles for Social Activism
In assessing work with people by external agents from the point of view of people's empowerment, we must ask whether *such agents are working to create autonomous people's organisations or promoting a dependence-relation between the people and themselves?* With a commitment to people's autonomy, we offer the following as a set of guiding **principles** for external activists to promote people's empowerment.

Return People's Self-esteem
People's indigenous lives are characterised by self-esteem. This has been or is being taken away by calling them 'poor' (I have myself been guilty of this error in my earlier discourses on people's participation), an identity that many people have internalised. *There cannot be any empowerment with a negative self-identity.* Men and women do not come into the world simply to solve their problem of 'poverty' nor to have it solved for them by others - they are born to show what stuff they are made of, by their personality and actions in whatever situation in life they face. People must think big about themselves, not small, in order to feel and exercise their power. Accordingly, social activism in terms of empowering people does not mean to project their relative material status as their principal identity; nor to work for 'poverty alleviation' with the people as 'beneficiaries'. Instead, it means to project the qualities that they possess, to seek to restore their self-esteem if they have lost it, and to work for the release of their positive potentials. This has implications for providing material assistance to the people for their economic betterment.

'Sharpen Each Other' (Uglolana)
The relation of external activists with people must be a **relation of equals**, both sides having much to learn from each other. The spirit is most aptly conceived as a spirit of *uglolana*, a word in the indigenous Bantu language of South Africa meaning 'to sharpen each other' (Rahman 1993). This concept rejects, on the one hand, radical pretensions of 'advanced consciousness' or 'revolutionary intellectuals' and, on the other hand, 'liberal' notions of the elite having the responsibility of 'developing' the people with the pretension of superior knowledge. *Uglolana* applied to the 'elite-people relation' calls for scientific and popular knowledge and intellect to interact with each other as equals.

Search for Positives in People's Life and History
Increasing people's self-esteem is of great importance for any external activist. External activists should search **with** the people the positives in their lives and his-

tory in terms of values, creativity, innovativeness, social mobilisation for assertion, constructive action, and their indigenous knowledge and wisdom. In light of the erosion of values that we are observing in today's societies an important part of this task may be to search for communal institutions of ethical power that existed or still exists in some local communities. These could be revived or strengthened and adapted to current conditions.

Solidarity Before Material Assistance

For people who form groups or organisations in response to external projects, offers of financial or material assistance may not necessarily develop the needed sense of solidarity on which people power – the collective strength of people – rests. A challenge to external activists is to animate the people to form **solidarity groups**, for mutual care and cooperation without a promise of immediate external financial or material assistance.

Monitoring People's Self-reliance

The principle of autonomy of people's bodies translates into the principle of people's **self-reliance**. In an elite-governed society, grass-root communities tend to develop an attitude of dependence on elite assistance and guidance which, in turn, strengthens elite domination. An NGO committed to people's empowerment must take the task of promoting people's self-reliance seriously, and initiate monitoring of progress toward a capability of its grassroots 'partners' to move on independently of outside support. This means identifying initial areas of dependence, and planning and implementing strategies to eliminate or progressively reduce such dependence and periodically review progress in this direction as a systematic task.

Liberating Education

Liberating education is widely evident and supported in NGO work. However, the practice for many NGOs leaves much to be desired. Words like 'conscientisation' and 'participatory research' are being 'co-opted' to transfer knowledge and ideas from outside. **Conscientisation is a process of critical self-inquiry and self-learning** and of developing the confidence and capability for finding answers to questions on one's own. It is not necessary for this to mechanically follow any method of 'conscientisation', Freirian or otherwise. Modern pedagogy of education has by now absorbed these contributions to liberating education and calls for the creative exploration, jointly by 'teacher' and learners, of ways to animate and promote collective self-learning.

In the modern world, alphabet literacy as a communication tool is essential for the people to overcome elite domination, and should be promoted with a priority within the pedagogy of liberating education. But social literacy is vital as a foundation of empowerment. Hence the core concept in liberating education is that of *self-reflected critical awareness* of the people of the phenomenon of social domination, a continuous process of understanding just as we ourselves are constantly trying to promote our own self-reflected understanding of this question. One's empowerment *vis-à-vis* society, in fact, begins with the critical understanding of this question – a basic *human* need as distinct from *material* 'basic needs' with which development discourse has preoccupied itself.

Work Toward Synergy and Promoting 'Voice of the People'

Many NGOs are working at multiple locations in a given country but their work may not be 'adding up' beyond the arithmetic. It hardly needs to be said that systematic **interaction** and **networking** between people's groups can add a synergy to such work with many positive outcomes. This includes contribution toward developing a 'voice of the people' over a broader space and also linking such people's networks with other progressive social movements (for example, for gender equality and environmental care). Interaction and networking between people's groups, *transcending individual NGO domains*, can promote such synergy over an even wider area. In many countries the aggregate work of NGOs taken together is creating the potential for such synergy but it remains largely unrealised. Some NGOs, however, actually exhibit an 'empire' mentality and do not favour networking by their grassroots 'partners' within their respective territories. Ironically, these same NGOs have in some countries networked themselves to form associations of NGOs to promote NGO power and to protect NGO interests as distinct from the interests of the people. In such cases the voice of the NGOs is heard more prominently than the voice of the people!

Assistance for Honourable Partnership

Economic assistance, if it meets its immediate objective, does enhance people's power. Hence it can strengthen their **social power** *if* this were linked to the formation and strengthening of autonomous people's organisations and the promotion of people's critical social awareness. Without these outcomes, economic betterment, rather than empowering the people, may facilitate a higher rate of exploitation (surplus extraction) by raising their productivity in an exploitative framework. This would increase economic inequality and hence the imbalance in social power.

We may go deeper and ask how economic assistance can be made less of a charity and more of an element of **honourable partnership**. While charitable work with the people may have humanitarian merit (or fulfil the giver personally (it has nothing to do with empowering the beneficiaries. NGO resources for economic assistance are scarce and any group(s) chosen for such assistance becomes privileged relative to those who are left out.

Notwithstanding their material status, people anywhere have an immense amount to *give* and can be an inspiration to the wider society by their values and by their deeds. Genuine respect for people entitles their external friends to challenge them, in return for the privileged assistance that they are to receive. We should challenge them in a series of ways:

- to demonstrate their innovativeness and creative problem-solving ability that can be of use or an inspiration to people anywhere,
- to show their value of solidarity,
- to show values of solidarity, mutual cooperation, share and care,
- to provide leadership in their neighbourhood in terms of community action and contribute to such action with *labour* if they have little else to contribute,
- to save part of the gains from external assistance to help others,
- to show a concern that other people placed in a similar situation as theirs are also assisted as they are assisted,
- to actively join *as partners* in the task of animating others in their neighbourhood towards a broader movement for people's empowerment thus releasing scarce NGO animators for work elsewhere.

Thus 'economic assistance' can acquire a deeper meaning as a genuine partnership toward a broader movement for a better society, enhancing also the social legitimacy of people's' empowerment beyond their partisan rights, and in turn empowering them all the more with social 'power' as well as self esteem. Anyone who has tried this knows that people who are challenged in this way will respond. They will want to give and not just take, and will respect you for respecting them.

Promote People's Power over the Market

It *is economic assistance without command over the market* that leaves open the possibility of continued exploitation. The solution to this lies in combining economic assistance with strategies for the people to develop **power** over the **market**; *as labour, as producers and as consumers*. Collective bargaining for wage labourers, promotion of self-employment to substitute wage labour, and cooperative exchange, and inputs from small producers as *collective entrepreneurs* are the kinds of strategy that we should promote. An NGO assisting people toward economic betterment by financial, material or technical assistance needs to reflect on how its assistance will contribute most. Their assistance could help the people to reap the maximum possible gain from such assistance, instead of merely inviting a higher rate of exploitation. In this bid people need organisational and management know-how, market information, as well as the use of modern tools of speedy communication, toward which NGOs can extend their services by assisting and equipping the people.

Concluding Comments

We have seen here that people should be empowered *vis-à-vis* what we see as unjust. And this is what gives us the legitimacy and strength to speak about people's empowerment. Likewise, the principles suggested above are based on the premise that the real power of people to confront the unjust comes from their *inner strength*, derived from their *critical, ethical and spiritual self-awareness*. Instrumental and material strength are not to be undermined, as they facilitate the exercise of this power, and toward this end autonomous people's bodies and collective initiatives to promote people's command over the market have been suggested as particularly important. But without inner strength these may be inadequate and also prone to co-optation or abuse.

On the morrow of this new millennium I invite the community of NGOs to reflect on how they may chart a path for their work that defeats the cheap labour ideology of the current call for globalisation. Let grassroots work be inspired not by compassion but by the deepest respect for the people. Let our endeavour for the new era be to enliven, empower and liberate the worthiest human spirit that resides in all peoples. Let our vision of globalisation be one of uniting and mobilising this spirit in all people across the globe, and let the contribution of NGOs toward promoting this expression of **people's power** be recorded in the coming pages of human history.

1.3 Empowerment and Women
Musimbi Kanyoro

Every day upon awakening I think about the empowerment of people and specifically, the empowerment of women and girls. I would like to use the YMCA as a case study to examine the issue of women's empowerment. Our latest poster says, *'Change begins with a simple idea, it begins with you and me, one is never too young and one is never too old to participate in the change'*. This is how we at the YWCA work as a movement.

The YWCA began here in Britain approximately 150 years ago. Its philosophy was that if women were to be taught useful skills, then other things which affect them also needed to be considered, such as accommodation and child-care. Women need support. For this reason, the YWCA began with setting up hostels and kindergartens. The YWCA in the United States is the country's largest provider of child-care for women. It acts as a support system for working women, whose children can be cared for safely whilst they go to work. In the YWCA, we seek to empower women but we also recognise the difficulties:

- We recognise that **inequality and inequity** do exist in terms of the participation of women in many areas of life.

- We recognise the absence of women in **decision-making** at every level, not because women are incapable of participation in decision-making, but because cultures and societies have been socialised not to include them. We believe that only women themselves can achieve the kind of change that they want.

- We recognise that the media has created an image of women in the world which is often negative and ill-informed. We encourage women to think about this and present themselves as they see fit.

- We recognise that the global economy **marginalises women in many different ways**. For example, in Africa, women are present in every aspect of agriculture, education and income-generation, but they do not have the resources or support to take advantage of their position within the economy.

- We recognise the critical importance of **global justice**. We recognise that there are many different conflicts in the world; we recognise the place of women in them, either as vulnerable people or as tools that have been used to satisfy other people's needs. We would like women to have a voice on global justice issues such as peace, economy and health.

- In the private realm we recognise specifically the silence that has existed for years about **violence in women's lives**. The YWCA and many other women's organisations believe that if women could talk openly about the violence in their lives this would be an act of empowerment in itself.

When we talk about the empowerment of women we must first create an environment where women are able to discuss the issues that hinder their empowerment. A prerequisite to empowerment, therefore, is stepping outside the home and participating in some form of **collective undertaking** that develops a sense of independence and confidence among women. Collective groups enable other women to hear each other and share their own life experiences. Through these life experiences they are able to form a collective picture of what it is that affects their lives. In this way an atmosphere of trust is created, rather than one of isolation and loneliness. This leads to a suggestion that one way of evaluating success or failure, is to look at how communities have organised themselves to deal with issues collectively. This is because collective power does make a difference and **collective power** stays with the community much longer than the particular projects that we design to meet immediate needs.

What is Empowerment?

Is literacy by itself a means of empowerment? I would argue that **literacy** by itself is only **partial empowerment**. In China, for example, as well as being taught reading and writing, women are also taught about various environmental issues which affect their lives, such as recycling and overcrowding. In Africa I have seen literacy programmes that have taught literacy in terms of democracy, participation and in terms of dealing with cultural issues that affect the lives of the people. I believe that knowledge and literacy, combined with something that changes your life, have a much more empowering effect than literacy classes by themselves. As Foucault said, *'Knowledge is power'*.

Empowerment has to undergo a series of **phases**, and one is the expectation that personal and collective empowerment will lead to **public action**, however small. We aim to make women not only experience power on a personal level but also in terms of being able to use that power in the public arena. Let us take the example of violence against women in Zambia. Women had asked for permission on a number of occasions to protest against the number of rapes and the amount of violence taking place in the country, since they wanted to raise awareness. Permission was refused. However, they continued to demonstrate, and as a result were arrested. Once they were arrested, rape and violence became public issues, which is what their initial aim was.

Many of the YWCA programmes for women usually tend to help women move from the private into the public realm, in terms of mobilising 'action' that is community focused. Women can achieve empowerment in many different ways. There is **emancipatory knowledge** that comes from women knowing what should be done. There is **economic leverage**, when women work on micro-credit systems, or as entrepreneurs. Economic leverage is a very important support for women to be empowered at the family level, which also enables them to achieve recognition elsewhere. Women's movements and women's groups provide the space for that empowerment, because just stepping out of the house, in some cases, is in itself a step towards empowerment.

Another important aspect is **political mobilisation** and this is the arena in which women take up the issues they deem important at the **policy level**. In the YWCA we believe that the policy level is very important and we pursue it via interventions at the United Nations and in a number of associations, in order for women to lobby their own government. We have lobbying groups in Washington, Brussels, Geneva and one is being established in Addis Ababa. Below is an example of effective lobbying at a national level.

> **Lobby Groups at the National Level:** The example is the YWCA of Britain. We have been working collectively as YWCA together on the issue of 'Third World Debt'. We are able to bring the issue of debt to the communities that we work with. The issue is translated into a language which people can understand. Why are we lobbying the Group of Seven? What is it that we wanted to achieve in July 2000 when the last meeting was held in Japan? We reduce this kind of material to a level where the audiences that we reach are able to deal with it. When we get this debate to the level that the people can comprehend – even if these people are not going to be there at the United Nations – they will understand why a certain decision has been made. This is a small but important step.

Furthermore, **advocacy** requires the empowerment of women at levels other than at the grassroots level. When academics, or wealthy women, undertake advocacy work on behalf of others, political leaders often tell them: *'We want to hear the voices of the grassroots women, not yours'*. Accordingly, they are completely marginalised. The women's movement has always advocated that in order to change policies and to improve conditions for women, women at every level will be required. Academic research is important. Political decisions are important. Therefore the inclusion of the public sector in mobilising women for political understanding of wider global issues is part of what we see as empowerment. When we do this we make sure that the women are able to hold their own governments, communities, district officers and their chiefs, accountable.

> **Concientisation in a coastal village in Kenya:** In a small village on the Kenyan coast there is a YWCA. I lived with the community for a while to learn if the YWCA had any problems. The women were not illiterate but they had been talking a lot about their own poverty and the income they derived from the coconut items that they made. They discovered that they got very little payment from the big lorries which came from Mombasa to pick up their curios. Then they went through a process of **concientisation** and tried to better understand the effort, time and cost of their work. They sent different people to Mombassa to learn what the lorry people were charging for the items bought from the village. Armed with the knowledge of what the lorry people were charging and of what they were being paid, they decided not to sell to those people any longer. Instead they agreed that they would find a way to hire a lorry, obtain money from YWCA and take the material to Mombassa themselves. This kind of concientisation is important: people discover for themselves what the problems or issues are and begin to think of a point of action.

Comment
What is needed is knowledge, solidarity and a better understanding of women's issues. Once these issues are known and understood, we have to challenge the structures of power that sustain gender inequalities. Like other women's movements, we feel that the empowerment of women cannot be measured by statistics alone. It is not a short-term prospect but a lifelong one. Therefore, when the YWCA works in the community, it is only over a long period that mutual trust and confidence are gained. This enables the YWCA to learn what people require. The leadership has to come from the community itself, so that people are able to see daily the leadership and trust it with the kinds of action that they would like to see happen.

The following slogan can be seen at the International Women's Tribune Centre:

> I am learning how to read so that I can read my own life. I am learning how to write so that I can write my own life. That's empowerment, learning literacy, not just for the sake of literacy, but for the sake of making a change in my own life.

1.4 Concluding Comment
Peter Oakley

If we are to monitor and evaluate a process of 'empowerment', then the starting-point must be a context-specific **analysis** of it as a dynamic process that lies at the heart of most political, social and economic relations. Without such an analysis we can never be sure either of the relevance of our purpose or of those forces or factors that could emerge to frustrate the intervention. We have noted above the complexity of the process that underlines the importance of this initial analysis. We have also read two convincing arguments in support of 'empowerment' as a fundamental ideology of working with poor and excluded groups and also in its crucial role in breaking the marginalisation of women. Both accounts are essentially personal statements based on many years of seeking to promote an 'empowerment' approach. Rahman has had a distinguished working life dominated by both powerful intellectual interventions to interpret complex grassroots processes and direct and active involvement in efforts to empower the poor. He rightly insists that all practitioners need to make that fundamental mind-shift and work to promote the innate abilities of poor people, rather than merely helping them to 'participate' in some externally-driven development initiative. Rahman's life has long been a crusade and the vibrancy of grassroots work in Bangladesh has been the product of his and many others' dedicated efforts. Musimbi Kanyoro's equally personal and committed statement is also the product of many years of dedicated effort to promote women's empowerment. And in the many different contexts in which the YMCA works, we can assume that the challenges are formidable. But Kanyoro strikes the same tone as Rahman in the sense of emphasising the importance of focusing on the strengths of women and not merely incorporating them into existing practice.

This review of the central concept of this book – empowerment – inevitably leads us to ask the question: 'If we state that our purpose is to **empower** a particular powerless or marginalised group, how can we know if this has been achieved?' In this respect we assume that an empowerment strategy is both a relevant and a realistic response to the problems of the marginalised group. Such a question inevitably takes us into the area of the 'measurement' of a process such as empowerment and the means that we would use to do this. We now turn to these issues.

CHAPTER 2
Empowerment and its Evaluation

2.1 Introducton

In earlier workshops on the evaluation of social development we explored in detail the approaches, methods and instruments relevant to the M&E of qualitative (and quantitative) processes such as 'empowerment'. In this respect the challenges of the M&E of empowerment are similar to those related to other processes such as, for example, 'participation', 'capacity-building' and 'democratisation'. Since the early 1990s there has been a steady build-up of literature related to the M&E of such qualitative processes as empowerment, with the result that we are now in a sounder position to attempt such evaluations (Marsden, Oakley and Pratt 1994; Valdez and Bamberger 1994; Davies 1995; Oakley, Pratt and Clayton 1998; Roche 1999). These and other texts have produced both a conceptual and practical knowledge base that has slowly begun to influence development practitioners. However, the practice at programme and project level has not yet caught up with either our increasing conceptual understanding of 'empowerment' or M&E systems capable of effectively tracking the process. Indeed it is true to say that most development agencies, while vigorously endorsing the promotion of 'empowerment', have singularly failed to develop methods to monitor its progress. Where progress has been made, it is usually in terms of a number of **indicators** that could be used to monitor the process. Such indicators are often expressed in a macro-sense and there is rarely any guidance on how they could be operationalised.

We stand at this moment, therefore, at a kind of *impasse* in terms of a widespread commitment to empowerment as strategy to break the massive silence and marginalisation of millions of poor women and men in the world. And yet we lack the tools to adequately understand it as a process. More concretely, development agencies are pouring resources into supporting the process but, beyond a few broad indicators, have little means of accounting for those resources. It is for this reason that we chose the concept of empowerment as the central focus of the Fourth Workshop. We hope that succeeding chapters will help us to construct appropriate methods and means to confront this impasse.

2.2 The M&E of Empowerment: Current Practice and Operational Dilemmas
Peter Oakley

Reviewing Agency and Practice
The concept of 'empowerment' has clearly entered the operational vocabulary of a wide range of development agencies. If we reflect on the development literature of the past decade we would probably conclude that this explosion of use took us all by surprise and there has been a sense that, almost overnight, we have become an 'empowering' set of actors committed to the 'empowerment' of the world's poor. It has now become almost an institutional obligation to commit oneself to promoting this process and, while the process does understandably have its critics, few publicly denounce it or suggest that it might be irrelevant to poverty alleviation strategies that are, after all, at the heart of most development policies. Empowerment, like 'participation', has become a 'hurrah' or 'feel-good' word and we bask in our commitment (Jackson 1995). More and more development agencies, from the UN to NGOs and other civil society organisations, are pledging themselves to 'empower' the poor through a range of different strategies, and several have gone into print to explain their particular approach.

Before looking at individual agencies, it is interesting to note the usage of 'empowerment' in the Copenhagen Declaration and Programme of Action, following the World Summit on Social Development. Empowerment is used several times in the Declaration and Programme of Action, and is closely associated with the notion of participation. Empowerment is seen in terms of people being able to participate in decisions that affect their lives. For example, the UN Summit on Social Development in 1995 called for all member governments to embrace the notion that 'empowering' people was a fundamental step in any development process. It called on all governments to:

- Recognise that **empowering** people, particularly women, to strengthen their own capacities is a main objective of development and its principal resource. Empowerment requires the full participation of people in the formulation, implementation and evaluation of decisions determining the functioning and well being of our societies.

- *Establish structures, policies, objectives and measurable goals to ensure gender balance and equity in decision-making processes at all levels, broaden women's political, economic, social and cultural opportunities and independence, and support the* **empowerment of women**. (UN 1995:10-20)

A more detailed examination of both the above statements and the Summit's declaration in full reveals that, although the term 'empowerment' is used liberally in the document, there is very little direct reference to the notion of power. Empowerment is not seen in terms of giving power to the powerless and reducing the power of the powerful. Instead, empowerment has been depoliticised and used to refer to a more pro-active and vigorous process of 'participation' couched in such generalised terms in order to temper interpretations that might effectively challenge the status quo. Essentially 'empowerment' is seen as some kind of gift at the disposal of governments who in their benevolence can use it mitigate the harsher realities of massive political, economic and social exclusion.

In a more operational sense the **World Bank** took the 'development community' by surprise in the early 1990s by its sudden discovery of the centrality of local participation in development processes that, ultimately, led the institution to address the issue of empowerment. In this respect a study of the relevant World Bank documentation must conclude that the organisation essentially equates 'empowerment' with 'participation' and sees the former as what we might call the ultimate stage of a process of participation within the context of the project cycle.

This was confirmed in a recent paper by the Bank documenting its experiences of using participatory approaches:

Participation was defined 'as a process through which stakeholders influence and share control over development initiatives and the decisions and resources which affect them'. Over time other distinctions have been made with regard to the continuum of participation. That is, the Bank began to recognise several stages of participation: information sharing, consultation, collaboration and, finally, **empowerment**. When projects do support participation, it is largely task-based and functional in nature, rather than the type of participation that empowers primary stakeholders to make their own development decisions. (World Bank 1998:19)

The above study of 48 World Bank-supported projects, all of which were considered to be participatory, made a distinction between participation as information sharing and consultation, and participation as empowerment. Participation as empowerment was seen in terms of project beneficiaries participating in decision-making or initiating their own activities. Only one project out of 48 was found to have been empowering in this sense. Most of the projects reviewed rarely engaged with the beneficiary population beyond the levels of information sharing and consultation. This has tended to confirm the view of the instrumental nature of much participatory practice in the sense of using participation to improve the implementation of pre-designed projects. The study found little evidence of capacity-building with beneficiaries or empowering them to initiate their own development activities (World Bank 1996). As with the UN Social Summit, what inevitably emerges from this statement and study is a similar depoliticised view of empowerment. What is absent in these statements by the Bank is a broader view of empowerment, beyond the project, that tackles local power structures and inequalities.

At the **multilateral** level UNDP has also been exploring the implications of setting its development objectives within a human rights framework and this has brought the organisation to suggest a deeper and more structural perspective on empowerment. Empowerment is no longer just about people participating in decisions that affect their lives but has an additional dimension through people asserting and demanding their **rights**. It is recognition that empowerment is not simply about giving people the opportunity to participate but rather it is about people actively claiming their right to take action.

> Human rights are enhanced when gender equity or poverty reduction programmes empower people to become aware of and claim their rights. Sustainable human development and human rights will be undone in a repressive environment where threat or disease prevails, and both are better able to promote human choices in a peaceful and pluralistic society. (UNDP 1998:5)

This is a more fundamental and dramatic challenge to the 'development community' in terms of empowerment and we await any assessment of its implementation as a development strategy. The evidence to date would suggest that UNDP has yet to come to grips with how it would assess its performance in seeking to promote the above process.

At the **bilateral** level, official donor agencies have similarly embraced this commitment to empowerment (DANIDA 1993; SIDA 2000). For example, the incoming Labour Government in Britain 1997 commissioned a White Paper on Overseas Aid Policy that took its commitment to 'participatory processes' one stage further. In the White Paper empowerment was stressed in relation to the position of women:

> The goal of achieving equality between women and men is based on principles of human rights and social justice. **Empowerment** of women is moreover a prerequisite for achieving effective and people-centred development. (DFID 1997:47)

DFID's 1999 Departmental Report then went further and focused on the notion of political empowerment. Unlike the other statements from donors that have been presented above, DFID's statement makes an explicit reference to power and poor people's exclusion from power:

> **Political Empowerment:** Political systems often have a democratic veneer. But in practice power may simply rotate between branches of the same elite. Poor people remain excluded from economic and political systems. Our new approach to tackling political exclusion recognises this to promote the freedoms of expression and association; access to information including free and effective media; a politically active civil society to make government more responsive; political parties which are representative and democratic and which reach out to remote and deprived areas. (DFID 1999:38)

The above reflects the growing influence of a **rights-based** approach to development within DFID's policy. This approach sees empowerment as fundamentally concerned with poor people being able to take their own decisions about their own lives, rather than being the passive objects of choices made on their behalf. The linking together of empowerment and human rights in policy statements is a relatively new practice and it is not clear yet how this will be operationalised at the programme level. A rights-based approach to poverty alleviation provides an overall framework which within which people claim and assert their rights; when poor people actively demand their rights, they are considered to have been 'empowered'.

Finally we examine briefly the **international NGO** sector and the extent to which it is committed to promote empowerment. Of course this is a large and widely varied sector and it is impossible to present a representative picture of this enormous universe. In particular the increasing number of NGO-sponsored publications that broadly take up the theme of empowerment is noticeable. Instead we shall take two examples to **illustrate** the NGO sector's promotion of empowerment. Given the nature of NGOs and their supposed purpose, one could reasonably expect to find solid evidence of a more politically and action-focused view of 'empowerment'. This would be framed in both intellectual and practical terms, particularly in relation to the rather limited view of 'empowerment' as some advanced form of 'participation' in donor-funded projects. In general terms this is the case (Franco et al. 1993; Strachan with Peters 1997; Bergdall 1998; Whitemore 1998; Smith 1999; Whiteside 1999). For example, DanChurchAid has made empowerment central to its support for development initiatives:

> As far as development assistance is concerned, this means a long-term contribution, often in the shape of integrated programmes with emphasis on the **empowerment** of the local target groups in order to enable them to influence

and decide on their own future. (DanChurchAid 1998: 20)

Furthermore, the *Oxfam Handbook on Development* has a clear statement on empowerment that relates it fundamentally to the issue of confronting powerlessness:

> **Empowerment**, in the context of development work, is essentially concerned with analysing and addressing the dynamics of oppression. Confronting the ways in which people internalise their low social status, with a resulting lack of self-esteem, and assisting groups and individuals to come to believe that they have a legitimate part to play in the decisions which affect their lives, is the beginning of empowerment. (Oxfam 1995:13)

The Oxfam view of empowerment explicitly rejects the notion that 'participation' in development in donor-funded development projects is a sign of 'empowerment'. Indeed it is emphatic that much of what passes for popular participation in development and relief work is not in any way empowering to the poorest and most disadvantaged people in society. (Oxfam 1995: 14)

Operationalising Empowerment

We can summarise much of the above by examining how development practice has come to differentiate between different **purposes** of empowerment. There is a noticeable symmetry in the purposes that are beginning to emerge and the ways in which they are being implemented across the agencies. In general terms a review of a substantial body of operational literature suggests that development agencies currently promote and support 'empowerment' initiatives with a number of different but interrelated purposes. In the literature, we can identify a number of key uses of the term:

Empowerment as Participation: This link between 'participation' and 'empowerment' is the strongest that emerges in the practice. The World Bank, for example, sees 'empowerment' as the ultimate stage of a process of local people's participation in a development project. This perception has broadened into the now widely recognised concept of 'participatory development' that has become the more common strategy for promoting 'empowerment'. Furthermore this has now been strengthened by the ever-increasing Participatory Rural Appraisal (PRA) techniques that have become for many the fundamental methodology of community-based empowerment. Essentially we have here a very project-focused view of empowerment and one that places enormous faith on this age-old instrument to deliver the goods!

Empowerment as Democratisation: This concerns the idea of empowerment in the broader political macro-sense. Northern donors have long lamented the lack of supposed democratic structures and practices in many countries and have seen a process of 'empowerment' as the basis on which such structures and practices could be built. As early as 1990 Korten was arguing for support for such broad-based processes as democratisation as a means to build 'People's power'. His cry has been echoed in development strategies across the agencies in terms of support for building civil society structures and supporting grassroots organisations.

Empowerment as Capacity-Building: In the past decade Capacity-Building (CB) has become a major thrust and key strategic objective of many development projects, particularly in terms of the empowering of local groups and organisations. CB has come to represent a hotly contested and broad spectrum of approaches. Some of these appear no different than 'training', while others stress the essential 'learning' basis of the approach, the critical importance of reflection and, fundamentally, the notions of ownership and autonomous action (Kaplan 1996; Eade 1997; James 1999). Whatever the perspective, there is currently a substantial amount of activity taking place around the term 'CB', most of which professes to empower the recipients (Herrera and Hansen 1999). For example, commitments to the strengthening of NGO and civil society institutions, in order that they might better negotiate with other more powerful stakeholders, are typically made in this vein.

Empowerment through Economic Improvement: It could be argued that greater amounts of 'participation', democratisation and capacity-building mean little unless poor people also have greater economic ownership and control. Hence the view that supporting poor people to gain access to tangible economic resources or in small enterprise development are essentially activities that can help to 'empower' them (Sahley 1995). Improving people's opportunities for generating greater income is a central component of many poverty alleviation strategies and could ultimately give them greater economic power. Similarly in the past few years increased donor resources have been poured into helping to set up small business enterprises, micro-finance and the general creation of entrepreneurial skills among the poor as the means whereby they can begin to rise out of their poverty (UNDP 1998).

Empowerment and the Individual: Finally, the consequence of poor people's involvement in activities such as those above should be to help build their own inner person and give them the confidence and experience to expand their horizons and not to settle for what they have. Much of this view is essentially Freirian in nature and derives from earlier ideas around 'awareness-creation' and the development of 'critical faculty' (Freire 1974). To be 'empowered', if such a process could ever be documented and communicated, is essentially an individual experience and lies at the basis of breaking down decades (centuries) of exclusion and the decision to join in action to cross the divide (see Taylor below).

The above illustrates how the concept of empowerment has been interpreted by a range of development agencies. In this respect it is true to say that the level of public commitment is impressive. Furthermore, this review reveals certain dominant notions of empowerment within development agencies. Firstly, there is an overriding view that links empowerment to some stage of a process of greater local participation in development projects. This has led to a clear and widespread project-focused view of empowerment that omits the broader context. However, some of the more recent statements have taken this broader view of empowerment as democratisation. What seems to be less evident, however, is the notion of empowerment as economic control and power, although interestingly 'women's empowerment' is often expressed in terms of their access to economic resources (DFID 2000). Democracy, participation and capacity-building may mean very little to the poor if they fail to bring with them tangible economic benefits. For many empowerment is seen as the key to tackling poverty and social exclusion, but the breakthrough will only come when it is translated into hard benefits. To date the evidence is simply not there that 'empowerment' can lead to widespread economic improvement for the poor. Indeed there is a suspicion that, in economic terms, it has had a differential impact.

All of the above practices, however, take place largely within the context of powerful donor recipient relationships. The former usually come equipped with established procedures and frameworks, often reducing everything to measurable results and reports. Into this package is built the notion of 'empowerment' that is often presented as able to be facilitated externally and deliverable. In this respect Taylor (below) suggests that the donors 'simply don't get it', nor understand what a process of 'empowerment' is all about. He points to the two fundamentally different worlds of the 'tangible' and the 'intangible'; development practice and M&E are dominated by the former while the development workers themselves are often involved in and wish to explore the latter. Wolfe (1996) comments in a similar vein and suggests that donors too easily foist their own interpretations of such terms as 'empowerment' on reluctant partners who are torn between the need for autonomy and ownership and the aid and protection they get from donors. There may be a conflicting world out there between what development workers do and perceive and what they feel obliged to report!

A Framework for the M&E of Empowerment

It is probably true to say that little progress has been made to date in terms of answering the question: 'In a process of empowerment, how do we know that a previously powerless group has been 'empowered'? Of course, the question is not as simple as that and it may be difficult to argue that there is an ultimate and finite state of being 'empowered'. However, given that across development agencies and the sectors there is now such a public commitment to 'empower' people as a result of a directly targeted project intervention, it is not unreasonable to ask how we may know when this has been achieved? Once we ask this question the matter then becomes one of how can we approach the issue and what methods and instruments we could use in the task. In this respect the situation is mildly encouraging in the sense that there has been considerable progress in the past decade with approaches and methods to the M&E of qualitative processes in development projects targeted at the poor and marginalised. Indeed in the field of M&E to date – apart from a small number of examples (Bergdall 1998; Whitemore 1998; Smith 1999) – we await a substantial exercise that would seek to monitor and explain the unfolding of a process of empowerment to guide us in 'evaluating' its impact.

Within the context of targeted development interventions, the measurement of the 'impact' of a process of empowerment essentially requires an appropriate **monitoring and evaluation approach**. To be able to do this effectively it is important to take note of the general lessons that have been learnt in monitoring and evaluating social development processes such as empowerment. The approach is based upon the development of a 'minimum but effective' system, which has as its objective the generation of a sufficient – but not an exaggerated – amount of data and information. This would allow a development agency to have a reliable understanding of the output, effect and impact of processes such as 'empowerment' that it is supporting. It is in this area that most of the interesting work on M&E is currently taking place. Essentially in the past decade there has emerged an alternative to the more conventional quantitative and results orientated approach to project evaluation. It is within the framework of this alternative 'model' that we must seek guidance on how to approach the issue of the M&E of a process of 'empowerment'. The increasing emergence of this alternative has begun to show us how we might go about the M&E of these qualitative processes and the relevant literature and practice have grown considerably in the past decade. It could be argued, however, that much of this energy and practice has been built more around the notion of making M&E more 'participatory', than adding substantially to our understanding of how we (beneficiaries and practitioners) could 'evaluate' the process, in the broadest sense of the term.

Much of the above is familiar territory and was explored in some detail in the 1996 Workshop. As we are all aware, broadly speaking there are two broad and contrasting approaches to monitoring and evaluation.

(1) The first can be called the **orthodox** or '**blueprint**' approach. This is the approach that most development agencies have traditionally followed and, to a large extent, continue to follow, but now with a supposed 'participatory'

quality. A detailed input output monitoring system, including the selection of indicators, is set up before the implementation of the project, and serves as the basis for monitoring for the duration of the project. While this approach is appropriate for monitoring the physical input and output of projects from a whole range of perspectives, it has major limitations when monitoring broader social development objectives such as 'empowerment'.

(2) An alternative **process approach** to monitoring has been developed in the past decade that is less prescriptive and more flexible and adaptable. Rather than define all the elements of the monitoring system at the start of the project, the system supposedly develops and evolves out of the ongoing experience of implementing the project. Monitoring lies at the heart of this approach and there have been some radical experiments designed to question some of the basic tools of project evaluation, as for example, the extent and nature of 'beneficiary' participation, the nature of indicators, broadening the range of instruments used and grappling with the elusive concept of 'impact'. Certainly the language of this 'process approach' is now widely spread but there is still the struggle between building it into the more structured 'blueprint' approach and genuine attempts to allow it to function in its own right.

Whatever the nature and content of an appropriate approach to the M&E of empowerment, if we wish to answer the basic question we will clearly need to do more than merely record activities and outputs. These are the means by which powerless people hopefully become 'empowered'. We need, therefore, to understand what happens and what **effect** and **impact** these may have had in both the immediate and the longer term.

While initially the M&E of empowerment will involve a detailing of effort expended and a description of activities undertaken, the crucial first stage in measurement will be to assess what has been the outcome of the project in terms of the **effect** it has had on the initial situation of powerlessness. By effect we mean the more immediate tangible and observable change, in relation to the initial situation and established objectives, which it is felt has been brought about as a direct result of project activities. Experiences with evaluation exercises with other processes such as empowerment have revealed that it is possible to construct an understanding between the different actors of what effect the outputs have had on the process. As with most development interventions, however, the major difficulty will lie with understanding the **impact** of a process of empowerment. In the overall process of M&E, impact assessment is the last stage and it is rarely reached. In this respect we can understand the sequence of outcomes in the following table:

Table 2: **Measuring Outputs, Outcome and Impact**

Point of Measurement	What is Measured	Indicators
Outputs	Effort	• Implementation of Activities
Outcomes	Effectiveness	• Use of Outputs and Sustained Production of Benefits
Impact	Change	• Difference from the Original Problem Situation

Source: A. Fowler (1997), *Striking a Balance*,

We shall return later to the difficulties related to evaluating a process of empowerment. In the first instance we should note two important aspects of any approach to the M&E of a process of empowerment:

Indicators

A major operational breakthrough of the past decade has been development agencies' increasing familiarity with and apparent use of qualitative indicators in the evaluation of processes of social development. The amount of discussion and numbers of examples in the literature on this matter are a reflection of this breakthrough. In this respect, therefore, there is no need to review here either the background information concerning qualitative indicators or indeed the basic issues relating to indicators such as **definition, characteristics, selection and use**. There is ample background material on these issues in works such as Casley and Kumar (1987), Marsden and Oakley (1990), Westendorff and Ghai (1993), and Gosling and Edwards (1995). The basic principles that indicators should be unambiguous, consistent, specific, sensitive and easy to collect are as valid today as they were when first suggested by Casley and Kumar in 1987. An initial general observation would be that, while there is an increasing familiarity with the 'language' of indicators and reference to them in project documentation, there is still a predominance of indicators which show material results, whereas in the unfolding of a social development process, results are not always predictable beforehand. Furthermore, many development practitioners almost certainly continue to have problems in identifying appropriate indicators.

The radical re-orientation of development interventions in the 1980s and 1990s saw the emergence of a new genre of **development objectives** that reflected new sets of priorities. If we were to review the development priorities of many contemporary agencies, we would probably find in their statements and literature references to the following as broad institutional objectives:

- Self-management and self-reliance.
- Organisational development.
- Awareness building.
- Participation and particularly the greater involvement of women in development initiatives.
- Democratisation.
- Empowerment.
- Strengthening of civil society.
- Building horizontal links between groups with similar economic and political power.

Table 3: **Examples of INDICATORS of Group Empowerment**

Before the Process	After the Process
• Individualism and lack of collective action	• Internal cohesion and sense of solidarity
• Lack of critical analysis	• Ability to critically analyse and discuss
• Economic, social and political dependence	• Internal structure and element of self-management
• Lack of confidence	• Collective activities
• Suspicion and isolation	• Ability to deal with and relate to others

Essentially we have arrived at a situation where currently our commitment to the above broad set of objectives is running well ahead of our ability to explain what effect or impact the vast resources that we have employed may have had. It is to rectify this that in the past five to six years several substantial exercises have been undertaken across both the NGO and the bilateral community (Riddell 1997; Oakley 1999; Roche 1999). While these have provided some very necessary insights into 'measuring the immeasurable', they have not built up the critical mass of analysis and practice that would help to make a break-through. Furthermore, there have been other significant initiatives in the past decade in terms of the M&E of processes such as empowerment that have helped to take us beyond output. Alas, they do not yet add up to any noticeable or significant change in the practice (Shetty 1994; Davies 1995; Goyder et al. 1998; Bergdall 1998; Diakonia 1999). Indeed much of the alternative energy that has been generated around M&E has helped to make the whole process more 'participatory'. While this is a most positive move and a vast improvement on common practice, it still has not helped to come to grips with the very real question of how we can be confident and explain when – for example – attempts to promote the 'empowerment' of a particular group have been successful or not? This whole question – along with processes such as some of the others mentioned above – continue to constitute a major challenge to development agencies across the board.

Analysis and Interpretation

If we can assume that some appropriate M&E approach has been set up, indicators agreed and monitoring undertaken, we then enter the largely uncharted territory of analysing and interpreting the 'information' collected. This involves determining what it tells us in terms of the 'empowerment' that we hope has taken place. In many of the earlier 'conscientisation' exercises, for example, this was done in an open meeting where all concerned shared their perceptions of what they felt had been the overall outcome. This was commonly referred to as 'systematisation', but it was often strong on the detail of activities and events and less confident in making judgements on what concrete changes might have taken place. This is a crucial stage if we are to be confident that all the human inputs have had a positive impact on the original situation. But it is a stage which few development interventions reach in any substantial manner. The critical areas of this stage include the problems of subjectivity, the slow pace at which processes like empowerment unfold, the need for a visual presentation of the process unfolding and the importance of regular interpretation. We are only just beginning to come to grips with this final but crucial stage.

Critical Issues in the M&E of Empowerment

For decades the 'development community' has temporarily sought refuge in one or other 'fresh' perspectives on development project interventions with an increasing anxiety to have some meaningful impact on the lives of the poor. In this respect it would appear that the slow build-up of momentum in the 1980s and 1990s that saw a substantial scaling-up and influence of the concept of 'participation' has now established a strong basis from which to fundamentally influence practice. Empowerment is the logical evolution of 'participation' and indeed it could be argued that the two terms are interchangeable when the term 'participation' is *not* limited merely to being a project beneficiary. However, in the rhetoric we continue to run far ahead of the practice and, crucially, we continue to largely overlook the 'learning' function of 'evaluating' project interventions. This is indeed a crucial point since we 'evaluate' processes of empowerment not simply to balance the accounts but critically to learn *how* it might effectively be brought about. Commitments to 'empowerment' abound but that is not enough. We *must* equip all the actors involved with the ability to track the process, understand how it works – if at all via project interventions – and document its progress. Powerlessness lies at the heart of most people's poverty. We cannot continue to loudly proclaim our commitment but at the same time settle for a few aggregated statistics or superficial assessments. If 'empowerment' in all of its dimensions is now central to the development policies of the 'development community', then the least that this community can do is to seek to come to grips with it as a live and real process.

We have seen that empowerment is essentially an intangible process that is best understood by those more closely involved in the immediate context. In this respect, as outsiders we need to ensure that we do not get lost in the morass. As Dichter (1992) has commented, we view the context from the 'high ground' while empowerment takes place in the 'swamp'. Power lies at the heart of what goes on in the swamp: the funding of projects, negotiated 'partnerships', targeting one group as opposed to another and in the effect and impact that projects can have on established patterns of access to services and resources. In this kaleidoscope of parallel and entwined processes, we somehow have to disentangle the notion of empowerment, to monitor it and to stand by its consequences.

At this juncture the problem becomes a 'technical' one. Notwithstanding any discomfort that we may have with terms like 'monitoring' and 'evaluation' within the context of a process of empowerment and the issue of donors and Northern agendas, we face the task of embarking on a process – empowerment – with a particular group and understanding the process as it unfolds. The practice and literature shows that this task has become quite widespread and also that the difficulties of monitoring the process are formidable. Essentially, we are contemplating 'measuring the immeasurable' and, most critically, we are moving 'beyond the numbers game' (Fetterman 1999). We have seen above how far we have come to date in terms of 'measuring the immeasurable'. We now have to ask the question 'Is it enough?' to allow us to monitor and seek to explain how people become 'empowered'.

The M&E of 'intangible processes' has come a long way since the early 1990s. The question is: 'How much further do we have to go in order to understand this complex process?' The evidence to date suggests the following as some of the critical issues that attempts to M&E a process of empowerment will need to confront:

- Recognising from the very beginning that there are severe limitations to working with such complex and sensitive issues as 'empowerment' if it is to be largely externally driven. Empowerment is not an 'add-on' or another input that is externally provided. Unless its whole dynamic and understanding is based on those most directly involved in the process, attempts to M&E it in the conventional ex post approach will flounder into generalisation.

- Grasping the concept and ensuring that both its understanding and its operational implications are clear: it is not a term simply to adorn project proposals!

- In conjunction with those who will be more immediately affected or involved, the preparation of a **contextual analysis** that is not merely an inventory of human and physical resources but one that examines already existing patterns of power and its distribution that presumably will be affected by any concerted process of 'empowerment' (Kaare and Nielsen 1999).

- It is not enough to enter the fray armed only with a set of broad **indicators**. Whatever is to be used to help structure an understanding of the process must be broken down into a small number of discrete organisational/ behavioural changes, actions and activities that will form the basis for monitoring the process. In this respect it could be argued that **action** will be a key indicator of a process of empowerment and should form the basis of its monitoring.

Table 4: **Indicators of INTERNAL and EXTERNAL Empowerment**

Indicators of INTERNAL Empowerment	
Objective	**Indicators**
Self-management	• Membership growth and trends • Clear procedures and rules • Regular attendance at meetings • Maintaining proper financial accounts
Problem-solving	• Problem identification • Ability to analyse
Democratisation	• Free and fair selection of leaders • Role for weaker members in decision-making • Transparency in information flow
Sustainability and self-reliance	• Conflict resolution • Actions initiated by group • Legal status • Intra-group support system
Indicators of EXTERNAL Empowerment	
Building Links	**Indicators**
With project implementing agency	• Influence at different stages of project • Representation on project administration

	• Degree of financial autonomy
With state agencies	• Influence on state development funds • Influence on other state development initiatives in the area
With local and social political bodies	• Representation of these bodies • Lobbying with mainstream parties • Influence in local schools and health centres
With other groups and social movements	• Formation of federations • Networking
With local elites and other non-group members	• Level of dependence on local elites • Degree of conflict • Ability to increase power
Source: Sketty (n.d)	

- As with most development interventions – and more so when we are dealing with 'intangibles' – the whole area of the **impact** of a process of empowerment may prove particularly elusive. But we should not be daunted by issues of, for example, attribution and subjectivity. In many ways the current concern for Impact Assessment has presented 'impact' as some kind of logical and definable outcome that we should be able to detect ultimately. It may be more appropriate to forget the whole term, concentrate upon effectively working with and understanding the process and, if there is to be any impact, it should begin to manifest itself in concrete actions and changes (Roche 1999).

- Clearly the monitoring of intangible processes demands **methods and instruments** that help us to move beyond the purely quantitative aspects of development and into the more contextual world of 'change'. In this respect there are some encouraging initiatives, largely built around participatory methodologies and the concept of 'beneficiary perception', that are beginning to show how we can effectively understand and monitor these processes and who will be involved (ActionAid 1999). What is critical is not to declare in your project proposal that you intend to 'empower' this or that group and wait to send in an evaluation team three years later to 'evaluate empowerment'. But this is what is happening!

We hoped that issues such as those above and others – would surface at this Fourth International Workshop on the Evaluation of Social Development. For the many reasons outlined in this introductory document, we opted to base the workshop on this contemporary and highly controversial theme. Since the last workshop in 1996, we have noted both the increasing frequency with which the term 'empowerment' was beginning to be presented as the ultimate objective of development strategies of poverty alleviation, and also the noticeable paucity of accompanying approaches and methods to promote and understand it. In this situation we felt that it would be appropriate to convene the Fourth International Workshop to address this situation. We would see the following as the **objectives** of the workshop:

- To review and analyse the process of empowerment and further our understanding of its critical role in helping to break entrenched patterns of poverty and exclusion.

- To provide the opportunity for an exchange of views and experiences among people who have been involved in promoting or supporting a process of empowerment with powerless groups.

- To examine current practice with the M&E of 'empowerment' and to identify how this practice could be strengthened and further developed.

We need a firmer grasp of this intangible process and its potential to promote effective change in favour of the powerless. In order to facilitate these different tasks we **suggest** below a number of the **key issues/questions** that might help us to structure our understanding of the issues involved in the M&E of empowerment. We stress that these are just examples of some key questions that we could ask:

- In the context of development projects which are intended to 'empower' the poor, what are the **key characteristics** and **factors** in the project context that we will need to identify and explain if we wish to understand the dynamics of power?

- What are the key **political, social and economic** differences between those with power and the powerless within a particular development context?

- What are the main characteristics of **powerlessness** that will have to be addressed if a development project is concerned with 'empowering' local people?

- What would be the **key elements** in any development intervention designed to 'empower' the poor?

- What are the **major factors** that can (a) **support** or (b) **constrain** the ability of a development agency to set up a minimum but effective M&E system in order to monitor and assess the impact of a process of 'empowerment'?

- What role do you think **community** or local **people** could play in the M&E of a process of 'empowerment'?

We now need to develop a clear and realistic understanding of this intangible process and its potential to promote effective change in favour of the powerless. Currently the 'development community' appears to be stuck with its linear view of development processes and with its highly systematised view of their development. The whole issue needs a push forward in terms of approaches to working with a process of empowerment that captures its essence, its vigour and its essentially radical nature, and do not merely treat it like any other development input.

2.3 Empowerment and its Evaluation: A Framework of Analysis and Application
Frits Wils

Introduction
This section offers a **framework** for the evaluation of empowerment. It considers both the role and relevance of underlying theories and also elaborates various operational or technical elements, while trying to link the former to the latter in an integrated approach. Such an approach fits well with the basic argument I will present. It suggests that NGDOs, like other development agents, are often not so strong when it comes to thinking about and explicitly formulating their development strategies – for example, what it is they are trying to achieve, how and with which particular target group. Hopefully, both Southern and Northern NGDOs will benefit from a challenge to become much more specific and explicit in formulating their *working hypotheses*, particularly in such a complex area as **empowerment**.

The discussion below is structured in the following way. First, I will 'clear the deck' and provide definitions of the basic concepts linked to a PME system for empowerment. I will then address what I call the 'muddle of empowerment' by distinguishing between empowerment as a means and empowerment as an end in itself. Only when all of this has become clear, will I focus on the planning, monitoring and evaluation of empowerment in detail. I hope that the unfolding framework will help participants to sharpen their awareness of what they are striving for in the field of empowerment. We will then be able to develop a better PME system for empowerment.

A PME System for Empowerment

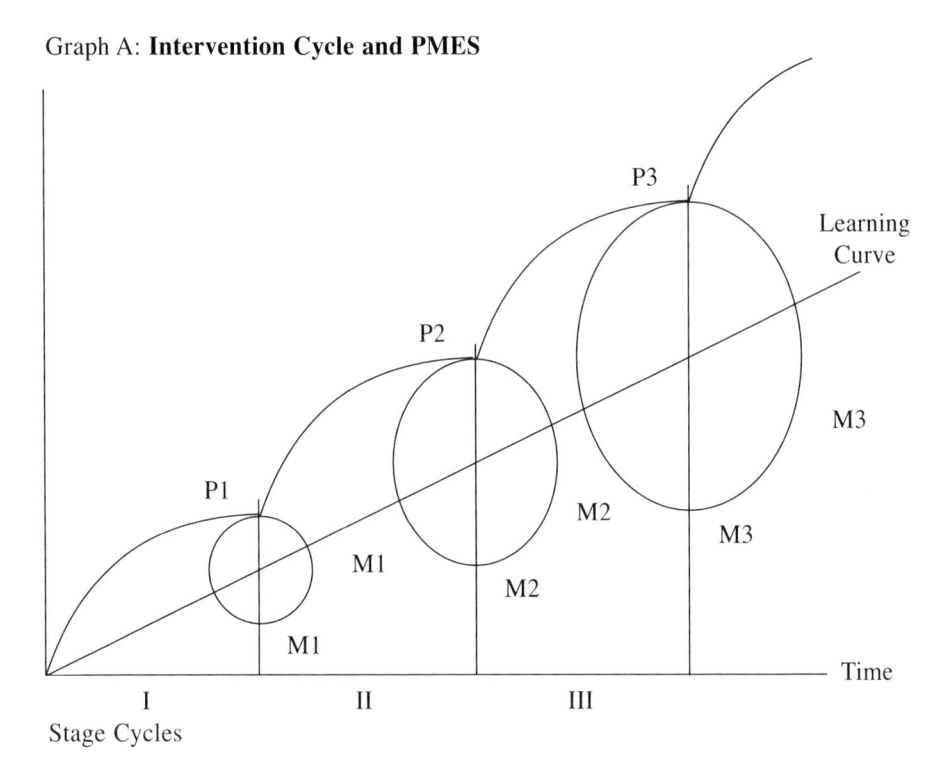

Graph A: **Intervention Cycle and PMES**

[Graph showing three stage cycles (I, II, III) along a Learning Curve axis of Time, with points P1, P2, P3 and monitoring markers M1, M2, M3]

Stage Cycles

Looking at monitoring or evaluation in isolation from planning makes little sense. We must assume that M&E has something to do with what we set out to achieve through our interventions; that is, with our initial general and specific objectives. Hence the concept of the PME system. Given the backward and forward linkages in intervention cycles, we would emphasise that it really is a *system*. A first problem that emerges in writing out a PME system is that NGDOs often do not have a clear idea, *ex ante*, of what **empowerment** concretely refers to. That is, how to formulate the planning or objectives of their intervention specifically. What does empowerment really entail? Not just in general, but in connection with a specific target group, in a specific location and context. All of these questions often only become clear in practice. Moreover, often the NGDO and the target group use a different discourse, especially at the beginning: the former may be one of empowerment, the latter one of survival. It is only through a *process of learning* (see Graph A), via intervention cycles, that we discover what the 'empowerment' of excluded groups and sectors stands for and what is viable in a particular period of time.

A problem that arises in the analysis of empowerment refers to the basic point that many doubt whether the premise of the *planning and promotion of change* is really a viable proposition. There is a lot of valid criticism concerning the linearity and attribution of causality, in the case of a simple goals means connection applied to complex fields of action. The critique applies particularly to the restricted project framework where NGDOs and donors alike share an immediate interest in the concrete measurement of the outcomes and effects of their work. Indeed, as we will see later, many unforeseen things do happen in processes of empowerment, whether on the part of the subjects of empowerment, or on the side of opposing interest groups. Nonetheless, the justifiable criticism of planning does not give licence for headless muddling, or a justification for sheer rudderless activism! We need to carry on, but on the basis of a *working hypothesis*. This is needed to help to find out – in a more or less organised manner – what the possibilities and margins are of viable interventions in the field of empowerment. Monitoring and evaluation plays a crucial role in this learning process: it provides us with the required feedback on the validity and viability of our working hypotheses and the relevant adjustments needed. In this sense, monitoring and evaluation represent indispensable instruments for applied action-research (Wils 1991).

Monitoring and Evaluation Defined

Graph B: **Logframe**

		Description	Indicators	Instrument	Assumption
Evaluation Related to Objective	General Objectives				
	Specific Objectives				
Monitoring Related to Intervention	Activities Programmes				
	Inputs				

A simple log frame is useful to briefly set out a series of concepts used in this introduction (see Graph B). Despite the many and well-known drawbacks of a log frame, it does permit a succinct and coherent presentation of general and specific objectives, and the configuration of means – Inputs and activities – to achieve those objectives. In this scheme of things, **monitoring** refers to the regular collection of information on:

- the extent to which the inputs and outputs of interventions are being generated as envisaged;
- the identification of factors that can help to explain the discrepancies (if any) between foreseen and actual inputs and outcomes; and
- the steps to be taken to adjust the programme for the next period.

Thus monitoring focuses on the field of operational interventions over which the agent – grassroots groups or NGDOs – can exercise more control. Monitoring examines whether the anticipated outcomes are being achieved and, if not, why not? Answers to such questions help an NGDO to adjust its programmes for the next period.

Such control is much weaker, however, when it comes to the activities that are the focus of **evaluation**. Evaluation examines the aims and objectives of an NGDO and the realities of the beneficiaries whose conditions it tries to change. In evaluation we go back to the upper half of the log frame – to the original objectives – and we see whether the results of an NGDO's intervention have brought about the changes envisaged. In practice quite a few NGDOs wittingly or unwittingly are largely, if not exclusively, engaged in monitoring – reporting inputs and outcomes – even when they think they're evaluating. Indeed, often NGDOs face problems when it comes to evaluation. Evaluation expects them to look critically and in a moment of systematic reflection at their work, from the perspective of their original objectives.

It is true that it is sometimes difficult to differentiate sharply between monitoring and evaluation. Evaluations are often carried out only every 3 to 5 years, and people are forced to wait a long time for an assessment of the effectiveness and impact of what they are doing. Hence, sometimes grassroots groups and NGDO staff are asked to include – already during their monitoring cycle – a judgement on the probability of achieving effectiveness or impact. Nevertheless, we will continue to differentiate, for the time being, between monitoring and evaluation: the former refers to programme implementation, the latter to the achievement of objectives. In both instances indicators are used. What do indicators refer to?

Indicators are defined at all levels: inputs, outcomes, effects and impact. They are necessary to check whether the anticipated outcomes are effectively being realised (that is the function of monitoring), and whether the anticipated changes are being achieved as laid down in the objectives. These indicators force us to specify during the planning stage those expected outcomes and changes, including the how and when their measurement will take place. This demands considerable insight and concrete experience on the part of the NGDOs and the grassroots groups with whom they work. And it is here that deficiencies are often found. All indicators must be defined in accordance with the well-known SMART criteria. They must *specify* the target group, its location and baseline condition. Only *measurable* indicators can be used. Indicators should be **agreed** upon as related to the outcome or objective involved. And indicators should be **realistic** and be put in a **time frame**.

A Definition of Empowerment

We cannot deal with the monitoring and evaluation of empowerment without first going back to planning: that is, the planning or programming of empowerment. First and foremost we need to look at the way in which empowerment has been **problematised**, if at all. We have already noted that NGDOs often fail to elaborate the 'what & why' of empowerment in some detail. Indeed, one of the most critical issues is that such an initial problematisation is an essential requisite for any coherent effort to intervene in processes of empowerment, as well as for the evaluation *ex post* of its outcomes. At this point we need a clear definition of 'empowerment' itself. What is at stake here? We need a simple core definition, a definition which can be replaced later by any other (argued) definition you would prefer for your own work. But for the purposes of our discussion here we need to make a choice.

Some define empowerment in terms of control over community resources (Korten 1987), while others define empowerment as being related to the means required for an escape from poverty (Schneider 1999). Another group of authors (Friedman 1992; Galjart 1987; Stiefel and Wolfe 1994) think of empowerment as involving *'participation in decision-making'* on matters important to the target group. This last definition seems to be the clearest when it comes to capturing the basic element of 'power' in 'empowerment': the power of decision-making. Decision-making is a central instance where power is applied, including the power to influence the behaviour and choices of third parties. In principle the subjects of empowerment – or as Tandon (1987) would prefer it, the 'self-empowered' – are those who normally are, or have been, *excluded* from such decision-making. Inclusion empowers them, gives them power in a socio-political context. Empowerment, therefore, though linked to social, economic or cultural dimensions is essentially a **political** strategy and process.

However, several things need to be clarified, such as the level of empowerment, the kinds of subject involved and what the decision-making in empowerment refers to. Clearly, the *context or level* – and with it, the related subjects – of empowerment differ enormously from case to case, from the level of interpersonal relationships involving gender and generation, to the level of households, local communities and neighbourhoods, to those of municipalities and districts, regions, societies and even the global system. The *subjects* of empowerment vary greatly too. For example, women and children, household members, community-based organisations, slum associations, or other social and ethnic groups.

What matters most is that the central **objective** of empowerment can vary considerably. Empowerment can concern decision-making over many different things, ranging from control over resources to holding one's own leadership and external agents accountable. For our discussion of the PME system of empowerment, such variations in the *level* and nature of empowerment are of great importance. They help define specific objectives of empowerment and the corresponding indicators of change, while meeting, of course, all the time SMART criteria. That is, in each case where empowerment represents a crucial objective of intervention, such variables as the level and subject of empowerment, and the objective of decision-making being sought, need to be spelled out in detail.

We should also note that, in principle, the subjects of empowerment can be either *groups or individuals*. An empowerment strategy is usually based on organised group interventions. These bring together those who as persons and as a collective should benefit from the effects of that intervention. Organised group action is needed because what empowerment usually tries to bring about is not a change of incidental arrangements. Instead, empowerment seeks to modify societal and institutionalised norms, customs and/or stratified relationships, often connected with class, gender, generation and ethnicity, that exclude certain kinds of people and sectors from decision-making. Nonetheless, though empowerment strategies usually use group-based actions in order to achieve access to decision-making, the final beneficiaries may be – especially when such access is given an institutional basis – both collective and individual members.

Indeed, given the complexities and paradoxes of participation (Cleaver 1999) – including its recurrent limitations and selectivity – one of the key issues in its monitoring and evaluation should always be how broadly and deeply the interventions are reaching those who are excluded. Furthermore, we should ask the questions, who exactly are getting effectively organised, and who are actively participating in decision-making? We are all familiar with differentials that are hard to eradicate: with the poorest who are rarely reached effectively; with leaders who benefit disproportionally; with the most excluded who are least likely to participate; and with organisations which help to disempower rather than empower the excluded. Monitoring and evaluation can and should play a crucial role in bringing out such differentials, and help lay the basis for adjustments in strategies, methods and tools.

Empowerment as an End or as a Means?

Another point that should be tackled before we can discuss empowerment itself in further detail, is the seemingly rather simple yet important question of whether empowerment is an **end** in itself or a **means** for something else. We can begin by summarising a simple but basic logical sequence that NGDOs often tend to follow when they refer to empowerment (see Diagram 1):

Diagram 1: **Logical Sequence of Empowerment**

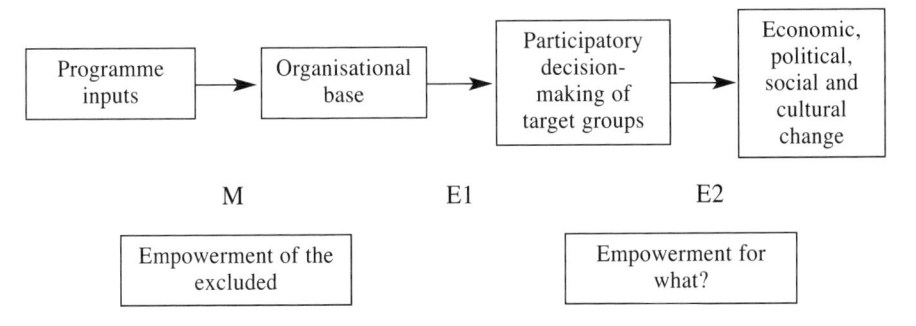

```
Programme     →  Organisational  →  Participatory      →  Economic,
inputs           base               decision-             political,
                                    making of             social and
                                    target groups         cultural
                                                          change

    M                E1                                       E2

Empowerment of the                          Empowerment for
    excluded                                    what?
```

Suppose we define empowerment as 'participation in decision-making' on matters important to the target group. In this respect NGDOs often see an autonomous collective organisational base as a requisite for such participation. In cases where empowerment is considered an **end** by itself, monitoring looks at whether inputs and actions did help establish such an organisational base (outcomes). Evaluation checks whether such a base is indeed autonomous and active (effects), and whether this in turn leads to the excluded obtaining effective participation in important decision-making (E1). If empowerment is not seen as an end in itself, but is viewed as a **means** (or a specific objective), then the question raised is, 'empowerment for what?' Monitoring then does the same thing as before, but in this case evaluation becomes a two-step operation that examines:

(i) whether an autonomous and dynamic organisational base leads to effective participation in decision-making (E1); *and*

(ii) whether such participation in turn leads to the political, social, economic or cultural changes hoped for (E2).

In technical terms the former would be an evaluation of effectiveness, the latter an evaluation at the level of impact. Note that in reality empowerment – that is, actual participation in decision-making – may not, and does not, automatically lead to such changes. Opposition from other stakeholders, lack of supporting allies or other factors may and do intervene. So it makes sense, at least in principle, to separate the two steps in the sequence.

It should be noted that when we maintain such a strict separation of steps in the logical sequence, the expected changes resulting from empowerment cannot and should not be brought back and included elsewhere in the sequence, either as a specific objective or as an indicator of empowerment. Indeed, in this case, the linkage between empowerment and its (other) objectives must be problematised, become an area of special interventions, and be elaborated in terms of specific objectives as well, with all the corresponding indicators.

It is, of course, also possible to set things up differently. One could argue that the expected changes – the crucial element in empowerment – can be considered as impact indicators of decision-making. The assumption then is that it is not the actual participation in decision-making itself that counts, but its impact. Indeed, I think that the usual practice of many authors and NGDOs is to take an instrumental view of empowerment. It is usually not seen as a good in itself, but as a basic requisite for other, often higher and more general, objectives, for example, to achieve equity, transformation of society or alternative development strategies. Most development agencies are interested in measuring the impact of empowerment, not empowerment itself.

However, if we fuse the functions of empowerment as an objective by itself and as a means for something else, we run certain risks. Or to put it in other words, it is confusing to consider empowerment *both* as a general and as a specific objective. Doing so entails the risk that empowerment remains a black box, a promising strategy yet mired down in an opaque muddle of goals and means. True, we can give different shapes to the (hypothetical) construction of a sequence or chain of steps in an empowerment strategy. Yet, whereas *in practice* steps may and do get mixed up, when we *problematise* a strategy of empowerment we are more likely to maintain clarity and transparency. Hence, one must be quite clear, from the start about the *general* overall objective. Is it empowerment *per se* or some other objective? In the latter case, empowerment is seen as a *specific* objective, the achievement of which will hopefully help attain the general one. This is the normal chain or sequence that NGDOs usually have in mind: it implies an instrumental use of empowerment. It makes sense, in this connection, to look again briefly at 'what matters in empowerment', involving answers to the question 'empowerment for what?'

Empowerment for What?

Table 5 summarises some of the main **changes** usually sought through the application of empowerment strategies, with some corresponding impact indicators. The list is provided more for purposes of illustration than as an exhaustive listing. It assumes that variables such as the subject of empowerment (in terms of class, ethnicity, gender, religion, etc.), the context or level of empowerment (such as interpersonal relations, household, community) and other SMART criteria have been specified. Obviously, the rather general indicators below need more detail for purposes of monitoring and evaluation.

Table 5: **Possible General Objectives Sought from an Empowerment Strategy**

	Objectives	Indicators
Socially	• greater equality of opportunities • access/use of services • higher social status	• greater choice jobs/occupations • shifts in division of labour/tasks • higher level of education • family more use health facilities • better habitat conditions • representation on prestigious • committee • shift in intermarriages • recognition by outsiders (visits)
Economically	• better economic condition • better access to economy	• higher income • own/control more assets • inputs use of credit • benefits from economic • programmes
Politically	• more effective power	• vote actively • occupy political/elective posts • intervene authorities (claims, protest) • intervene in markets (conditions) • intervene in allocation of resources • participate as citizen in governance • get shifts in programmes/policies
Culturally	• identity more accepted	• own programs including special conditions voice/view sought in community • music, language recognised

Note that NGDOs – and communitarians like Etzioni (1998), Korten (1987) and Friedmann (1992) – like to enunciate in their mission statements such broad objectives of empowerment as the 'transformation of society', 'redistribution of power in society' and 'emancipation'. Obviously, such lofty objectives should be defined by the NGDO operationally, in terms of more concrete and measurable elements or dimensions (with their corresponding indicators) and in accordance with SMART criteria.

To conclude, critical to the whole exercise of the M&E of empowerment is to clarify exactly what the NGDO's thinking is about the empowerment of a particular target group. The crucial point is that greater effort has to go into our thinking from the very beginning, and in close dialogue with the target group. The general statements that one finds in NNGO documentation on the subject of empowerment are rarely helpful, either to the NGDOs or to its grassroot partners.

Frames of Reference of Empowerment

Focusing more directly on empowerment, as a general and even as a specific objective, what do NGDOs usually refer to when thinking and acting in this field? What ideological and theoretical frame of reference do they apply, explicitly or implicitly? Discussing these questions involves, once again, returning to the planning of PME systems, prior to undertaking any monitoring and evaluation. Consider Diagram 2, which sets out a rough typology of theories of development, according to how the problem of exclusion is analysed, the sort of response deemed necessary and the foci of empowerment being applied.

Diagram 2 brings out the connection between general theories, on the one hand, and empowerment on the other. These general theories or paradigms are well known and hardly need much comment. They present different analyses of development and underdevelopment. In some, more than in others, a basis is laid down for empowerment as a crucial phenomenon appropriate for development and change. In most cases an empowerment strategy is seen as needed or desirable. There is no analytical basis for empowerment in a 'conservative' modernisation theory, which stresses individual rather than structural or systemic causes of (under)development. Such theories emphasise individual progress, driven by economic motives. In an interactionist, Weberian, Marxian or feminist framework, the empowerment of the excluded is an indispensable vehicle for their advancement.

We have tried to work out the overall linkages between the broad theories of society and development, and what NGDOs tend to articulate in their institutional mission statements. Clearly, there are many NGDOs that do not subscribe to a theoretical analysis of (under)development. Many relief and service-oriented NGDOs stay aloof from such an approach. Together with NGDO observers such as Clarke (1991), Fowler (1997) and Biekart (1999) we may regret such a limitation, in as much as NGDOs have often made considerable impact in the political field.

We should note, however, that sometimes we do find *in a project-related framework* a reference to the need for organising and 'empowering' the beneficiaries. In a moderate and *instrumental version*, the organised participation of beneficiaries in the PME system of the project cycle is recommended for well-known reasons of efficiency and sustainability, namely, better fit between demand and supply; more willingness to contribute labour and payment to implementation; and support for the operation and maintenance of project results. In a more *value-based version*, such active participation of project beneficiaries is considered a 'democratic right' of people whose resources and future are at stake. The latter version is often (and not surprisingly) associated with higher levels of participation than appear in the first, 'instrumental' version.

Another point relates to the role of empowerment in the access of the poor and excluded to both the *market and state*. In a neo-liberal framework – similar to the modernisation theory – the responsibility for service provision and Income and Employment Generation Activities (IEGA) is to a large extent diverted to the poor themselves, as well as to the NGDOs supporting them. In practice the poor are expected to become increasingly organised in groups and associations to intervene in the market-place *directly* as **consumers, workers and producers**. But they can, and do, also intervene in the market *indirectly*, via the state, acting as **citizens**, to claim their right to participate. In all cases they become organised and 'empowered' in a legitimate manner. Organised private initiative is used by the excluded to access both market and state, and to help redress inequities by 'levelling the field', at least to some extent.

But let us go back to a more general level. It is clear that the general theories referred to in Diagram 2 vary in the kind of broad goals they envisage and in the *short- and long-term objectives of empowerment that* they seek. Whereas more radical theories tend to give priority to a redistribution of power at higher (regional and national) levels – a view held by NGDOs in Brazil and Bangladesh – a reformist approach seeks more limited but nevertheless real changes, for example, in income, access to services, voting power and policy formulation. Moreover, whereas a Marxian analysis will emphasise the central role of class-empowerment, an interactionist approach will also stress the importance of *religious, ethnic and other bases of identity, as well as the perceived legitimacy of state authority, traditional elites and citizenship*. NGDOs are often unavoidably influenced by such general theories. In practice, however, things are more complicated. NGDO empowerment scenarios have to make choices and select their objectives and entry points. They are then faced with complex and multiple affiliations, often more complex than those envisaged by the theories which influenced them. Yet they must find ways to deal with such intervening variables when it comes to raising consciousness and building up organisations. Their capacity to problematise and manage an empowerment strategy in a complex setting will manifest itself in the way they justify the ensemble of intervention methods and strategies applied.

All that has been discussed so far will reveal itself immediately when one looks at the planning of empowerment and at its later stage evaluation. An NGDO's frame of reference will manifest itself in the sort of specific and general objectives that it has identified and in the justification thereof. Also in the kinds of indicators it uses in order to see whether these objectives are being achieved, and the manner in which such M&E information is gathered. This could be done in a participatory fashion with a team more or less mixed in terms of social, technical and political experience and with terms of reference that involve contacting different kinds and levels of stakeholder. In short, in order to understand what a specific NGDO and its grassroots organisations are trying to do, it is important to examine whether there is (explicitly or implicitly) a frame of reference underlying their work, or whether there is just a mixture of loose conceptual and strategic elements. Such an examination would help to provide coherence and a sense of direction.

Empowerment as a Field of NGDO Intervention

NGDOs' underlying frame of reference – whether explicitly formulated or not – is also linked to the empowerment *strategy* that an NGDO tends to apply in its interventions. Strategy here refers to the general choice of routes, stages and steps to be taken, and to the more concrete components to be put in place, through inputs and programmes of activities in each of these stages. This is all with the purpose of progressively building up empowerment as a process, and to develop 'empowered' groups at the end of it. In Diagram 2 we can see that *strategy-wise* the general theories vary a great deal, as for example, in their preference of *where to begin*. Though all stress the need for grassroots mobilisation and organisation of the excluded, 'vanguard' and 'populist' strategies reserve a crucial role for guiding elites. Feminists, by contrast, tend to underline the crucial importance of a process of joint critical self-reflection at the grassroots level, and on the meaning and implications of the existential condition of being a woman, as a point of departure for subsequent steps.

Another strategic option of an NGDO is whether to apply an *access strategy* or a *parallel strategy*. The former is based on empowerment of the poor so that they learn to claim access to legitimate entitlements, such as land, forests and targeted government programmes. This strategy is often applied in India. It implies linking organised or empowered excluded groups to public and/or private sources of benefits. A parallel strategy tends to be less empowerment-oriented, though it may also stress empowerment to some extent. The lesser variant consists of an NGDO developing its own broad-based service programs focused on its target groups, as often practised in Bangladesh. Such parallel schemes of NGDOs may, however, eventually be mainstreamed and transferred to the government. A more empowerment-oriented version seeks to democratise society and the economy, including a system of service provision under the control of the grassroots themselves (people's banks, marketing cooperatives and community schools). Indeed, this strategy can be considered even more empowerment-based than an access strategy which, after all, tends to create dependency on the state.

Most empowerment strategies share certain components or *stepping stones* (see Diagram 3). Practically, we always find ingredients like raising *awareness* or *consciousness*, the development of dynamic and accountable leadership, the need for an *ideology* or a platform of 'legitimate' claims, as well as the necessity for higher-level *apex organisation* and *allies*. Indeed these components, as we will see below in further detail, represent recurrent elements in the empowerment-scenario of many NGDOs.

Factors Influencing the Choice and Shape of Interventions

Diagram 3 provides a general frame of reference for the analysis of an NGDO's empowerment strategy. It makes clear that the connection between an NGDO and empowerment is not simple and straightforward, but is mediated by a set of intermediate 'intervening' variables, ranging from broad contextual to more proximate ones. First comes the sort of *problem analysis* made by an NGDO, referring back to the sort of overall theories set out in Diagram 2, and influencing an NGDO's response, as laid down in its mission statement. Then comes the *contextual setting*: the baseline situation of the excluded group or sector involved as the subject of the empowerment strategy. Next follows the general position of the NGDO sector in the society concerned, especially its legitimacy and space for action in the field of empowering the excluded. Such contextual conditions vary notably from country to country and obviously define parameters within which the NGDOs act. Next, we have *the NGDO's own resources and limitations* in the field of empowerment. Relevant here are its human resource base and experience. This includes the organisation's connections to relevant public and private power elites at micro- and macro-levels, and the geographical scope of its (direct and indirect) outreach. This whole configuration of variables will have a marked influence on the choices and shape of an NGDO's intervention strategy in the field of empowerment. For example, using the typology mentioned earlier, these variables help explain why Indian and Bangladeshi NGDOs are often markedly different. The former tend to rely on an 'access' strategy, whereas many of the latter prefer a 'parallel' strategy. The Indian State has from the 1950s onwards been developing and implementing a wide range of poverty alleviation programmes, whereas the Bangladesh regimes have been far more limited in this respect. They also help account for the tendency of more conservative NGDOs engaged in service provision who do not apply an empowerment strategy, while more progressive and especially radical NGDOs, by contrast, often attribute a pivotal role to it.

NGDO Intervention in the Field of Empowerment

In Diagram 3 we can see that an NGDO's *own intervention strategy* consists of the kinds of elements or stepping stones which many NGDOs share. But as indicated in the accompanying monitoring column, some of these elements may or may not be present in any given strategy and if present, the expected outcomes in each case may not have been forthcoming. Moreover, the sequence of steps depicted may not be neatly followed. As we saw, Freirean and feminist NGDOs may prefer to start working on awareness and consciousness-raising before building up organisations. Marxian-oriented NGDOs may want to start with the latter and build consciousness through organised collective action. Likewise, quite a few NGDOs have avoided government agencies; working with grassroots groups in isolation, they have indeed, fostered an aggressive posture towards public authority. Nowadays this is changing. Many NGDOs promote grassroots organisations with solid internal capacity for participatory planning, monitoring and evaluation, and an effective external dimension for bargaining with public and private agencies. Such options are obviously also related to whether the NGDO is applying a parallel or an access strategy.

Finally, we draw special attention to what we can call the 'institutionalisation of the results of empowerment' in the fields of (i) official registration and administration, (ii) planning and procedural inclusion (iii) funding eligibility for public finance. In research carried out at Habitat, we observed a notable gap between the 'bottom-up' work of public agencies and NGDOs on the one hand, and 'top-down' reforms like decentralisation and local government on the other (Wils and Helmsing 1998). Sometimes, as in the case of populist mayors in cities such as Quito and Lima, participatory planning gave sectors traditionally excluded the ability to influence the local governance processes for the first time. But in many cases where government is decentralised, no legal or institutional provisions were made for a more systematic and sustained inclusion of the excluded. For example, in many cities CBOs of slum-dwellers are not officially recognised or given a place in administrative or planning platforms and procedures. Special intervention programmes are needed here to effectively promote such institutionalisation, such as joint work between grassroots associations with lawyers, NGDOs and politicians to develop proposals for policies and actions in the area of municipal legislation.

Monitoring NGDO Interventions and Evaluating their Effectiveness

On the right side of the intervention bloc in Table 5 we have added a monitoring column, as well as sets of evaluation indicators corresponding to the various components and steps of an empowerment strategy. **Monitoring** refers to:

(i) the extent to which the inputs and outcomes of interventions are being generated as envisaged;

(ii) the identification of factors which help explain the discrepancies (if any) between foreseen and actual inputs and outcomes; and

(iii) the steps to be taken to adjust the programming for the next period.

In this sense, monitoring refers to the lower half of the log frame, under control of the intervening NGDO. It basically serves to see whether the presumed logic works of the log frame works in this bottom half, for example, whether the inputs do lead to the outcomes as intended. As we know, often they do not, or not to the extent we would have liked them to, owing to such factors as shortage of experienced manpower or a lack of interested participants in the community. At other times, however, outcomes exceed expectations.

In principle, the comparison between envisaged and actual outcomes – together with the effort to account for discrepancies – form the most valuable part of the project-learning process. They are also indispensable requisites for flexible intervention management. Even such a simple tool as monitoring the percentage of anticipated inputs and outputs achieved is helpful. For example, an NGDO checks whether the planned number of consciousness-raising courses was given, the teaching materials on entitlements and human rights were being produced, meetings with local officials were carried out, and so on. Suppose notable discrepancies were found; for example, not enough consciousness-raising courses. To what is this due? Lack of interested social promoters, lack of course leaders, no collaboration of schoolteachers in making space available? Such an analysis will help show what sort of problem exists: possibly the wrong approach, maybe the wrong pedagogical method? NGDOs are often better at enumerating their inputs and outputs than at indicating whether these were in accordance with earlier targets, let alone explaining why this happened. Nonetheless, one can already see a visible improvement in NGDOs, once they have managed to rise beyond *mere description* and begin *analysing* their work at this behavioural level.

When it comes to **evaluating effectiveness**, we can examine to what extent all these interventions have really helped to achieve the specific changes that the NGDO and its stakeholders had set out to achieve. In other words, evaluating effectiveness seeks to assess whether the presumed logic of the project works in the next stage of the log frame. This phase links the lower half of concrete interventions to the higher and more abstract half of the objectives. Note that, as in the case of monitoring, evaluation also compares anticipated with actual effects and tries to account for discrepancies between these two. Here again, much can be learned. The evaluation should consider the effectiveness of the separate steps as well as their interrelation and combined effects. The analysis may show that the assumed logic was faulty (for example, in relation to the expected response of the excluded or of antagonistic power groups). Other factors may have intervened, or steps been overlooked. The NGDO and its grassroots groups will learn much about the correctness of their strategy and its viability in the context in which they find themselves.

It is assumed – as indicated in the effectiveness indicators under the evaluation column of Diagram 3 – that an NGDO does not just wish to promote grassroots organisations and leaders for their own sake. It is assumed that such organisations, in turn, will lend the excluded a dynamic and autonomous *organisational base* of their own, which is recognised and accountable. Likewise, the anticipated effects of inputs and activities in the area of consciousness-raising, especially when combined with the effects of organisation, presumably consist of actively voicing claims to authorities, based upon entitlements and human rights. There should also be protest against violations of such rights, leading to a decreasing incidence. All efforts of an NGDO to help increase the *capacity* of the excluded will hopefully lead to the autonomous formulation of their own sets of demands and priorities, laid down in their own plan of action. The NGDO should also have helped to implement such plans, with the active contribution of the excluded in the operation and maintenance of the results.

Apex-organisation building is meant to help networking and establishing alliances to connect vertically with powerful public and private agencies. It is also a vehicle for bargaining and lobbying for the interests of excluded groups at higher levels. Actions in this field are meant to *link the micro- to meso- and macro-levels*. Hopefully these actions will lead to the existence of second and third level associations; sets of networks and allies, negotiations with power holders; and lobbying with relevant public bodies. Note that the PME capacity plays a crucial role in this connection: it helps provide the first as well as apex organisations of the excluded with a strategic instrument to take and maintain the initiative in claim-making, bargaining and lobbying. Without such platforms and agendas of their own, people are easily manipulated by those who offer them only limited benefits. Such PME capacity (should) include the drafting of proposals which are viable, technically sustained and which can be defended at higher levels and before a wider audience.

The last step or component – *the institutionalisation of results* – deserves more special attention. NGDOs are too often satisfied when they are achieving effects, even at the meso- and macro-level, in terms of certain policies and programmes. The sustainability of such results, however, depends very much on their institutionalisation in terms of special legally-based rights, procedures and chartered establishments relating to the excluded. Empowerment of the excluded should lead to their formal and effective inclusion in a democratised governance system, not owing to the goodwill of a particular progressive mayor or national regime, but anchored in law and official procedure. Evaluating the effectiveness of an empowerment strategy should, therefore, in my view, explicitly extend to this component or step. Provided, of course, that the NGDO included such an objective in its programmes of active intervention in the first place!

Empowerment Strategy and Impact Evaluation

Empowerment is seen as the active participation of the excluded in decision-making, that is, the general objective of the strategy and related interventions undertaken jointly by an NGDO and other organisations representing the excluded. Let us suppose that the specific objectives of empowerment were largely being achieved. The excluded would then dispose of dynamic, autonomous organisations associated in an apex association. They would be strengthened through a network of allies, and a platform of demands and proposals of their own and be enriched through their new bargaining and lobbying capacity. Would such achievements then lead to the sort of impact that is being sought? Of course, during the problematisation stage the where and what of such important decision-making must have been defined from the start to formulate impact indicators. Does it refer to the community, neighbourhood, city or national levels, or even to interpersonal relationships? And insofar as the 'what of decision-making' is concerned, indicators should refer to real changes, in terms of an authentic and effective inclusion of the excluded. For example, to a capacity for autonomous organisation and action as related to decision-making; to joint responsibility for budgets; a plan for the usage of assets; and to an explicit recognition in law by third parties.

Another problem is to keep empowerment as an objective independent from what we called the *institutionalisation* of its results. Indeed, one might consider the effective institutionalisation (legal and *de facto*) of participation of the excluded in decision-making as an impact indicator of an empowerment strategy. But this must then be laid down in these terms in the original problematisation. In this case some redefinition would also be needed, of what the specific objectives would be of an intervention meant to develop legislative and policy proposals for new procedures and platforms. The products or outcomes of such programmes would presumably lead to debate and public attention, which in turn would help generate institutionalised inclusion in decision-making.

NGDOs are like 'Alices in Wonderland'; they define their own world. But like Alice, in doing so they must retain sufficient transparency and coherence in the construction and flow of argument to lend themselves to correction and adjustment. Out of the ensemble of elements presented here, each NGDO forges its own tools in accordance with its own frame of reference and concrete situation. Hopefully, when held up against the light of the frame of reference developed here, the profile of particular NGDO empowerment strategies and interventions will become more visible. This includes both their stronger and weaker elements, their contextualisation and the need for further operational elaboration.

The Methodology and Organisation of a PME System

In the case of empowerment it would be quite recommendable to apply participatory methods both in problematising empowerment and in the formulation of the PME system. This is not just because it is the excluded themselves who should be the first and foremost subjects and agents of their own empowerment, but also because the whole exercise has an enormous learning potential for them. This could reveal the gains and the losses which could be made in situations marked by – sometimes serious – risk and uncertainty; the excluded move, after all, in a world of power and interests. The burden of responsibility for risk-taking, in the end, remains that of the excluded themselves. This is a moral point, but there is also a pragmatic argument. The sustainability of empowerment strategies and its results under conditions of vanguardism is limited. This is something experience has demonstrated time and again.

The crucial role of **participation** in planning, monitoring and evaluation is once more underlined. A participatory PME system is a basic vehicle of empowerment for the target group. It helps ensure mutual accountability between an NGDO and its grassroots counterpart; and acts as a sort of guarantee for sustainability of project results. It is interesting that when we researched processes of NGDOs promoting the self-reliance of rural-poor groups in India, a participatory PME system was found to play a very strategic role. More than anything else, it enhanced the empowerment of the target group *vis-à-vis* the NGDO, and rendered self-reliance a strategic objective of the population itself (Wils and Archarya 1997). This self-reliance also implies that the target group came to accept, in accordance with what had been agreed from the start, full responsibility for the operations and maintenance of the project.

Another point has to do with the periodisation and timing of the monitoring and evaluation of empowerment. In view of the tremendous variety of objectives, it is difficult to generalise each level and issue involved. It seems hardly realistic, however, to expect that the empowerment of women, outcastes or children, will be easy. It is absolutely necessary to break down a long-term process into manageable proportions or stages. There will be much need for continuous shifts and adjustments, informed by evidence from the (participatory) monitoring and evaluation system. Moreover, monitoring and evaluation may have to be combined, possibly more than in other fields of action. Although certain programmes do lend themselves well to regular monitoring – such as leadership and cadre training – other kinds of activities do less so. This applies, for example, to building-up an apex organisation, helping to establish alliances, or the promotion of a bargaining and lobbying capacity. These are complex and difficult challenges, demanding flexibility and skill for understanding politics and tactics, which are not simple to acquire. Nonetheless, such complexity gives no license for activism or *ad hoc*-ism, and it remains necessary to retain a grip on the complicates lines of activity. Evaluations may well have to be carried out more frequently to see whether interventions do or do not begin to generate the sort of effects and impact that is hoped for.

Final Comment

The last comments relate to the NDGOs' mission. NGDOs may, and do, have comparative advantages in the political field. That is where they have already had a noticeable impact, such as in human rights, gender, the environment and minorities. The empowerment of those most immediately affected has often been the most decisive factor in tipping the scales of decision-making in their favour. This argument enhances the relevance of investments made by NGDOs and those supporting them, such as INTRAC, in the field of empowerment. Hopefully our discussions can help NGDOs to clarify their ideas concerning what they want to achieve in their country, sector and locality. That is where evaluation should begin. Northern NGOs which aim to support Southern NGDOs face great problems, because they will need to bridge the gap between their own highly generic institutional objectives and the concrete reality of their partners. Region, sector and group-specific frames of reference could help bridge that gap. Indeed, these would help facilitate and accelerate the learning process that is so badly needed. We already know more about service delivery, but less about income and employment generation. We know even less, however, about the much-needed strategies and processes of empowerment and related civil society building. Let us face the challenge of these facts.

Diagram 2: **Theories and Paradigms in Relation to Development, and to the Response Needed** (including whether empowerment is needed (+/-) and if so, with what focus).

Theory/ Paradigm	Analysis development (causes obstacle/push)	Response needed	[- - - - - - - - - - - - - - In mission statement of NGDOs - - - - - - - - - - - - - - -] Focus of empowerment (also +/-)
Modernisation	Values/motivation x Use of opportunities	Change value/motivation Create opportunities (e.g. credit) Training skills	- Often no emphasis on empowerment - (-) Assistance/ relief - (-) Services without organisation beneficiaries - (+) With organisation (for efficiency and sustainability) - (+) With organisation (for participation and democracy) - (-) IEGA without organised access (as workers, consumers or producers) - (+) With organised intervention state/market
Interactionist	Motives and opportunities Stratification of class, status; power Struggle interest/ideas Legitimacy versus protest	Combination of motivation and opportunity Organised social movement Charismatic leadership	- (-) IEGA without organised access (as workers, consumers, producers) - (+) IEGA with organised intervention state/market - (-) Training/education without organised (individual recipients) - (+) Organised struggle as workers, consumers or producers - (+) Organised struggle for citizenship, rights, claims - (+) Organised struggle for new policies
Marxian	Class exploitation/oppression under capitalism and a bourgeoisie state	Class-consciousness Leaders, vanguard and allies	- (+) Class in & by itself]for redistribution ownership and power - (+) Organised class struggle] & for new class/state relationships
Gramsci/ Freire	Ideological hegemony	Liberation from hegemony	- (+) Organisation and counter ideology - (+) Pedagogy of the oppressed and organisation
Feminism	Patriarchy under capitalism	Consciousness raising Redistribution of power	- (+) Struggle at all levels (interpersonal, HH, community etc.)

Diagram 3: **Elements of NGDOs' Empowerment Strategy and Related Monitoring and Evaluation Indicators**

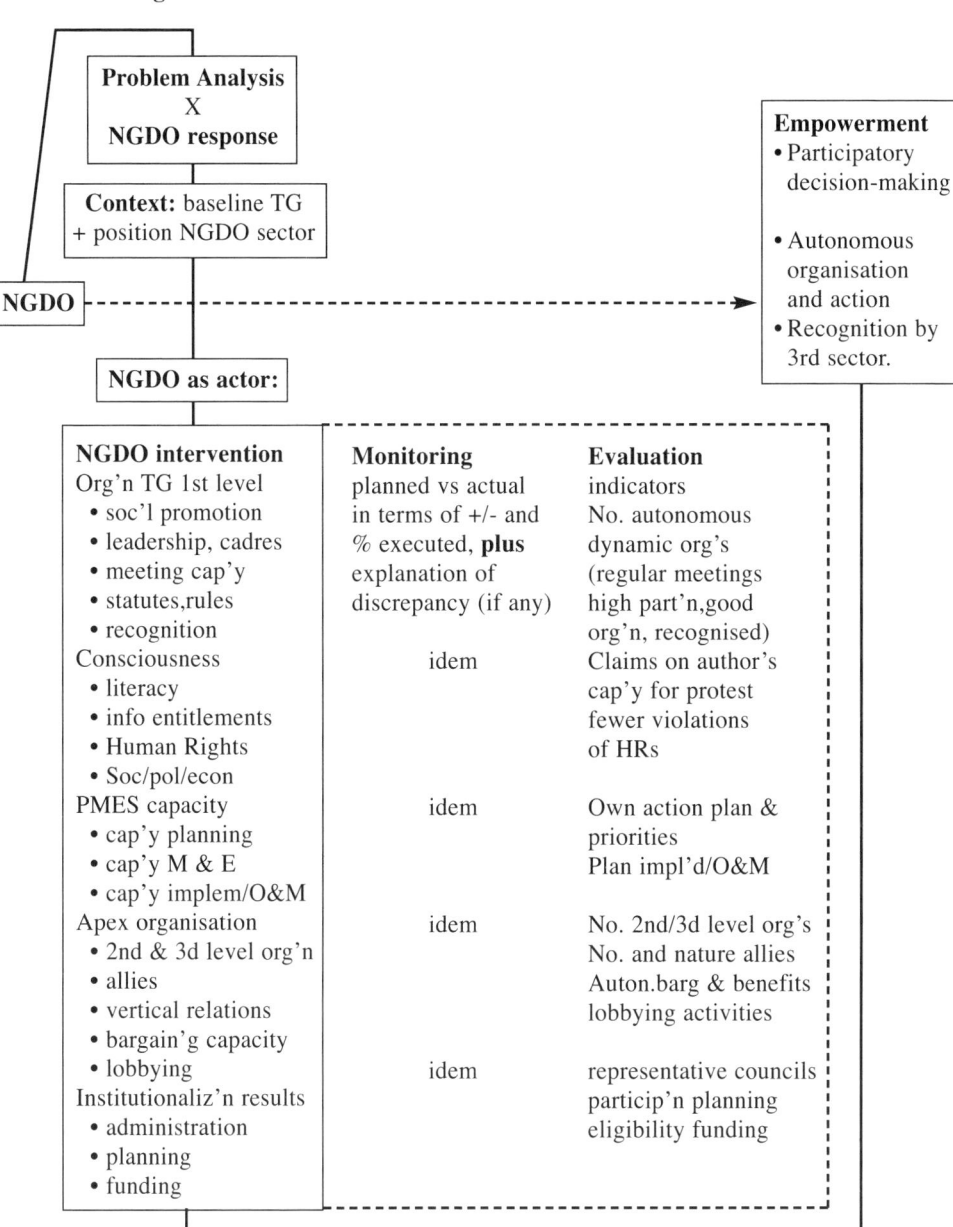

Problem Analysis X **NGDO response**			**Empowerment** • Participatory decision-making
Context: baseline TG + position NGDO sector			• Autonomous organisation and action • Recognition by 3rd sector.
NGDO as actor:			
NGDO intervention Org'n TG 1st level • soc'l promotion • leadership, cadres • meeting cap'y • statutes, rules • recognition	**Monitoring** planned vs actual in terms of +/- and % executed, **plus** explanation of discrepancy (if any)	**Evaluation** indicators No. autonomous dynamic org's (regular meetings high part'n, good org'n, recognised)	
Consciousness • literacy • info entitlements • Human Rights • Soc/pol/econ	idem	Claims on author's cap'y for protest fewer violations of HRs	
PMES capacity • cap'y planning • cap'y M & E • cap'y implem/O&M	idem	Own action plan & priorities Plan impl'd/O&M	
Apex organisation • 2nd & 3d level org'n • allies • vertical relations • bargain'g capacity • lobbying	idem	No. 2nd/3d level org's No. and nature allies Auton.barg & benefits lobbying activities	
Institutionaliz'n results • administration • planning • funding	idem	representative councils particip'n planning eligibility funding	

NGDO →

CHAPTER 3
Institutional Approaches to Evaluating Empowerment

3.1 SIDA: Sweden
Ylva Lindstrom

SIDA is a Swedish government development cooperation agency, providing in total approximately eight billion Swedish Kronor, out of which up to 900 million kroner is set aside for support through Swedish NGOs. In a letter of appropriation decided upon yearly by the government, it was stated that these funds should be used to promote the development of a vibrant and democratic civil society and to strengthen local partners through capacity-building.

What is the Importance of Empowerment as an Objective of Development and What Steps are Being Taken to Institutionalise its Understanding?
Our interpretation of the term empowerment in relation to NGO programmes is linked to the issues of **democracy** and **participation**, focusing on organisational development and capacity-building. We believe that popular movements, associations, societies and organisations are of a fundamental importance in developing countries. They are important as arenas for democracy as well as alternative service providers to the state. SIDA believes that NGOs are important agents in social and political interaction and development. NGOs can serve as vehicles for mobilisation and collective action and thus counterbalance other forces in the state or the market.

The funds set aside for the NGO-programme are allocated to 13 large Swedish development NGOs, of which half are umbrella organisations representing smaller Swedish NGOs. In total, close to 300 Swedish organisations receive SIDA funding for their international development cooperation. The organisations are active in more than 100 countries, with the number of projects amounting to approximately

2000. SIDA has issued various guidelines for these 13 NGOs. For example, it has guidelines on how a local organisation should be structured in order to be able to receive support, how monitoring and evaluation should be carried out and on reporting methods. The guiding **principle** is to **support** and **develop** the **knowledge, understanding and skills** of the partner organisation to enable it to assume ownership and carry forward the development. This activity should be the result of a local initiative and supplement the knowledge and resources that exist locally, and both men and women should be active in describing the problems and formulating the goals. For example, SIDA funded organisations' work is to a large extent focused on strengthening the capacity of **women** to increase their self-reliance and the right to determine choices in their life, through the ability to gain control.

What Steps have Been Taken to Try and Build the Evaluation of Empowerment into SIDA's Existing M&E Systems?

As a donor, SIDA does not monitor and evaluate the projects and programmes it supports. The responsibility of carrying out evaluations lies with the individual organisation. The responsibility of SIDA is to ensure than the NGOs have appropriate systems and methods for carrying out these evaluations. However, SIDA is willing to meet the request of an organisation by making resources available should an NGO want to develop its monitoring and evaluation systems. For the purpose of safeguarding the quality of the organisation's work in this respect, SIDA uses two instruments to check the quality of the M&E systems within its partners. Firstly, SIDA uses capacity evaluations, which cover most aspects of an organisation's external and internal functions. Secondly, it checks the quality of M&E systems through audits, focusing on the financial functions and control as well as formal and informal decision-making and control. The studies that we have made so far show that most organisations have a basic monitoring system but that they lack a proper system for evaluations. Evaluations are of course done, but on an *ad hoc* basis, and usually upon completion of the project, and not regarded as part of the monitoring process of a programme.

Other steps include SIDA staff making field visits and attending seminars arranged by the organisations, to learn how they deal with the concept of monitoring empowerment. A guide on organisational evaluation and development has also been published on behalf of SIDA, in cooperation with representatives of Swedish NGOs. The purpose of this is to introduce ways to work with organisational analysis and organisational development. To support the organisations in their work, SIDA also arranges seminars with external consultants like INTRAC around these key issues.

> External Consultants: SIDA has initiated the use of external consultants on evaluation together with several Swedish NGO framework organisations. The aim is to find ways to measure impact in terms of qualitative change of support to capacity-building on an aggregated level. The strategy is to develop a system that can both satisfy SIDA's need to report back to Parliament and the public on results, and the organisations' own defined need to be able to measure results. The work has only recently started, and is expected to be carried out during 2001 and 2002.
>
> To start the process, SIDA arranged a seminar to examine a model on how to measure and report on development progress, based on an interrelationship between goal-setting, accountability (demonstrating and justifying actual performance to those stakeholders who have legitimate claim on the organisation), effectiveness and assessing performance. The development performance is understood as achieving changes defined by those whose lives and circumstances should improve because of NGO initiatives. These changes, which were negotiated between Swedish NGOs, partners and communities, are defined and presented on a scale with negotiated indicators and measures that are useful for all partners.
>
> Earlier this year Sida also invited a representative from Diakonia (one of the major Swedish organisations receiving support from SIDA), who has compiled a handbook on how to measure and evaluate results and effects of interventions aimed at strengthening democracy. They suggest that this be done by measuring democratic structures and democratic culture according to a number of indicators and questions related to these indicators.

What are Some of the Methodological Problems in the M&E of Empowerment?

In-built systems for evaluation and monitoring are mainly focused on evaluating a project after its conclusion. The evaluation is related only to outputs, and not to results – which of course are also more complex to measure, especially on an aggregated level. With regard to the project on measuring development progress, it is obvious that SIDA will have a major methodological problem if its intention is to monitor and evaluate the impact of 300 partnerships, and even more so if its intention is to monitor the impact of a few thousand contributors. The aim of the project is to ascertain if there are any possibilities of finding common indicators regarding capacity-building and organisational development, the common denominator of all the organisations with completely different aims, which can be aggregated. This is a very complex task, and we are well aware of the fact that if we are successful in this task, the system will not be a very precise one.

3.2 Monitoring Empowerment within ActionAid: A Partial View
Rosalind David and Charles Owusu

When the mighty sun sets, the stars can shine.

Empowerment is one of the more frequently used words in the development lexicon. International NGOs (INGOs) have long sought to 'empower' women, men, boys and girls to gain more control over their environment, their lives, their political arena and ultimately their own development. Project proposals have for years detailed how development interventions will 'empower' individuals and community groups to achieve greater self-reliance and long-term security. Despite such proposals, however, INGO monitoring and evaluation systems generally fail to measure the benefits of the empowerment process. This section seeks to explore how ActionAid – one of the largest British INGOs – is currently developing its systems to facilitate greater understanding of the development process.

What do we mean by empowerment? In the development discourse it is frequently used to describe something bestowed by one person (usually the external agency) on another. However, as Rowlands eloquently argues, it is equally – and perhaps more frequently – a process that can be self-driven. Individuals and groups are deemed to be empowered when they are able to maximise the opportunities available to them without constraint (Rowlands 1997). In other words, empowered people have choices. As Shetty (1991: 9) writes: 'Individuals are empowered when they are able to critically analyse their own environment and enjoy a feeling of control and awareness'. As a concept, empowerment has many dimensions: political, social, cultural, personal and organisational. In development terms, an empowering process should enable people to have genuine control over their own development.

ActionAid and Empowerment: What We Say

For ActionAid, the empowerment process is a key element of development. ActionAid's strategy Fighting Poverty Together (1999–2003) aims to address the fundamental causes of powerlessness. Our first strategic objective is to 'strengthen the capacity and power of poor women, men, girls and boys at grassroots level to claim and achieve their basic rights...'. As an organisation we are committed to 'work closely with the poor and marginalised *people and with organisations to build their confidence and enable them to organise themselves to stand up for their rights*' (ActionAid 1999: 11). Changing the lot of poor and marginalised people means changing society, and supporting people at all levels – international, national and local – to exercise their rights.

Such an ambitious strategy has demanded significant organisational changes which attempt to bring internal processes and systems in line with organisational objectives, and crucially, processes which aim to 'foster an empowering organisational culture for staff members and teams' (ActionAid 1999). After all, how can we enable the empowerment of others if we are not empowered ourselves?

In this section we will examine ActionAid's present monitoring and evaluation (M&E) systems (and their deficiencies) and explore what we currently know about the empowerment process in isolated contexts. We will then discuss the changes afoot within the organisation and consider how these changes are expected to provide a framework for a more holistic understanding of the development process.

Current Monitoring Systems

ActionAid's Planning and Reporting System (APRS) has been the subject of much debate recently. This system has emphasised upward reporting, accountability to donors and sponsors and an over-reliance on ActionAid's own interpretation of change. Large, wordy reports have tended to describe project activities in great detail while giving less emphasis to the wider outcomes, impacts and changes perceived by the groups of people with whom ActionAid and ActionAid's partners work at different levels. One staff member in India has said of the system *'only when the mighty sun sets can the stars shine'*. The tyranny of written English, the perceived pressures of detailing variances between planned and actual activities, and the inordinate amount of time staff and partners spent writing reports has to some extent stifled creative understanding of development processes.

In spite of this dominant planning and reporting system, ActionAid does have some understanding of how its work is supporting an **empowering process** in different areas. Such examples are by their very nature locational and context (specific, and on the whole are confined to two dimensions: **personal** (or individual) empowerment and **group** empowerment.

Personal Empowerment

ActionAid's work in REFLECT is one of the areas in which we have some knowledge of the complex changes engendered by the development process. Reviews and evaluations using participatory processes have attempted to understand how participatory literacy programmes have led to a feeling of greater self-esteem and self-worth, particularly among women. REFLECT processes encourage participants to analyse their own circumstances in a structured manner with a view to generating solutions to the problems they face. These processes support the systematisation of people's own experience-based understanding and validate it through the development of literacy tools.

However, simplistic statements about the relationship between education for women and gender equality may fail to capture the complexity of the social processes involved. An analysis of women's empowerment in REFLECT circles in Uganda suggests that participation in REFLECT is only life-changing for women when it gives them skills or social assets which supports their own ongoing strategies for gaining status and respect within established hierarchies of gender and class. Usually these strategies are ones of accommodation and conformity rather than challenge and change; for example, semi-literate women in Uganda present themselves as more efficient and dutiful housewives than illiterate women. However, they may then use this culturally sanctioned claim in order to bid for a greater influence over household budgeting. This supports the finding, repeated in innumerable qualitative evaluations of adult literacy programmes, that gains in self-confidence are the key outcome reported by women themselves.

The reality poor women face outside literacy classes is a highly constrained and conflictual one and we understand relatively little about how well, or in what circumstances, women are actually able to translate confidence into real gains in their social or economic power and well-being. Nevertheless, the research in Bangladesh and Uganda has yielded certain findings. Two broad aspects of personal change have been identified by women in REFLECT circles in Uganda and Bangladesh. These are greater negotiating power and commercial skills, as explained below.

REFLECT Negotiating Power: Maps and tables used in REFLECT become tools for generating new interpretations of reality and for building consensus. When women use graphics to abstract and dissect local concerns, they are learning to take a distanced, impersonal and 'objective' perspective on these matters and to present them as shared problems demanding public action. In other words they are learning how to talk in the style of the male authorities: village elders, local officials, NGO staff and religious authorities. Being able to use written text and numerical records to objectify reality is one thing that helps women master the skills of 'public' discussion. Being able to call on external sources of authority (which could be anything from scientific knowledge of the causes of disease to quotations from the Bible) is seemingly just as important. Thus one REFLECT circle in Uganda proudly labelled themselves the wahanuli, the expert discussers! REFLECT gives women a 'safe' place to practice all of these skills and the egalitarian, learner-centred setting ensures that nearly all learners eventually come to participate fully in discussions within the circle.

For poor women, traditionally excluded from the public arenas where men make decisions and women are commonly dismissed as ignorant gossips, these skills have powerful implications. In Bangladesh some of the learners and female facilitators were approached to stand as candidates for local office after the Government introduced a quota of reserved seats for women at the local level. Others – including young, unmarried women without public influence – were recruited by candidates to canvass for them door-to-door. Workers on a tea estate in Sylhet not only found the confidence to confront supervisors over the long-standing practice of under-weighing their produce, but were also able to persuade the bosses to introduce a fairer system. The power of these skills and the degree of authority and credibility that these women have achieved is shown by the fact that some are now teaching their husbands what they learned in the circle – a complete reversal of gender roles.

In Uganda women found it revolutionary that for the first time they were able to speak freely in village and church meetings; many were elected to positions of responsibility on the parish councils. In their homes, some dared for the first time to open up discussions with their husbands on family planning or the sharing of domestic chores and the division of profits from the crops that the women grow.

Women Mastering the Market-Place: Aside from these 'political' skills in public decision-making, practical numeracy and accounting skills are of central importance in Bangladesh, a highly commercialised society in which practically everybody is a small trader or entrepreneur of some kind. The market-place is another 'public' sphere and most Bangladeshi women cannot engage in money transactions on their own account. As a result they are in the dark about how their male relatives are managing the income that they generate. For them numeracy is a question of power, and keeping written records of expenditure is part of a strategy for increasing their managerial control over resources. REFLECT responds to these concerns by developing numeracy skills out of an analysis of power relations. For example, making a 'workload calendar' which shows how much time women and men spend on different chores is not only an exercise in time-reckoning and calculation but also an analysis of gender roles. Also making an 'income and expenditure tree' often shows how much men are spending on alcohol and tobacco. As they develop analytical abilities, women are able to expand their financial influence and independence in a variety of subtle but significant ways. For example, some of the learners in one rural area started giving their husbands precise instructions about what to buy, what quantity and at what price, instead of simply sending them to buy fish or rice. Others have organised collectively to try and stop their husbands spending so much money on alcohol. Over the longer term many hope they will be able to persuade their husbands that education is of such value to women that their daughters should be able to continue school to secondary level or beyond.

A Note of Warning: While there are numerous examples of REFLECT processes engendering positive changes in people's lives, there is always a danger of overstating the case. Firstly, it should be noted that the changes, noted in REFLECT work, depend on women's ability to appropriate and exploit the prestige attached to being literate. Indeed, 'empowerment' of this kind has been observed in literacy programmes the world over and may also arise in a literacy course where learners do nothing but chant phonetic syllables for months on end. Secondly, it's a truism that development workers are prone to find empowerment only in development projects, and that other influences are regularly missing from their understanding. As an anthropologist working in Uganda on REFLECT points out, *'our blindness to the context often leads us to radically overestimate the potential of out own interventions'* (Fiedrich 2000).

Source: Extracts from Anne Jellema (1998), 'Women's Empowerment through REFLECT', in *Gender and Women's Rights*. London: ActionAid.

Group Empowerment

A second dimension in which ActionAid has some experience of analysing empowerment is its work in support of capacity-building for civil groups in several country programmes. As in the case of the REFLECT work above, our understanding of multidimensional change processes is partial and highly dependent on the ability of staff and partner organisations to use participatory methodologies in order to understand qualitative change processes. Participatory use of hypothetical indices, scales and other forms of diagrammatic representation have been important in achieving some understanding of fluid change processes. The following two examples from Nepal illustrate two aspects of group development:

- supporting internal capacity-building of a group, or change in the group's capacity, organisational skills and coherence;
- supporting a group's effectiveness in engaging in the external environment: increased effectiveness in taking forward issues affecting civil society.

Sindhupalchowk Tenancy Movement, Nepal: The issue of tenancy rights as a priority advocacy issue was first identified through a series of PRA exercises conducted in 1994 and repeated in 1997 with seven village development committees (VDC) of Sindhupalchowk in Nepal. The exercises revealed that of the 5232 households in the area (of which about 40% were tenants) only 5% had formal tenancy rights; the remaining 95% of tenants had no such rights and lacked any document or proof to claim such a right. The most productive land in the area is owned by a handful of landlords who have a large number of tenants working for them.

Source: Ramesh Khadka (1999), 'Claiming the Land: Grassroots Advocacy in Nepal', in *IA Exchanges*, London: ActionAid.

The Campaign: Raising Awareness of Legal Rights: In 1995, ActionAid Nepal supported two local community-based organisations to organise a legal awareness-raising workshop for a group of tenants from seven of the village development committees in Sindhupalchowk. Facilitated by lawyers from Chautara, the tenants were made aware of national legislation and rights relating to land and tenancy issues. At the end of this training programme the tenants formed a tenancy-awareness committee called Mohi Jagaran Samiti (MSJ). With ongoing support the committee was able to approach the District Land Reform Office (DLRO) to claim their tenancy rights.

Since then there have been numerous rallies, follow-up awareness-raising workshops and press conferences organised by the farmers. The campaign has generated wide media coverage in Nepal, drawing in many supporters, including some government ministers.

Since the campaign started 258 tenants have filed claims with the district court and more than 110 cases have already been decided in favour of the tenants, with the rest under consideration. This is a tremendous achievement for the tenants as they are now legally entitled to half of the land they have been cultivating. Tenants are now also aware that they should obtain proof of payments made to their landlord. Some landlords have volunteered to give land to tenants. However, others have put up strong resistance, with some landlords setting up their own committee to safeguard their interests.

Internal Capacity-Building: There were both positive and negative impacts from the campaign, which are listed below. The campaign did much to help build the capacity of civil groups to take action, and increased the space within which such groups can act in Nepal. The tenancy committee has remained very strong and committed throughout the campaign and has helped form other committees at various levels to fight their case as well as address other injustices that occur in their area. They are now confident in organising rallies, workshops and even press conferences in the capital city. They have also learned to approach and influence policy-makers. In the process they have acquired a good knowledge of legal rights and the procedures of legal discourse. More importantly, there is now awareness that solidarity can bring about change.

The campaign has increased people's awareness of the structural causes of inequality and poverty. Obtaining their legal right to the land they cultivate has created more assurance for their future livelihoods and food security than any previous technological assistance would have done.

As part of their campaign strategy, tenants enlisted the support of political leaders. Some local-level leaders helped them but those at central level paid very little attention. These leaders have, however, paid a price in recent elections, as

tenants were able to affect the results by mobilising voters.
Landlords routinely threatened their tenants during the campaign. They tried to break their solidarity by promising some returns, and in some cases were able to influence tenants to break away from the campaign. This created some friction among the tenants.

Effects on CSRC and ActionAid Nepal: This was a learning experience and a capacity-building experience in advocacy for both agencies. It made staff realise that advocacy is possible at the grassroots level and that policy can be changed in favour of the poorest.

It also provided a good example of how rights, when properly secured, can help alleviate poverty and provide security more effectively than technological interventions.

A Word of Warning: This instance, like all others, requires qualification. In this case, support to the CBOs helped increase knowledge, confidence and ultimately the groups' ability to gain tenancy rights for some farmers. It should be noted, however, that rights were only granted for men and not for women. As Kabeer points out in her paper on the impact of micro-credit on women in Bangladesh, the idea that empowerment *'can be reduced to any single aspect of process or outcome carries with it the danger of ignoring other significant and valued changes'*

Source: Kabeer (1998),'Money can't buy me love?' IDS.

Problems, Dilemmas, Omissions and Changes

The two case studies above illustrate how, in some areas of ActionAid's work, we have been able to capture a fragmented understanding of the changes induced by certain development interventions. In both examples, participatory processes were central to the facilitation and analysis of change. Indices, scales and other forms of diagrammatic representation were used in the analysis of benefits from the process.

These examples are, however, all too untypical. While ActionAid has been trying to develop more participatory, innovative processes to understand change (for example through the use of participatory video, oral histories, drama and other participatory tools) our internal reporting has, as explained above, been dominated by the static upward demands of the ActionAid Planning and Reporting System. The tyranny of upward reporting has diminished the time or space for creativity and innovation. Planning and reporting has in some areas taken months of 'front-line' staff time each year – staff who would otherwise be working directly with partners or community organisations. Internal incentive systems have been skewed so that reports have taken precedence over developing methodologies for understanding change. Indeed, participatory processes, which have managed to explore qualitative processes such as empowerment, are rarely explained in formal reports.

As a result, our overall understanding of empowerment (like that of most INGOs) is partial. Our understanding has been 'project' or activity focused. Our systems capture activities in detail rather than capturing the change processes of how (and if) the work of ActionAid and its partners is contributing to larger development processes. There are huge and extremely important areas of our work that we do not fully understand, for example:

- changes in cultural dimensions, and how these impact on women's roles and rights;
- access to and control over knowledge – though key to the empowerment process – is rarely captured in M&E systems;
- ability of people to have more control over their development choices and what this means in their lives;
- development of civil society and the changing role civil groups play in holding decision-makers accountable.

Clearly there is much work to do. As mentioned above, ActionAid is trying to bring systems in line with its new strategy, *'Fighting Poverty Together'*. One key task has been to rewrite the Planning and Reporting System which has now become ALPS (Accountability Learning and Planning System). Changes to this system have been dramatic, and when fully implemented should have significant implications for monitoring and evaluation, particularly the development of participatory M&E. The new system (currently only in draft form) emphasises downward accountability to the poor and marginalised people with whom we work. It reduces on reporting requirements for country programmes and emphasises annual processes of participatory reflection and review at all levels with stakeholder groups. It attempts to validate participatory processes by encouraging staff and partners to write up diagrams, matrixes and visual representations of the ideas expressed by women, men, boys and girls. The system also aims to promote creative ways of understanding change processes, for example through participatory video and oral history. In time such processes should open up the space for more creative and hopefully more honest assessment of change.

Changes to a system create trade-offs. One immediate difficulty that ActionAid will face is the need to produce additional formal reports for donors and sponsors. Some major institutional donors still, unfortunately, require reports against 'logical frameworks,' which inevitably constrains analysis and reinforces a 'project' perspective. As one Kenyan development worker pointed out some years ago, *'the*

important issues always seem to fall between the boxes'.
 In addition, institutional change inevitably takes a long time. ActionAid's revised ALPS requires fundamental changes in our approach. These changes will need to go hand in hand with the organisation 'fostering an empowering organisational culture for staff members and teams' (ActionAid Fighting Poverty Together 1999-2003:21). This is not something at which Northern NGOs have traditionally excelled. Though most agencies have used the rhetoric of participation for many years, institutional systems have rarely created space and support for staff to work in truly empowering ways. Ironically, while most Northern NGOs have written about empowerment in their development literature, most staff within them have suffered from centralist attitudes and disempowering restructuring processes and language from the head office. In addition, NGO staff have often imposed their own meanings and frameworks on clients by using culturally inappropriate forms of communication to discuss and explain complex social, economic and political issues. Change therefore cannot happen overnight; it will take years.

However, with the introduction of the new planning and reporting system, ActionAid staff should slowly begin to find that they have more time to engage, listen to and work with the concerns of poor and marginalised groups. Annual review processes should be guided not by reporting requirements but by a real desire to work with stakeholder groups to understand how and whether interventions are supporting complex development processes that contribute to people's ability to have more control over their lives. It might be a long time before we capture these vital processes in reports; the important thing, however, is that they are happening.

3.3 Empowerment and DFID
Colin Kirk

The Department for International Development (DFID) is a relatively new aid agency, set up in 1997. Its policies are outlined in the 1997 White Paper 'Eliminating World Poverty: A Challenge for the 21st Century'. In the paper, new approaches are outlined and new targets set for country and institutional strategies. DFID's aim is the elimination of poverty in poorer countries and, along with other bilateral donors, it has set a target of reducing this poverty by 50% by the year 2015. It is DFID's goal that the objectives shall be pursued through the promotion of **sustainable development**. In particular this will be done by:

- building development partnerships with poorer countries;
- working more closely with the private and voluntary sectors, and the research community;
- working with and influencing multilateral development organisations;

- working with other government departments to promote consistent policies affecting poorer countries; and
- using knowledge and resources within DFID effectively and efficiently.

DFID's specific objectives are:

- **Policies and actions which promote sustainable livelihoods.** In particular, DFID aims to contribute to sound policies and pro-poor economic growth; the development of efficient and well-regulated markets; access of poor people to land, resources and markets; good governance and the realisation of human rights; the prevention and resolution of conflicts and the removal of gender discrimination.

- **Better education, health and opportunities for poor people.** In particular, DFID aims to contribute to lower child and maternal mortality; basic health care for all, including reproductive services; effective universal primary education; literacy, access to information and life skills; safe drinking water and food security, and emergency and humanitarian needs.

- **Protection and better management of the natural and physical environment.** In particular, DFID shall aim to contribute to the sustainable management of physical and natural resources; efficient use of productive capacity, and protection of the global environment.

DFID's goal is to have explicit recognition of **empowerment** in long-term development partnerships with poor countries; good governance and the realisation of human rights; and the removal of gender discrimination. Empowerment is about human rights and a rights-based approach to development. Furthermore, DFID believes that:

> Given the necessary support, the poor can be the means as well as the beneficiaries of sustainable development. Where poor people have rights and choices, they are able to make good use of them.

The international development targets of DFID are designed to provide milestones against which progress towards the goal of poverty elimination can be measured. In general terms these are as follows.

Economic Well-being:

- A reduction by one-half in the proportion of people living in extreme poverty by 2015.

Human Development:

- Universal primary education in all countries by 2015.
- Demonstrated progress towards gender equality and the empowerment of women by eliminating gender disparity in primary and secondary education by 2005.
- A reduction by two-thirds in the mortality rates for infants and children under age 5 and a reduction by three-fourths in maternal mortality, all by 2015.
- Access through the primary health-care system to reproductive health services for all individuals of appropriate ages as soon as possible and no later than the year 2015.

Environmental Sustainability and Regeneration:

- The implementation of national strategies for sustainable development in all countries by 2005, so as to ensure that current trends in the loss of environmental resources are effectively reversed at both global and national levels by 2015.

The above broad objectives/indicators are essentially quantitative and measured on that basis. However, they also include objectives that are less quantifiable but that contain qualitative processes that demand different approaches to their assessment. These include democratic accountability, the protection of human rights and the rule of law. DFID is working to develop appropriate means to monitor such objectives. A strategic overview of DFID's approach can be seen in Diagram 4. This is based on the overview of DFID's policies and purposes as outlined in the White Paper and is based on the establishing of **targets** in an upward direction that leads to the establishing of overall aid policy. Accountability is also shown as an upward process from the programme and project base of aid through to the UK Treasury and Parliament. This overall framework is the basis for the determination of a range of institutional and country level strategies to ensure the effective implementation of DFID's development objectives.

Lift a Billion People by 2015 out of Poverty by Ensuring:

- Economic growth, equity and security.
- Better health for poor people.
- Poverty eradication and the empowerment of women.
- Human rights for poor people.

- Environmental sustainability and the elimination of poverty.
- Addressing the water crisis: healthier and more productive lives for poor people.
- Making government work for poor people.
- Education for all: the challenge of Universal Primary Education.

Country Strategies:

- Building partnerships with governments and people in poor countries.
- Working closely with other donors and development agencies.
- Ensuring consistency of policies.
- Measuring the effectiveness of our efforts, alongside others, against the IDTs.

Country Performance Reviews:

- Annual Portfolio Reviews.
- End of cycle Strategy Reviews.

Institutional Strategies:

- Work closely with multilateral department institutions.
- Strengthen their commitment to poverty elimination.
- Strengthen M&E systems for greater efficiency and effectiveness.

Institutional Portfolio Review:

- Annual Portfolio Reviews.
- End of cycle Strategy Reviews.

A key objective of DFID's aid policy is the defence and promotion of **human rights**. This objective is achieved through effective **participation** that enables people to claim their human rights through development that promotes all human rights for all people and encourages everyone to fulfil their duty to the community. It is also about **obligation** in strengthening state policies and institutions to ensure that obligations to protect and promote all human rights are fulfilled. In this objective the new frameworks and new tools being used include:

- Participatory Poverty Assessments.
- Participatory Human Rights Assessments (to be developed).
- Social policy checklists/matrices.
- Matrices for mapping country programmes.

Evaluating an Aid Recipient's Social Policy

A government's social policy should be assessed against our social development objectives of enhanced well-being and greater equality of opportunity and choice. Such an assessment would include the extent to which the aid recipient government is committed to the following **objectives**. As an aid agency DFID is prepared to provide assistance to help enhance national capacity to achieve one or several of these, depending on the particular circumstances. Assistance could be to government institutions and/or to organisations or groups outside government. The objectives relate to purposes and actions of governments and are not weighted. DFID will provide assistance to a government that:

- encourages self-activity by representative civil society institutions in shaping economic and social policy and provision;
- establishes enabling policies, such as appropriate legislative frameworks, to ensure a range of choice in agencies of provision with commitment to private as well as public sector capacity to satisfy needs;
- gives high relative priority in public expenditure to equitable and economically sustainable social sector provision;
- provides specific and targeted public interventions to meet and promote livelihood and other social needs of deprived and disadvantaged social groups, designed on the basis of consultation with the groups concerned;
- implements socially cohesive fiscal policies, consistent with economic efficiency;
- ensures that public entitlement does not discriminate on the basis of gender, religious or ethnic distinctions;
- promotes equal opportunity in access to employment and product markets and does not assume that citizens' public or domestic roles and responsibilities are determined by biological criteria such as sex, race, age or physical ability;
- provides for citizens' entitlement to be protected from public and domestic violence and ensures that individuals and groups are free from arbitrary authority, whether imposed by government or others;
- collects and disseminates data which allow for the public assessment of the status of social and economic policy objectives and the monitoring of changes over time.

Diagram 5 shows the two pillars of DFID's aid policy – Partnership and Ownership – as the basis for producing meaningful and sustainable results.

Empowerment (or a 'rights-based approach') is central to the emerging frameworks for international development. These frameworks aspire towards being holistic, long-term locally owned partnerships, focused on good governance and accountability for achievement of real world results. Therefore, arrangements for M&E need to move upstream from project-level to assess and address policies and strategies at international, national and sector levels. Convergence of statistical and participatory methods of qualitative and quantitative information is needed at all levels. Undoubtedly new M&E tools are needed and increased M&E capacity is needed at all levels: development agencies in government and in civil society. Upward accountability needs to be complemented by mutual accountability to partners and by direct public accountability to citizens. Empowerment lies at the heart of DFID strategy and its **evaluation** is a major challenge. The evaluation of empowerment is critical for several reasons:

- Evaluation for empowerment ensures meaningful accountability.
- Evaluation as empowerment should be done through participatory M&E methods.
- Empowerment for evaluation: through capacity-building and effective programme and project level collaboration.

At DFID we are now building into our M&E systems more appropriate means to capture and record qualitative processes such as empowerment and in this way we hope to be able to judge the impact of DFID's rights-based approach to development.

Comment

The above examples would appear to underline the current state of affairs in terms of evaluating empowerment. Essentially the M&E of empowerment must begin at the programme or project level. This is vividly illustrated by ActionAid's approach at that level. This NGO sees 'empowerment' as central to its work at the village or community level and so has begun to develop relevant approaches in conjunction with local stakeholders. The two bilateral agencies, however, are non-operational or work largely through 'larger structures' – that is, substantial sectoral programmes or other such operations – in which the opportunity to focus on the specific demands of monitoring a process of 'empowerment' is usually not available. Hence their approach is far more generalised and not built on specific field level operations. They represent the dilemma of most bilateral aid agencies – their inability, except by proxy through development agencies operating at community level, to effectively engage with complex issues such as how to monitor and evaluate a qualitative process. Yet perhaps theirs is a different role; that of supporting and promoting more operational development agencies to explore and develop such issues. The positive thing is that both Sida and DFID recognise the critical role of **power** in any development context and also the importance of understanding *how* powerless people might become 'empowered' as a result of an external intervention. The presentations of both bilateral agencies confirm that the 'power issue' has been recognised at this level – subject, of course, to interpretation – and that there is support at this level for development initiatives that place power at the centre of their approach. Bilaterals and NGOs agree on the critical issue of 'empowerment' but they work within different operational boundaries that permit them to actively promote an empowerment approach in their different ways.

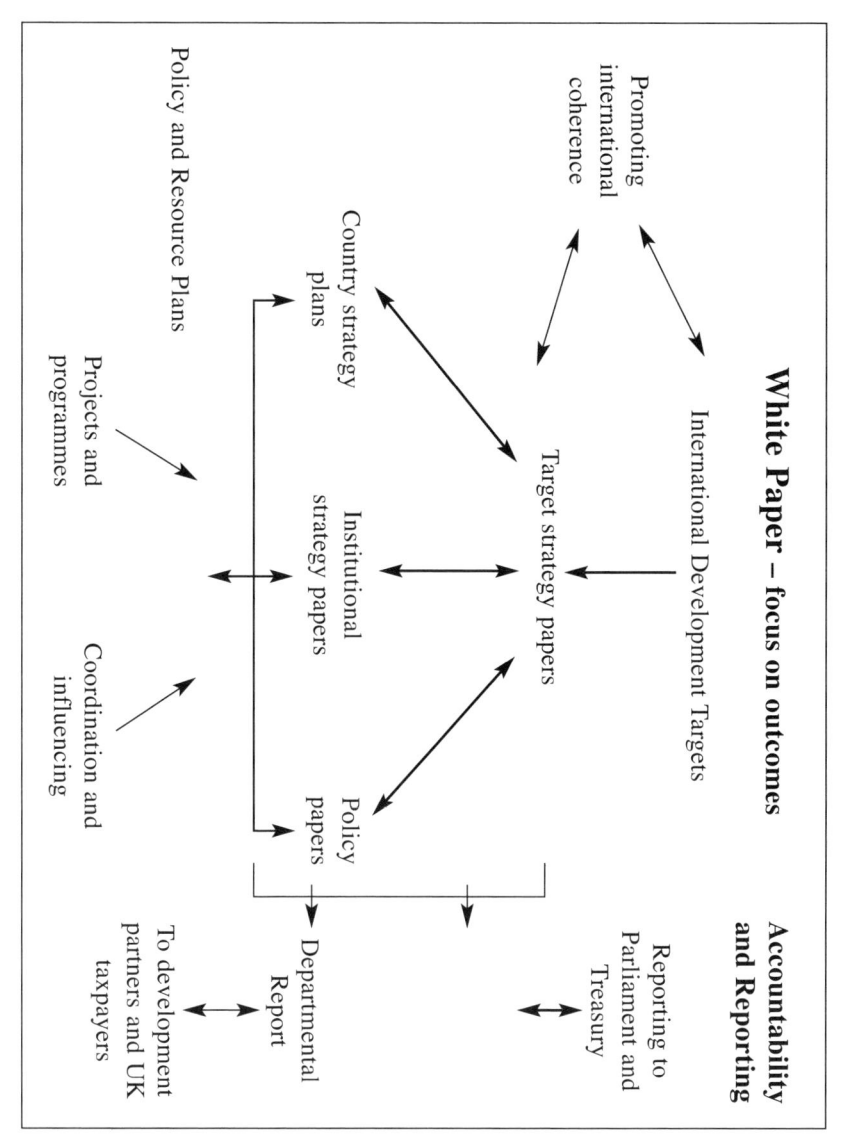

Chart 4: DFID's Strategic Overview

White Paper – focus on outcomes
- Promoting international coherence
- International Development Targets
- Country strategy plans
- Institutional strategy papers
- Target strategy papers
- Policy papers

Policy and Resource Plans
- Projects and programmes
- Coordination and influencing

Accountability and Reporting
- Reporting to Parliament and Treasury
- Departmental Report
- To development partners and UK taxpayers

93

Diagram 5: **The Two Pillars of DFID's Aid Policy**

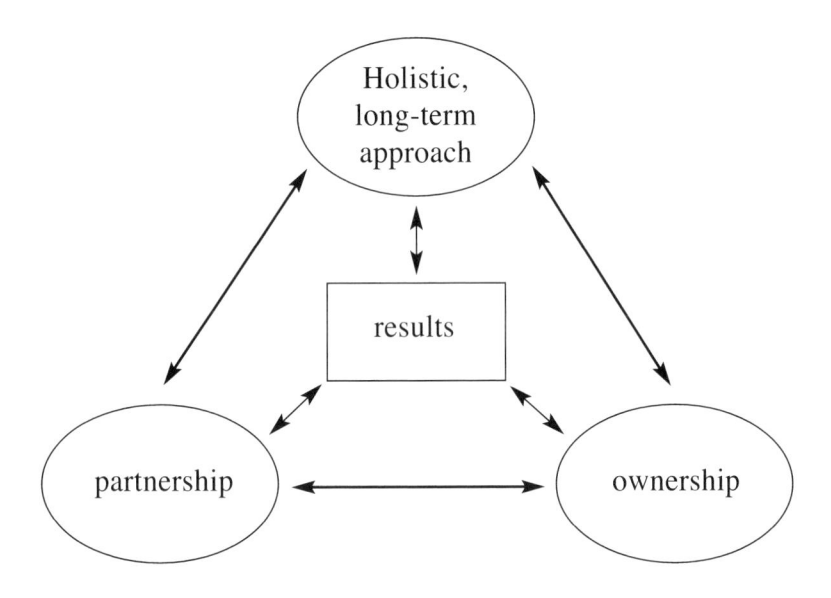

```
              Holistic,
              long-term
              approach

                 ↕
              results

    partnership  ←→  ownership
```

Source: Adapted from World Bank 1999 Annual Review on Development Effectiveness

CHAPTER 4
Regional Reviews of the Evaluation of Empowerment

An innovation of the Fourth International Workshop on the Evaluation of Social Development was the inclusion of four regional workshops within its overall preparatory process. These were convened in Bangladesh (Asian sub-Continent), Tanzania (sub-Saharan Africa), Nicaragua (Latin America) and Jordan (Middle East). Each of the four workshops followed a similar approach and content, and was based on a substantial **Resource Document** that INTRAC had prepared beforehand. Around 40 participants attended each of the four workshops. These participants came not only from the host country but also from other countries in the region, and expatriate staff of several Northern development agencies. The four workshops followed a similar pattern on inputs from the facilitators combined with group discussions that related the core concepts of the Resource Document – the Concept of Empowerment, the M&E of Empowerment and Methods and Instruments – to the regional context. While the concept of 'empowerment' was not new to most of the participants – always bearing in mind problems associated with its translation into other languages and interpretation in other cultures – for most it was the first time that they had explored the concept operationally and from the perspective of its evaluation. At the end of each of the workshops two of the participants were invited to attend the Fourth International Workshop and present the findings of their regional workshop, which we present below.

4.1 African Regional Workshop: Arusha, Tanzania
Grace Mukasa and Sering Falu Njie

The African regional workshop on the monitoring and evaluation of empowerment was held in Arusha, Tanzania, in February 2000. The workshop followed the programme structure outlined below:

- an analysis of the concept of empowerment;
- an examination of a framework for the monitoring and evaluation of empowerment;
- an examination of methods and techniques for the monitoring and evaluation of empowerment;
- a discussion of participants' experiences of the monitoring and evaluation of empowerment;
- gender and the monitoring and evaluation of empowerment;
- an introduction to case studies on structuring and designing an approach and system for the monitoring and evaluation of empowerment.

The programme centred around group work, together with more formal inputs on key themes presented by the facilitators. Participants were encouraged to bring with them their own experiences of the processes of empowerment and efforts to monitor its progress. As with the three other regional workshops, the objectives of the Arusha workshop were:

- to review the concept of empowerment and the issues related to its monitoring and evaluation;
- to examine and assess the current practice of empowerment and its monitoring and evaluation from an African context;
- to undertake a practical exercise in designing an approach to the monitoring and evaluation of empowerment.

Below is a summary of the main findings and discussions from Arusha. It follows the basic structure of the workshop: to examine the concept of empowerment, the issues concerning its implementation in Africa and a review of current practices in the region.

The Concept of Empowerment

Participants examined a range of definitions of the concept of empowerment within the context of planned social change. Empowerment can reveal itself as part of many development programmes, be they **rights-based, capacity-building or self-management**. In each case it is a progression from dependence, through independence to interdependence. They concluded that empowerment is a process of *'enabling people to take responsibilities for their own development and to be able to take charge of their lives in a sustainable way'*.

In the context of East Africa, participants stated that powerlessness has its roots in **political, community, religious, educational, cultural, social and economic hierarchies**. In this sense powerlessness was defined as an inability to voice opinions, take part in decision-making, access economic resources and information, identify and analyse problems, and to take responsibility for one's personal management. Powerless groups were defined as women, children and the disabled.

The key political, social and economic differences between the powerful and the powerless were said to be: the ability to influence politics and decision-making; the capacity to organise; an awareness of one's rights; access to resources; authority; security; personal confidence and skills.

Given this analysis, participants felt that in order to become powerful, individuals or groups must become involved in decision-making, more aware of power structures and increasingly skilled. The implications for development organisations is that they must become more sensitive and flexible *vis-a-vis* the dynamics of power. They must become more culturally specific and more informative towards their target groups, while being better able to clarify their roles. Several participants cautioned their colleagues regarding the viability of mainstreaming these aims. They expressed a concern that organisational sustainability is a major constraint for the work of empowerment, to which, in all cases, the issue of ownership over the empowerment process is critical.

Issues Surrounding the Implementation of Monitoring and Evaluation Systems for Empowerment in Africa

During the workshop the facilitators were keen to distinguish between **macro- and micro-factors** affecting the implementation of the monitoring and evaluation of empowerment. One break-out group decided that an understanding of the macro-context required an analysis of key institutions such as donors, governments and the international aid system. These actors can effect the monitoring and evaluation of empowerment through donor conditionality, legislation (laws that govern the operations of NGOs) and by setting global trends in the development agenda.

Participants noted that South–South dialogue is currently building up their understanding of the international context, whilst increased advocacy by Southern networks is helping to influence international systems. These initiatives include the civil society programmes of several African countries, which have enhanced the capacity of NGOs to engage with and influence governments and donors. However, participants also recognised that the capacity of NGOs to comprehend and influence macro-developments remains limited. NGOs require further capacity-building and a clearer common vision. Referring to the micro-context (the specific roles of development organisations and their projects at the local level), workshop attendees undertook an exercise to design an effective M&E system to monitor and assess the impact of empowerment processes.

From these discussions several key issues emerged which reflect the experiences of the participants. One attendee stated that since development workers themselves are powerful actors at the local level, there is a need for the practices of empowerment to be mainstreamed within local development organisations. The relationship between empowerment and organisational processes was later expanded upon by one participant, keen to explore the links between individual empowerment and organisational capacity-building. Other participants felt that development workers should be aware that empowerment is a continuously evolving process, while the complexities of implementing an empowerment agenda warrant a detailed understanding of the nature of empowerment and its indicators.

There was agreement amongst participants concerning the need for NGOs to strategise their relationship with powerful groups, who may affect the outcomes of their projects. Several participants felt that since power in a development context often centres around giver(receiver relationships – between weak recipients and powerful providers (dependency), or between weak providers and powerful extractors (exploitation) – NGOs should conduct a self-analysis of their own roles. One participant proceeded to say that NGOs are themselves part of an institutional hierarchy of power, linking international, national and local-level structures.

Key indicators of the existence of empowerment were then examined. Having identified these indicators, participants were asked what they thought would be the key steps to be taken in order to operationalise them. The participants decided that once a practical M&E system had been designed, data should be collected, stored, analysed and interpreted in conjunction with key stakeholders.

The role of the community in the M&E process was seen as helping to: develop the indicators of empowerment; design the M&E system; assess the effects of change; have ownership over the project; conduct self-monitoring and evaluation; and assist in data collection, analysis and storage. The key factors supporting and constraining the implementation of empowerment systems by development organisations in East Africa are shown in Table 6:

One group of participants also set out to examine issues around the implementation of M&E systems from a gender perspective. They concluded that obstacles to gender-sensitive M&E programmes in Africa have included: cultural barriers; the complexity of social dynamics; and competition amongst NGOs. To nurture a more gender-aware M&E system the group stated that NGOs must approach participation qualitatively, rather than as a numerical exercise. Members of the group were also keen for the gender composition of project teams to be more balanced.

The Practice of Monitoring and Evaluation for Empowerment: Methods, Techniques and Tools

Participants were later asked to assess a series of case studies – from Nicaragua, Egypt, Tanzania and Bangladesh – in which the M&E of empowerment processes had been applied. From these case studies the workshop attendees learned various macro- and micro-level lessons concerning the implications of attempting to implement M&E of empowerment systems in particular contexts. Much of this learning was thought to be location-specific, but in each case participants concluded that the

Table 6: **Factors Supporting and Constraining the Implementation of Systems to Monitor and Evaluate Empowerment**

Supporting Factors	Constraining Factors
Equal participation	Lack of donor support
Knowledge of community	Outsider imposition of M & E system and design
Skilled staff	Unfavourable political, social and economic environment
Shared aims and understanding	Untrained staff
Design and use of appropriate systems	Inadequate follow up and a lack of time
Appropriate time frame	The perception of powerful stakeholders that empowerment threatens their position
Donor support	Inability to identify key indicators and reliance on quantitative techniques
Adequate financial resources and equipment	Inadequate learning resources on the topic of the M and E of empowerment
Flexible programming	

economic situation of an area, the definition of empowerment used, and the politics of government decision-making were critical factors. More specifically, the participants felt that to be successful, the M&E of empowerment projects must gather accurate and precise information, pay attention to local community structures and ensure the appropriate level of participation for each stakeholder. In order to achieve these goals, participants stated that local organisational capacities must be built. Moreover, at a meso- institutional level, NGOs activities needed to be better co-ordinated.

Following the more general discussions above, the latter section of the workshop focused in detail on specific methods and tools appropriate to the M&E of empowerment. The participants reviewed a range of systems, methods and techniques which, in their experience, have been usefully applied.

Participatory Rural Communications Appraisal (PRCA) and PRA: This method focuses on communications and feedback and aims to promote two-way learning processes. The problems associated with this method include the length of time needed to conduct the exercise, and ethical concerns regarding its participatory nature. The success of PRCA often depends upon good facilitation, and practical training is required.

Networking: This approach has been enhanced through advances in information technology; although peer-to-peer exchanges continue to be important, they are time-consuming and costly. Qualitative data from exchanges is useful to triangulate research findings and can promote group solidarity.

Social Audit: Social audits were originally used by the private sector. The technique has been criticised for raising expectations where no real mandate for social audits exists. Moreover, the objects of social audits can feel threatened. Social audits are also time-consuming.

Participatory Voluntary Self-Monitoring (PVSM): PVSM is an experiential learning method that encourages adult learning. The indicators provided by the method can, however, be unclear. PVSM is most appropriate for illiterate beneficiaries.

4.2 Asian Regional Workshop: Rajendrapur, Bangladesh
Subrata Chakrabarty and Amjad Nazeer

The Asian regional workshop was held in Rajendrapur, Bangladesh, in November 1999. A total of 47 people participated from six regional countries. The workshop centred around group work, together with a number of more formal inputs on key themes presented by the facilitators. The workshop's programme was based upon the following structure:

- an examination of the concept of empowerment;
- a review of participants' experiences of the monitoring and evaluation of empowerment;
- an assessment of the systems used for the monitoring and evaluation of empowerment;
- an assessment of the indicators, methods and techniques used for the monitoring and evaluation of empowerment;
- an exercise to design an approach and system for the monitoring and evaluation of empowerment; and
- a review of case studies of the monitoring and evaluation of empowerment,

looking at problems, indicators, methods and tools;

Before summarising the main discussions of the regional workshop, we will refer to a number of critical issues in relation to the M&E of empowerment that participants raised:

- Attitudes and programmes concerning empowerment vary greatly, depending on whether we regard empowerment as instrumental to achieving project goals or, more profoundly, as an aspect of social transformation.

- The experiences from the workshop suggest that we are more aware of the constraints to good monitoring and evaluation of empowerment than of the supportive aspects. We need more sharing of experiences of positive examples.

- There are still problems in knowing the limits of empowerment programmes when the external environment is restrictive; this makes its monitoring and evaluation difficult because of the dominance of external factors.

- The identification and operationalisation of indicators in relation to the empowerment objectives has been difficult.

- There is still little evidence to suggest that client groups are selecting indicators.

- There is still a need for more exposure to methods for collecting baseline data and relating this to monitoring and evaluation.

- Where empowerment goals are more specific, such as in relation to a target group (e.g. street children), it is easier to start selecting indicators of empowerment.

- During the workshop it was surprising that there was not more discussion of linking empowerment at 'community' level to wider macro-level issues.

- There is still a need for greater clarity about empowerment. Often the problem is that we try to force a traditional community development project into an empowerment model rather than fundamentally changing our approach to development.

- Although we recognised the importance of context-specific issues, the overall framework of M&E, as symbolised by the one used for the case study exercises, seems to have been generally acceptable.

The Concept of Empowerment

Participants at the Asian regional workshop considered resources, gender, age, ethnicity and affiliation to key institutions to be the main characteristics of empowerment. The workshop identified a number of additional factors linked to empowerment, including: patriarchy, unequal distribution of resources, corruption, lack of education, lack of awareness and unequal social opportunities. In the context of South Asia, NGOs, the government, donors and other stakeholders have recognised empowerment as an objective of development. The 'powerless' (identified as women and the poor) are the target groups of different development projects. However, achievements in this regard are still not significant.

Participants defined **power** in terms of (a) information and knowledge, (b) linkages to associations and networks and (c) psychological issues. Power was seen to manifest itself in access to and control over resources. Participants analysed empowerment by examining its economic, social and political constituents, on the basis of key differences – be they religious, cultural, educational, legal, biological or gender-based – identified between 'powerful' and powerless' groups. The **economic** elements included: income potential, asset base, education, bargaining, technology, confidence, choice, influence, access, control and satisfaction. The **social** elements were linkage, religion, culture, education, law, health and gender. The **political** elements were association, representation, decision-making, influence, mandate, legislation, confidence, choice, influence, access, control and recognition.

The characteristics of **powerlessness** in South Asia were seen to revolve around access to and control over: information, educational and health services; household resources; representation in decision-making bodies; and position within social and religious hierarchies.

Issues Related to the Implementation of Monitoring and Evaluation Systems for Empowerment in South Asia

The participants identified three levels by which empowerment has been attempted in South Asia. At the level of the individual, empowerment has been addressed through the processes of **self-management**, but it can also be tackled at the level of the organisation through **capacity-building** and at wider institutional levels. At each of these levels participants stressed the need for particular approaches to the M&E of empowerment to be tailored to the local socio-cultural context. Moreover, in all cases the question 'Who is building whose capacity and for what purposes?' must be addressed.

Table 7 is an indicator of the current level of M&E of empowerment within South Asia. It outlines the key supporting factors and constraints experienced by organisations in the region.

Table 7: **Factors Supporting and Constraining the Implementation of Monitoring and Evaluation Systems in South Asia**

Supporting Factors	Constraining Factors
Beneficiary participation	Lack of communication between stakeholders
Common understanding of project aims between stakeholders	Lack of commitment from project leaders who perceive M&E to be a 'policing exercise'
Good Participatory Implementation Plan (PIP)	Lack of understanding of the project aims by the stakeholders
Skilled and trained staff	Lack of importance attributed to M&E within the organisation
Adequate financial resources, equipment and time	Lack of financial resources, equipment and time
Good accountability system	Lack of skilled, trained staff and quality control
Commitment from management	Too much information to establish clear indicators
Detailed clear indicators	Lack of participatory processes
Flexible programming	Lack of support from donors
Co-operation from donors	Management rigidity concerning targets
Proper Management Information Systems MIS)	Log frames developed by those without under standing of field realities
Good co-ordination of programme	No proper MIS
Appropriate M&E design	Short-term projects
Clearly articulated project goals	Lack of understanding on concept of empowerment and the M&E of empowerment

The problems associated with the implementation of empowerment in South Asia have led some commentators to question how much real social change actually occurs in the projects and programmes that currently pass as empowerment. Are development organisations actively pursuing empowerment agendas, or are they simply focusing on less politically contentious issues, such as micro-credit? One participant noted that in Pakistan, for example, the public sector and media continued to question the legitimacy of NGOs, with the exception of those defined within the narrow limits of a charitable organisation. Some groups in Bangladesh also question the major role that NGOs play in that country.

Development projects in this region have focused on empowerment, but development practitioners have faced tremendous problems in their attempts to operationalise it. At the Asian workshop empowerment was seen as a **location-specific issue**: the definition and indicators of empowerment vary from one location to another. In addition, the indicators of empowerment vary according to the perspective of different stakeholders. Although empowerment may vary from one location to another, common themes for the achievement of empowerment were cited as being: organisational capacity-building, changes in individual psychology and behaviour, greater access to information and services, a greater understanding of beneficiary needs on behalf of NGOs; institutional development and advocacy.

The Practice of Monitoring and Evaluation for Empowerment: Methods, Techniques and Tools

Participants of the workshop assessed several methods and tools associated with the operationalisation of empowerment. Each method or tool was assessed in terms of its capacity to strengthen the practices of the M&E of empowerment:

PRA-based PME: The use of PRA-based PME has been increasing in Asia. In the experience of participants, this has been a successful process since it enables the target group to monitor its own development, while considering the opinion of all additional stakeholders. However, some participants found it a time-consuming process that requires a highly skilled, experienced practitioner. It was felt that there was a need for good facilitation.

Survey or Questionnaire-based M&E: This is a quick and structured method for collecting and analysing quantitative data. However, it is less participatory and more expensive than other, more participatory approaches. The target people do not have any ownership of the findings. It was suggested that there was a need for strict supervision and quality control to strength this M&E method.

Focus Group Discussions: This is a commonly used method in M&E. It can be cost-effective and can provide in-depth information quickly. It was felt by participants that the facilitator must be experienced with good record-keeping and analysis.

Interviews: This technique is widely used in Asia. Participants felt that it has the flexibility and scope necessary for easy compilation and in-depth analysis. The drawback of this method is that beneficiary participation is limited. To strengthen the quality of this M&E method, there is a need to improve the understanding of the interviewers and to ensure proper communication and integrity during the interview.

Log Frame: This method is based on the rationalisation of expected results and performance indicators, which are simple and participatory. It is an effective method to monitor the time-bound project. Practitioners may need extensive orientation, however.

Participatory Video: In this process, all conversations are recorded and played back at the government level to illustrate what is wrong and what can be done within a particular community. In some cases, PRA has been incorporated within this method to visualise the baseline situation for future M&E. However, it appears to an expensive and time-consuming method.

Visual PME: This is a very visual tool that comes under a number of names. One organisation in Bangladesh calls it Participatory Analysis and Continuous Education (PACE). In this method, preparation by the facilitators saves time and ensures quality. It generates dialogue among participants, which can lead to empowerment. Excellent facilitation skills and knowledge of PRA is essential to implement this PME system.

4.3 Latin American Regional Workshop: Managua, Nicaragua
Brenda Bucheli and Mirtha Ditren Perdomo

The Latin America regional workshop, held in Managua, was organised by INTRAC with the support of the Nicaraguan NGO CRIES. A total of 48 participants attended the event, from countries throughout Latin America and Northern Europe. As with the three other regional workshops, content centred around group work, together with a number of more formal inputs on key themes presented by the facilitators. The basic **objectives** of the workshop were to:

- explore the concept of empowerment and its use in the analysis of poverty;
- understand and document participants' experiences of empowerment and its evaluation; and
- examine ways in which the M&E of empowerment can be operationalised.

The Concept of Empowerment
Before analysing the concept of empowerment in the context of development interventions, participants first grappled with the translation of empowerment from

English to Spanish. The Spanish term for empowerment, 'empoderamiento', implies that power is something that is provided by a benefactor to a beneficiary. This assumption was thought to have its roots in Latin America's long history of paternalism. However, attendees strongly disagreed with this usage in the context of development interventions today. Indeed there was a strong feeling among some participants that international donors had introduced this understanding of the term.

A consensus was eventually reached amongst participants that the term **'participacion social'** or social participation should be used, since this better reflects the original sentiments of the word in English; that is, empowerment as the **promotion of self-management**. With this definition in mind, participants stated that any development project or intervention should attempt to create conditions favourable to the empowerment of its beneficiaries. They believed that the target population should itself be the protagonists of empowerment, while the role of NGOs is simply to facilitate this process.

The facilitators then asked participants to describe the key characteristics of a development project that need to be identified in order to understand the dynamics of power, and hence the nature of empowerment. The key characteristics mentioned by respondents – in the context of Latin America – included: the attitude of project leaders; the degree to which local leaders represent the target group; the degree to which beneficiaries have access to information and resources; and the level of political and religious polarisation within the community. Additional factors that may influence power relationships in Latin America included: culture; paternalistic social structures; patriarchal social structures; direct repression; lack of opportunities and access to education; a state that does not prioritise basic needs; and historic trends, such as post- and neo-colonialism.

In order for development practitioners to foster empowerment, the workshop participants agreed that the characteristics of **powerlessness** needed to be defined. In the experience of participants these were stated as follows: the absence of social consciousness; inadequate organisation; a lack of self-esteem; poor access to resources; insufficient training; poor leadership; a lack of knowledge; repression; and dependency. The major differences between powerless and powerful groups in Latin America were then categorised by participants into political, social and economic domains. Participants felt that groups such as women, children, the poor and the disabled, were less powerful than other social groups. This was largely because of their lack of access to knowledge; legal systems that favour the rich; their lack of skills to access important decision-making processes; the monopoly of the rich of influential public positions and their control of the media that allows them to manipulate public opinion.

There are also several key social differences between powerful and powerless groups: lack of access to basic resources, education and training; food insecurity; little or no management training; and a fatalistic attitude. Economically powerless groups are more likely to be unemployed; less likely to own land or property; and lacking in access to finance and financial management skills, including information.

Monitoring and Evaluation Systems for Empowerment

Once the workshop participants had analysed the nature of power and established a clear meaning for empowerment, they proceeded to examine the M&E of empowerment and the ways in which such qualitative processes can be implemented as part of a development intervention. In the first instance it was felt that any development intervention should include an analysis of the context that would examine the nature of power and its distribution and use before the intervention began. Furthermore, empowerment can be understood in terms of three broad categories of intervention. Firstly, empowerment processes can be seen as an approach to **capacity-building** among poor people. Secondly, interventions attempting to empower beneficiaries may seek to develop and strengthen relationships or **networks** between marginalised groups and other stakeholder bodies. In the final instance participants conceptualised empowerment in terms of projects or programmes which attempt to provide **access** to economic resources for the poor. However, it was also felt that the term 'intervention' itself implies a relationship of domination and imposition between the benefactor and the beneficiary. It is important to be clear that the powerless are not necessarily the economic poor, but also include women and the elderly. It was suggested that the key elements of an intervention seeking to empower supposedly 'powerless' groups were as follows:

- Target populations should decide upon the nature and means of their empowerment.
- The intervention should work towards **sustainability**.
- The **empowerment process should be gradual**, taking into account the fact that organisational time-frames and the needs of the community do not necessarily match.
- The process should be **flexible** and address community initiatives and decisions.
- Attention should be paid to the implications of international and national structures in the analysis of local power relationships.

Although the M&E of empowerment has not yet been mainstreamed within development organisations in the region, several participants stated that many development practitioners are currently leaving assistance programmes in search of projects that promote democratisation and the strengthening of civil society. In this sense, some development practitioners at least are actively looking for effective ways in which to promote empowerment in Latin America. For the most part, participants felt that empowerment is a difficult process to measure. They stated that this was because the term is not sufficiently understood, and that many indicators are themselves nebulous and require analysis of large quantities of information. Participants were cleare, however, concerning the steps that should be taken after key **empowerment** indicators are selected. There was agreement that once each indicator has been defined, suitable methodologies and instruments must be selected for data collection and analysis. Following the validation of these instruments, the monitoring of the indicators could begin. A quality M&E system must incorporate feedback mechanisms during the data collection phase to enable inappropriate indicators to be adjusted.

The definition of indicators is a dialectic process that goes from concrete to abstract issues and vice versa. It is also seen as a **dynamic process** that should be analysed, systematised and adjusted. It was suggested that indicators should be concrete, measurable, and contextualised and that there should be a mix of qualitative and quantitative indicators. It was also felt that the number of indicators should be in accordance with the management capacity of each project. Since, clearly, the M&E of empowerment is a complex process, agencies need to 'size-up' their capacities before undertaking such a demanding task. In their assessment of the implementation of an M&E of empowerment system, participants focused on the implications for particular marginalised groups, namely women and children. In respect of women, the group explained how equality of opportunities in respect of gender is often difficult to achieve. Women's projects cause suspicion and distrust in Latin American since husbands and partners can perceive the intervention to be a threat. A member of the workshop described how, in an attempt to improve this situation, some organisations in Latin America have begun to work with men to try to address issues surrounding gender.

In an effort to manage problems associated with the 'gender-awareness' of M&E systems, it was suggested that practitioners should develop training programmes based upon women's needs, requirements and opportunities. Some participants felt that women should be trained in technical areas, in addition to personal relations and organisational issues, areas that are traditionally considered to be feminine activities.

In terms of the implications of the M&E of empowerment for a target population of children, it was felt that legalistic interpretations of children's rights needed to be modified. A move towards a more ideological dimension, promoting social responsibility, should be made. This would involve a switch from a focus on children as an object for protection to a vision of children as the subjects of their own rights. It was pointed out that it would be necessary to develop adequate concepts and methodologies to promote children's participation, in order to consider both the rights of the child and the adult.

4.4 Middle Eastern Regional Workshop, Amman, Jordan
Munif Abu-Rish

The Middle East regional workshop on the monitoring and evaluation of empowerment was attended by 55 participants from nine regional countries. The event was hosted by JOHUD, the Jordanian Hashemite Fund for Human Development. During a preliminary discussion, each participant described the type of issues and areas of the M&E of empowerment that they thought should be addressed by the workshop. These are summarised below:

- develop a clear understanding of the concept of empowerment;
- identify effective tools for the measurement of empowerment;
- develop an understanding of the concepts of M & E;
- enhance participants' understanding of the role of networking and communication strategies in development processes;
- improve participants' understanding of the relationship between regional, national and local processes of empowerment;
- expand upon the relationship between production projects and empowerment; and
- focus on gender and empowerment issues.

The Concept of Empowerment

Participants began their analysis of the concept of empowerment by identifying the key characteristics of power. These attributes were grouped into five categories: economic, social, political, cultural and institutional. **Economically**, participants felt that several factors were most important in the analysis of power: distribution and ownership of property and income; level of unemployment; possession of skills; access to commercial networks; access to infrastructure; degree of regional economic differentiation; attitude of household head; and gender and the division of labour.

In terms of **social** factors, it was felt that demography, gender, hierarchical social structures, the nature of the state, social services and problems with disaffected youth were the major social problems affecting power relations in the Middle East. In terms of the political factors, the level of political participation, the representativeness of political parties and the role of community leaders were identified as crucial.

Traditional practices and attitudes and religion were also described as cultural impediments to empowerment. More significantly, the institutional framework for developmental activities in the Middle East was criticised. Workshop participants asked where the regions community-based development initiatives were, and how far they had encouraged grassroots participation?

Participants then proceeded to examine the main characteristics of powerlessness in the Middle East. A lack of education and access to social services, unemployment, repression, an inability to access appropriate information, and a lack of political awareness were thought to be important indicators of powerlessness. With a fuller understanding of the nature of power and powerlessness, participants were able to discern the key political, social, economic and cultural differences between the powerful and the powerless in the Middle East. Major political differences included ideology, levels of participation in decision-making forums, the capacity to establish pressure groups, degree of freedom to express oneself, influence over the legal system and the level of women's representation.

Looking at the key **economic differences** between the powerful and the powerless in the Middle East, participants referred to levels of poverty, the distinction between labourers and owners of the means of production, and access to productive resources (which vary according to both class and geographic location). Major social differences between the powerful and the powerless were stated to be: geography; social class; ethnicity; health; education; gender; and family size and structure. The cultural differences described included language and diversity of values.

Monitoring and Evaluation of Empowerment

The objective of the second phase of the workshop was to describe the workings of an M&E of empowerment system. Participants were asked to describe what they thought were the main elements of a development intervention designed to empower the poor. Their responses included the following:

- A needs assessment of the target group conducted prior to the project planning and implementation phases.
- Continuous feedback and evaluation.
- Clear project aims and indicators.
- A communication and dissemination strategy for project outcomes.
- The liberation of development projects from donor influence.
- Full beneficiary participation in the planning and implementation stages of the project.
- Cultural sensitivity.
- The appropriate use of available local resources.
- Specification of the project's methodology.
- Project flexibility.
- Effective training of staff.
- Co-ordination and networking with other stakeholder organisations.
- Identification of local counterparts.

Participants were subsequently asked to name the major factors both supporting and constraining the implementation of the M&E of empowerment in the Middle East by NGOs. The responses of the group are summarised in Table 8.

Table 8: **The Implementation of the M & E of Empowerment in the Middle East**

Supporting Factors	Constraining Factors
Staff commitment	Availability of information
Clear goals and vision	Capacity to manage information collected
	Staff skills
	Financial resources and equipment
	Lack of local and regional co-ordination

In discussions following the construction of this framework a number of comments were made concerning the nature of **NGOs** in the Middle East. It was made apparent during the workshop that the shift within the Middle East from a tribal to a semi-industrialised society has induced various fundamental changes that contextualise the work of NGOs. NGOs in the region were identified as having two roles: one focusing on the provision of services and the other centred around issues of empowerment, through, for example, the promotion of democracy and the strengthening of civil society. Participants stated that many Arab NGOs have now begun to shift their understanding of development from that of service provision to empowerment. However, some argued that such a transition should be analysed with a degree of suspicion since the majority of NGOs continue to under-resource proper monitoring and evaluation processes. It would appear that the only reason for this sudden NGO interest in M&E was donor pressure.

The Middle East regional workshop concluded with a series of recommendations designed to improve the ways in which M&E systems could focus on empowerment.

- Development practitioners should receive more training in the processes of M&E.
- Evaluation would be seen as a continuous process.
- NGOs should network at local and regional levels.
- NGOs should clarify their independence from governmental organisations.
- The private sector should support NGOs.

- Civil society organisations should become more aware of empowerment.
- NGOs should develop a communications strategy between stakeholders.
- Women's decision-making capacities should be enhanced.
- NGOs should focus on capacity-building.
- Donors should allow NGOs to implement their project in a more flexible manner in accordance with local reality.
- Interventions attempting to empower would take the needs of the community as a starting-point.

4.5 Synthesising the Findings of the Four Regional Workshops

Given the divergent contexts in which the four regional workshops took place, it would be both simplistic and erroneous to seek consensus and present a series of consolidated findings. Power is central to any interpretation of a process of 'development' and yet it cannot be universally described. The contemporary distribution of power in any country or region will have historical, cultural and ethnic roots and these must be understood individually and not as part of some global pattern. In this respect we can note, for example, the historical dimension of powerlessness that emerged in each of the regional discussions as well as more contemporary understandings of those factors that can perpetuate this state. But we can also note a number of common themes in each of the regional reports: for example, the political, economic and social nature of powerlessness and the importance of understanding powerlessness in terms of discrete social groups – women, children and the elderly. While respecting the context-specific nature of each of the four presentations, we can extract from them a number of common threads.

The Concept of Empowerment

It is clear from discussions during each of the four regional workshops that definitions of 'empowerment' remain contested. The original Spanish translation of the term *empoderamiento* implies that power is something that can be provided by a benefactor to a beneficiary. This understanding bears a close relationship to the practice of many current development interventions in that weaker recipients receive goods or services from more powerful benefactors. If a consensus emerged it was that development practitioners should move towards a definition that sees empowerment as a *'process of enabling people to take responsibility for their own development'*. In this sense empowerment is a continuously evolving process of social participation and the promotion of **self-management**. Understandably participants took a distinctly operational approach to their understanding of empowerment while forcibly recognising the critical influence of context. Despite difficulties of defining empowerment, the concept can be used at the level of the individual, the family, the community and the organisation. Participants consequently conceptualised empowerment as an essential part of both **rights-based** and **capacity-building** development programmes.

Another theme running through the four workshops was that empowerment has both general and specific characteristics. Participants stated that 'powerlessness' has its roots in political, economic, social, religious and cultural hierarchies and is most likely to affect women, children and the disabled. As a result, workshop participants defined the effects of powerlessness in similar terms for each region. These were (a) an inability to take part in decision-making, (b) inadequate access to economic resources and information, (c) a lack of organisation, (d) the absence of social awareness, (e) a lack of confidence and skills, (f) poor strategic networking and (g) an inability to communicate effectively.

However, there was a strong argument in each of the four regions that the local effects of each of these characteristics can vary widely. In Latin America, for example, paternalism was said to be more pervasive than in Asia, while anti-democratic state tactics were emphasised by participants at the Middle Eastern workshop. The implications for of these variations for the M&E of empowerment are that the indicators of empowerment will be specific to the local context.

Monitoring and Evaluation Systems for Empowerment

At each workshop a clear distinction was made between macro- and micro- factors affecting the implementation of the M&E of empowerment. Referring to the macro-environment, the four workshops concluded that an analysis of the project's institutional context – namely its donors and governmental authorities – must be conducted during the first stages of the project's design. The micro-factors that can influence the M&E of empowerment are localised influences upon project performance. Although many localised differences inevitably exist, Table 9 generalises the key micro-factors affecting the M&E of empowerment across the four regions.

Each of the four workshops detailed the main elements of a development intervention designed to empower the poor. These included: a needs assessment of the target group; a communication and dissemination strategy for project outcomes; full beneficiary participation in the planning and implementation stages of the project; clear specification of the project's methodology; and identification and co-ordination of local counterparts. It was also argued that good M&E systems incorporate feedback mechanisms during the data collection phase to enable inappropriate indicators to be adjusted. A second recurring finding was that, where possible, NGOs must approach the M&E of empowerment in a qualitative way. Participants agreed that empowerment is a long-term, often discontinuous process that is essentially difficult to measure. Taking the workshops as a whole, several common approaches to achieving empowerment emerged:

Table 9: **Factors Supporting and Constraining the Implementation of Monitoring and Evaluation of Empowerment in Africa, Asia, Latin America and the Middle East**

Supporting Factors	Constraining Factors
Beneficiary participation	Lack of donor support
Knowledge of the target group	Absence of participation in the design and implementation of M&E systems
Skilled and trained staff	Unfavourable political, social and economic environment
Common understanding of project aims between stakeholders	Lack of communication between stakeholders
Design and use of appropriate system	Lack of skilled, trained staff and quality control
Donor support	The perception of powerful stakeholders that empowerment threatens their position
Commitment from management	Inability to identify key indicators and reliance on quantitative techniques
Adequate financial resources and equipment	Inadequate learning resources on the topic of the M&E of empowerment

- Capacity-building
- Behavioural change
- Building self-esteem and self-management
- Encouraging full participation
- Awareness-raising
- Institution-building
- Advocacy and networking

Given the universality of much development practice based on externally funded development programmes and projects - with the same broad group of development agencies – it is not entirely surprising to find that workshop participants identified the same kinds of factor. In many ways the weight of externally funded development interventions has helped to universalise practitioners' perceptions of issues and problems. The twin concepts of the workshops – M&E and empowerment – are both external constructs and accordingly discussions on them touched on many of the same issues. Indeed it is difficult not to conclude that the four workshops 'forced' an issue that was not intrinsically emerging in the four regional contexts. This is not to say that 'power' is not recognised by development practitioners across the contexts and at the heart of any interpretation of 'underdevelopment' or 'poverty'. What the regional workshops appear to have (rightly) concluded is that the whole concept of empowerment as what a 'benefactor does to a beneficiary' is not readily translatable into different contexts. Empowerment is not a single activity but more of an approach to working with powerless people – who know themselves that they are powerless and who do not need somebody to tell them so – in a manner that enables them to undertake the things that they feel might change their situation vis-a-vis other economic and social groups. Hence it was difficult in the workshops to develop the notion of 'empowerment' as opposed to stimulating debate on issues relating to 'powerlessness' as being at the heart of poverty. The usefulness of the workshops was that they confirmed the centrality of 'power' in terms of explaining the massive gulfs that separate socio-economic groups in the same context. They also confirmed that development agencies could usefully listen to key informants and observers in any context before they set up their empowerment programme!

CHAPTER 5
Perspectives on the Evaluation of Empowerment

5.1 So Now They are Going to Measure Empowerment
James Taylor

In recent years donors and international agencies in the development sector have successfully promoted and insisted on the implementation of strategic planning, monitoring and evaluation models and methodologies. There have been many positive spin-offs as activities have become more strategic and measurable, and organisations have become more accountable. But there is growing concern amongst practitioners regarding the limitations inherent in these seemingly sophisticated, but unavoidably reductionist, methodologies. Even if one ignores the harm done by non-developmental methods used to introduce these methodologies, we cannot overlook the alienation and disempowerment that the language and convoluted logic of these systems causes. Moreover these logical framework-type systems have a more fundamental shortcoming, particularly if they are to be used to measure empowerment.

Their weakness emanates from the fact that they are best suited to measuring that which is most easy to measure, namely: the delivery of products and services. But if the sector has learned anything, it is that there is no direct casual relationship between the delivery of products and services, and development. If we are starting to recognise that empowerment is the ultimate objective of development interventions, we will have to accept that it cannot be delivered like water pumps, health programmes, or training workshops. Equally it cannot be measured in the same way.

Furthermore there is deep ambivalence about whether to welcome the interest of those who have the power to enforce new methodologies and approaches in the **measurement of empowerment**. The dominant, competitive, market-driven global paradigm dictates that power is used to the benefit of those who already have an advantage. The view of practitioners closer to the periphery is that those at the centre are about to take control of that which is most important to them. There is a deep fear that in order to measure it effectively, empowerment will be reduced to the level of the next deliverable development, provided by the powerful through capacity-building workshops, training programmes, and participatory projects. Those at the centre must understand that they have the ability to reduce empowerment to the next 'flavour of the month'. Those closer to the periphery have the responsibility to resist it, and to provide an alternative.

This chapter explores an approach to measuring empowerment as one crucial element of an integrated development practice that has empowerment as its ultimate purpose. As a practitioner from the South, I will challenge convention, and highlight the universality of the need for empowerment, by using an example of some development work that I once did in the North.

Case Study: The setting is a generally wealthy borough in north London (UK). Within the borough there are a number of large council-owned housing estates inhabited by predominantly unemployed single-parent families. I was employed as a community worker by the Social Services Department to work on one estate, which my employers had identified as having unacceptably high levels of 'social problems'. These problems included child abuse, vandalism, substance abuse, family breakdown and mental health issues. The flats that people lived in, although not that old, let in winter and cold air around poorly fitting windows, and were generally in a poor state of repair. Despite housing well over a thousand people, there were no communal or recreational facilities on the estate.

During my initial period of getting to know the people and their needs I was struck by their general sense of powerlessness. The little energy that the occasional tenant displayed was in the form of anger towards the authorities. I eventually managed to get a small group of single parents sufficiently motivated to get together to share some of their common problems. One example of the extent of the dehumanising situation became clear to me when they shared how desperate they became in the school holidays when they sat cooped up with their young children indoors all day. Two of the parents found humour in the fact that they had both stumbled onto the same solution to the situation. When it became intolerable they would open a valium capsule prescribed for them by their doctor, and sprinkle the contents over their children's breakfast cereal; the kids became much less troublesome, and more manageable as a result.

As part of my analysis of the situation I identified and observed a number of relationships that I considered central to it. Amongst these were the way in which the tenants related to (and felt about) themselves as individuals, how they related to each other on the estate, and how they related to the rest of the borough (in particular the local authority which was their landlord). The overwhelming quality in the nature of all of these relationships was the sense of being a victim. As the community worker it was not that difficult to build a picture of the quality and nature of these relationships. Essentially no one really believed in themselves or in their own ability to do anything about their situation. They did not get together around issues of common concern except occasionally to moan about them, or go to the pub to forget about them for a brief while. Their relationship with the Borough Council was a combination of acrimony, apathy, fear and frustration that collectively led to avoidance. When it was no longer possible to avoid each other, the relationship very quickly became conflictual, with the Council inevitably drawing upon its power and authority as landlord to achieve its objectives.

The other relationships central to the whole process were those between the development agent (myself, representing the Social Services Department of the Borough Council) and the tenants on the one hand, and the rest of the Council (the Housing Department in particular) on the other. The relationship between myself and the members of the community was a complex one. One aspect of it was determined by the fact that in my mind I was a young, recently qualified, relatively inexperienced community worker working in a foreign country. To the community members I was a member of the Council who represented authority to them. Coming from the Social Services Department as I did, I was seen as a social worker and there was an expectation that I would bring resources and solve problems for them. Within my own Social Services team I was the only community worker in a team dominated by social workers who expected me to engage in some form of therapeutic group work that directly addressed the 'social problems' identified. In the broader relationships within the Borough Council, the Social Service Department was expected to assist the Housing Department by taking care of the social problems on the housing estates, which made them difficult to manage and maintain. The general relationship between the Council and the members of the community was characteristically welfarist in nature, complementing and supporting the people's feelings of powerlessness and victimisation.

Even though this example comes from a period before attempts to measure empowerment, issues of **power** were central to my community development practice at the time. I was conscious of the nature of existing relationships, and had a good idea in my mind of some characteristics of the ideal relationships that we were striving towards. With this understanding, analysis and objective in mind I set to work to involve tenants from the estate in initiatives that would start addressing their most strongly felt needs. This involved three years full-time, in-depth community work. It started tentatively with a committee of four women organising a holiday play scheme that entertained a small group of children for four days. It gradually grew into regular holiday play schemes, a latchkey club for after school care, an adventure playground, a Tenant's Association, a community centre with a crèche and pensioners club during the day, and various activities for adults and youths in the evenings. The Tenant's Association eventually managed to get the Housing Department to replace all the windows on the estate and repair and maintain the buildings. This was achieved through a sustained campaign involving petitions, protest marches, negotiations and finally consultations and joint supervision of the work carried out.

But what of empowerment and its measurement? As always it was easier to measure the 'products' delivered through the process, such as new facilities, new community structures, and the number of children and elderly persons involved in programmes. The Social Services Department also had a lot to measure in changes to reported cases of 'social problems'. But in attempting to **measure empowerment** we have to look beyond these more simply measured achievements.

I do believe, however, that it would not have been difficult to measure empowerment had we chosen to do so. Indicators of changes in relationships abounded. The simple increase in the numbers of people believing that they could make a difference could be measured by the numbers involved in committees and community initiatives. Shifts in the relationships between people on the estate could be detected in the fact that they were now getting together, and in what they had achieved through their efforts. The ability of people to gain access to and control over resources, previously beyond their reach, was evident in improved maintenance of their dwellings and the building of the community centre. The shifts in power relations were nowhere more evident than in the transformed nature of the regular exchanges between the Tenant's Association and the Housing Department, which had evolved into one of regular consultation and collaboration. The possible consolidation of this shift was imminent when I last got news, in that one of the original four women (who didn't know what to do with her children) had entered politics and was running for election into the Borough Council.

Another place where the shifts in relationships were very evident was in my relationship with the system in which I was intervening (the community) and my relationship with the system out of which I was operating (the Social Services Department and the broader Borough Council). Through the process of empowerment the community had learned about its rights and how to exercise them. They had organised themselves and mobilised against the Council (my employer). Their relationship with me had shifted from expecting me to solve their problems to making demands of me to assist them to achieve their own objec-

> tives. This obviously put a lot of pressure on me from both sides. It was not easy to justify to my employer why it was important for me to assist the community to mobilise in protests against them. Equally it was difficult for the Social Services Department to explain to the Housing Department that they should be grateful that their tenants were becoming more empowered, and that in the long term this would assist them in managing the housing estate more effectively. It is my contention that these difficulties are a part of the empowerment process. It is inconceivable that real empowerment can take place to the point of shifting power relations without those involved experiencing some level of pain or at least discomfort. These are also indicators of empowerment that need to be included as part of the measurement process.
>
> It would not have been difficult to describe in more detail what the relationships were like 'before' and 'after' the development intervention. Stories told by the people themselves, about how their experience of their relationships had changed, would have added even more weight to the argument. In practice, I do not believe that it is that difficult to measure empowerment; the difficulty lies in achieving it. Case studies of obvious shifts in relationships over such a relatively short period of time are rare. (I must admit even to the possibility of this one becoming just slightly idealised through the passage of time!)

As a South African practitioner the above example might have been a strange one to choose. My own country is being looked upon by the world as one of the most inspiring examples of empowerment in recent times. And it is true – we could measure it, but we don't have to – we know it. But we also know that it is an ongoing process. We are at times almost overwhelmed by a sense that we have just begun. For this reason it might be important to learn to measure empowerment more accurately to ensure that the process does not falter.

Development and Empowerment

As highlighted in the case study, genuine developmental practitioners are not simply engaged in delivering resources and services to those in need. They are initiating processes that result in people exercising more control over the decisions and resources that directly affect the quality of their lives. In order for someone to exercise more control, someone else will inevitably have to relinquish some control. A practice with the changing of power relations as its ultimate objective has to be built not only on a coherent understanding of what development is, but on an understanding of development in which empowerment is the foundation.

Development is an innate and natural process found in all living things. It is important to understand that as development workers we do not bring or deliver development, but **intervene** in development processes that already exist. Whether the intervention is in the life of an individual, organisation, community or country, it is critical to realise that the process of development is already well established. The first challenge facing the development practitioner is to understand the development process in which she or he is intervening: to know where the individual, the organisation, the community, or the country is located on its own path of development. This is necessary to understand where it has come from, how it has changed, and what is impeding its further progress. The second, more demanding challenge, is to intervene in the process in a way that facilitates development rather than undermines it.

The process of locating an entity on its own path of development and understanding the implications of the point it has reached is obviously not a simple process of quantitative measurement. To understand development as a process the practitioner must be able to identify the different developmental phases. These phases are characterised by substantial shifts in the nature and quality of relationships. The terms used to describe the phases (dependence, independence and interdependence) are drawn from the essential character of the different types of relationships. It is in these developmental shifts in relationships that empowerment is to be measured. In using the case study it becomes clear how these terms are helpful in describing the changes in the power relationships between the Tenants Association and the Housing Department, or the way in which the woman who entered politics related to her world.

Measuring Empowerment

On the bases of the above understanding of development, practitioners intervene in existing complex development processes. Through whatever resources, projects, or services they bring, they aim to affect change in the power relations of their beneficiaries. These shifts do not come about as a result of the efficient delivery of the resource or service, but through the developmental process employed. Measurement is but a part of this process. As mentioned above, the process begins with the ability to make developmental assessments, to analyse and understand the situations in which you are intervening as living, dynamic, changing processes that have a rich history, a present reality and a future potential. A central component of this assessment must include qualitative and descriptive pictures of the formative relationships surrounding the subject of the intervention. These descriptions form the baseline against which empowerment will be measured. The developmental practitioner must be able to isolate and describe different types of relationship by building a relationship vocabulary and developing the ability to apply it accurately.

Another important application of **relationship assessment** is to distinguish between external and internal relationships. As important as the nature and quality of relationships with others is the quality and nature of the relationship with one's self. Although this may sound strange at first, we do relate to ourselves. We feel and act in certain ways towards ourselves. Our relationship with ourselves constitutes our basic orientation towards the world. Essentially, we can feel assertive or victimised; competent and in control, or perpetually undermined and exploited not only in specific relationships with others, but within ourselves. The ability to assess these internal relationships, and measure change over time, forms another important part of development practice.

Having created a textured picture of the nature and quality of the critical relationships that constitute the system, in which the practitioner is intervening, the next step in the developmental process is to identify the nature of the **change** required. The preferred future relationships and their power dynamics must be described, and observable indicators that will reflect the desired changes identified. Once the difference between the existing relationships and the preferred future relationships is clear, a plan for the intervention can be devised and implemented.

In the case study there are simple descriptions of the relationships that individuals have with themselves, those between the tenants and the Council, and chose between the tenants themselves. Because of a developmental approach, the projects and programmes were not simply designed to deliver services to the community as effectively and efficiently as possible. The services were delivered through processes that involved the recipients in ways that increased their control and shifted their relationships. In retrospect, empowerment can be measured simply by comparing the original relationships to the ones that existed at the end of the three years. A more meaningful evaluation, however, could have been achieved if projections of 'empowered' relationships had been made, and indicators developed, at the planning stage.

When understood as part of an integrated development implementation process, the measuring and monitoring of empowerment does not present itself as an insurmountable obstacle. But, as previously pointed out, much that is done in the name of development falls far short of shifting power relations towards increased interdependence. If those who are the focus of the intervention are not directly involved in assessing their past and determining the picture of preferred future relationships, the process is not developmental. Developmental processes are participatory in nature. Monitoring and evaluation processes that contribute positively towards empowerment, rather than undermining it, must also be participatory. Another complication in the monitoring of complex social processes such as empowerment is the fact that it is difficult to represent the changes in numbers, percentages, graphs or tables. For this reason it is necessary to describe the changes in a narrative form. If 'logical framework' type planning and monitoring methodologies are being used, the boxes (delineated spaces left open to be filled in) will need to be made a little bigger. Development practitioners will need to develop the art of describing relationships before and after their intervention. They will need to learn to tell the stories of change.

In summary then, the essential **elements** of a developmental approach to the monitoring and evaluation of empowerment should include:

- an integrative, systemic, relational understanding of the world;
- an understanding of development as an innate natural process that results in shifts in the relationships between the elements of the system;
- the ability to undertake participatory developmental assessments, which locate the subject on their own path of development, and identify and describe the nature and quality of existing formative relationships;
- identification of those relationships that most need to change, in order to allow the developmental process to progress;
- creation of an image of the preferred relationships with observable indicators of successful achievement;
- the measurement of the change essentially involves using the indicators as a means of identifying whether the change has occurred and the ability to describe the changes in a narrative form.

Forces Working Against Empowerment and its Measurement

Non-developmental Paradigms

After 400 years the scientific paradigm continues to dominate our world. This rational reductionist world-view promotes a particular approach to measurement as one of its most central practices. This form of measurement is based on the belief that anything can be reduced to its essential ingredients, understood and controlled by man. (In relation to the scientific paradigm I use the terms 'man' and 'mankind' consciously in recognition of the eco-feminist view that the rational scientific phase has been particularly, perhaps even peculiarly, male in its orientation.) This paradigm is human-centred, with mankind dominating. In this paradigm, science assists in understanding nature in order to dominate and exploit it to meet the needs of man. The achievement of the scientific age has resulted in enormous gains in humankind's independence from many of the life-threatening vagaries of nature. Science and competition have combined to fuel a growing ingenuity and productivity that has produced solutions to an immense array of real and imagined human needs. It has developed an economic system that rewards those who are most efficient and competitive in exploiting and then adding value to natural resources, and also most effective in identifying (or creating) and then meeting human needs. The ability to understand and measure things dispassionately, objectively and scientifically is a central tenet of this paradigm.

However, the competition, domination and exploitation that characterise man's relationship with nature, and man's relationship with man, are no longer unquestioningly accepted. The present paradigm is being fundamentally challenged, initially by those who realise that man's present relationship with nature is simply not sustainable. The development sector has played its part in attempting to moderate the very worst excesses of man's competitive, dominant and exploitative relationships with nature. It has had significant success in forcing environmental issues into the mainstream discourse. This voice from the periphery is increasingly being strengthened from other sources, not least of all from within the scientific discipline itself. The new sciences are beginning to provide glimpses of what might well be elements of an emerging new paradigm. Amongst development practitioners there are many who believe that the present dominant paradigm is coming to the end of its usefulness.

It is increasingly being suggested that the scientific, human-centred (anthropocentric or self-assertive) view of the world – despite its past successes – has resulted in distorted understandings and practices that are becoming increasingly threatening and dysfunctional. A new emerging eco-centric (or integrative) view puts humankind not as the central controlling and exploitative force in the world, but as an interdependent part of it. Table 10, from Fritjof Kapra's book, *The Web of Life*, summarises some of the essential elements of the new paradigm:

Table 10: **Elements of the New Paradigm**

Thinking		Values	
• self-assertive	• integrative	• self-assertive	• integrative
• rational	• intuitive	• expansion	• conservation
• analysis	• synthesis	• competition	• co-operation
• reductionist	• holistic	• quantity	• quality
• linear	• non-linear	• domination	• partnership

In pursuing an exploration of the measurement of empowerment it is vital to be conscious of the paradigm out of which we are approaching the subject. If we approach it out of the scientific paradigm, which seeks to reduce everything to its simplest elements, the tendency will be to avoid the complex interrelational, systemic nature of society. We need to locate the process of empowerment within a paradigm that is based upon an emerging interdependent understanding of the world. The scientific approach leads us towards viewing poverty as a social problem that needs to be isolated, analysed and measured, so that it can be taken to pieces and fixed. To date this approach has been singularly unsuccessful. A view of the world as a complex system made up of interdependent relationships will lead our thinking and practice in a very different direction. We will then start viewing poverty as being in an interdependent relationship with wealth, and we will understand that the one will not shift without the other shifting too.

Non-developmental Development Practice

The old scientific paradigm and its complementary competitive market-driven economic paradigm have resulted in a 'delivery type' understanding of development and empowerment. In true market style, those at the periphery of society with unmet needs are viewed as potential consumers who cannot afford to pay for the goods and services they require. It is assumed that poverty at the margins can be eradicated by those at the centre by finding the most effective and efficient means of transferring some surplus. It is further assumed that anything that has made a positive contribution to developed societies will aid the development of those that are 'under developed'.

Welfarist thinking has been behind attempts to make transfers from the 'haves' to the 'have-nots'. In keeping with this logic, the obvious place to measure efficiency and effectiveness in the delivery of the product is at the point it reaches the recipient. We know now, beyond doubt, that the successful delivery of products and services has no direct or predictable impact on the power relations between giver and receiver. There is at least as much evidence of the delivery of development programmes and projects creating and fostering dysfunctional dependency, as there are examples of them contributing to increased independence or interdependence. Any meaningful attempt to measure empowerment will have to go beyond measuring the transfer of resources (be they physical, financial or human) to the least powerful. If empowerment is to be measured as changes in relationships, then the change will need to be detected in both sides of the relationship.

A Top-down Development Approach

A top-down developmental approach results in the whole development/aid system being thought of as a set of relationships that collectively form a conduit through which goods and services flow from the 'South' to the 'North'. It is often referred to as the aid chain. The mental picture created is of a number of organisational links between the North and the South; between the 'haves' and the 'have-nots'. Images abound that weak links within the chain result in widespread corruption and mismanagement of funds.

The first fallacy that this view of the aid chain perpetuates is that, on balance, resources flow from the more wealthy to the less wealthy, and that the flow is one way. We know that in fact the opposite is true. Differentials in power and in the world's consumption needs ensure that the flow of resources is from the poorer to the wealthier countries. It further perpetuates a belief that the more resources you can get to the poor the better. It completely denies the devastating and dehumanising impact of creating and fostering dysfunctional dependency. It implies that development practitioners are simply required to be delivery technocrats, moving development goods from donor to recipient; as if the value lies within the goods themselves. This view sees no need to fund a development sector with specialist competencies to assist the poor. It does not view the development sector as a disciplined field of practice, which needs to be adequately resourced to meet demand. This understanding of the aid chain perceives real value to be found only at the 'top' of the hierarchy. Despite all the advances in participatory development theory and practice, this view of development continues to shape the activities of the sector.

At best, this conceptualisation of the aid chain might have some value and validity when the need is to respond rapidly to disaster relief situations. As a point of departure for measuring empowerment it will lead to a dead end. Its simplistic linearity and assumed altruism belie the complexity and interdependent nature of the relationships that maintain the status quo between the different strata of society. At the very least we need to join the two ends of the chain together in order to accommodate the most rudimentary elements of interconnectedness and interdependence inherent in society. We need to accept the most fundamental principle of systems theory, which points to the fact that no single element of a system can change its relationships within the system without change occurring in all of the other relationships in the system. This has major implications for where we should be measuring empowerment. If I play a significant role in the empowerment of others, it is inconceivable that I will remain unaffected in my relationship with them. In order for them to develop I need to develop. In order for me to develop I will need to shift my relationships with those who have power over me.

If the **powerless** are really going to change their relationships in society, there will be consequences for others. If development practitioners are seriously committed to empowerment they cannot focus their attention only on those less powerful than themselves. For a start, they have to take their own development and relationships seriously. They operate at the interface between the 'haves' and 'have-nots'. They work within systems that have more power than themselves, and intervene in systems which are relatively less powerful. As facilitators of changed power relationships they need to envisage shifts in the relationships between the systems in which they operate, as well as those in which they intervene. In other words, if development practitioners are only seeking to facilitate change in those less powerful than themselves, they will never themselves be engaged in that which they are expecting to measure in their recipients. The agents of development will not have experienced empowerment in their relations with those more powerful. They will also not have moved from the old top-down paradigm that has contributed to entrenching the power relations that it is now pretending to shift.

If development practitioners are to contribute to and measure empowerment at all, they need to measure changes in the **relationships** on either side of themselves in the interconnected development chain. If it is worthwhile measuring empowerment, all those in the chain who are committed to development must be involved in its measurement, placing themselves at the centre of the relationships they are measuring. This includes the official Northern development aid agencies, Northern and Southern NGOs, CBOs, and the governments of donor and recipient countries. If everyone in the chain is engaged in the process the chain itself should develop over time as the relationships change within it.

Towards a Practice that is Empowering

Because all monitoring and evaluation systems are best at measuring that which is easiest to measure, it is vital that these systems do not start dictating and defining what empowerment is. It is all too easy for this to happen. If those who control the finances in the sector start demanding that empowerment be measured in a certain way, the methodology would control the definition of that which it is intended to measure. Any efforts and resources that go into measuring empowerment must be applied in ways that build up competent development practice in the sector. The following general conclusions are presented as a challenge to anyone committed to this end.

- Those who do not see themselves as central to the power dynamics they are attempting to measure are not likely to contribute much through their efforts. The act of measuring someone else's empowerment is potentially disempowering.

- Those who do not approach their own development seriously and consciously, and are not prepared to experience the crises of change, are not going to be effective in facilitating empowerment in others.

- Those who do not see it as part of their task to empower themselves in their relationships with those who control the resources are perpetuating the status quo and therefore cannot claim a commitment to development.

- Empowerment has to be planned into the way in which the services and resources of development are delivered. Empowerment lies not in that which is delivered but in the process of delivery; not in what is delivered but how it is delivered.

- Empowerment is detected in changes in the nature and quality of relationships over time.

- Changes in power relations are a definitive part of the development process; there is a tendency to progress from dependency through independence towards increased interdependence.

- If not incorporated as an integral part of a conscious and concerted development practice, monitoring and evaluation are likely to first diminish and then undermine empowerment by reducing it to easily measurable elements that become a meaningless parody.

- The monitoring and evaluation of empowerment should lead to learning, which should lead to improved development practice. If it does not, it is counter-productive!

The measurement of empowerment must not be allowed to become something that the more powerful do to the less powerful. It should become a regular and meaningful measure of the **shifts** in the **power relationships** between development practitioners (or agencies) and the interved systems. It must also be applied to the relationships between those most marginalised and those who limit their access to resources and ability to make decisions. The measurement of empowerment needs to be promoted by development practitioners who are prepared to apply their analysis to themselves and their own relationships.

5.2 Does Empowerment Start At Home? And If So How Will We Recognise It?
Rick Davies

Where to Look?

Oakley (1999) has provided a helpful overview of common approaches to empowerment in development, and the key issues involved in monitoring and evaluating empowerment. In the first section of this overview, which focuses upon the concept of empowerment, James (1999) refers to a growing scepticism about the use of the concept:

> Notions of sharing power, of stakeholders, of participation and representation and so on seem to refer increasingly to the self contained the world of projects themselves: the external structures of land holding and subsistence economy which have perhaps been disrupted, of political and military formations which have shaped and still shape the forms of social life in a region, tend to fade from view in the world of development speak.

Contrary to James, I would like to argue in favour of such a focus, and even argue that perhaps as a trend it has not gone far enough. The reason for taking this line is a concern about a similar type of myopia than James is concerned about. Organisations can easily become caught up in their own rhetoric, regardless of which end of the political spectrum they place themselves at a more self-critical examination of organisational behaviour may be useful.

I would suggest that the most appropriate way to assess achievements with empowerment is to start at home with the organisation that wants to empower others, referred to hereafter as an NGO. We should start by examining an NGO's immediate relationships, especially with the people it is trying to empower. We should also look at relationships between staff within that NGO and that NGO's relationships with its own donors and supporters. There are three reasons for taking this position. Firstly, economy of effort; all of this information should be close at hand, and thus much easier to access than information about their client's relationship with other individuals and organisations. Secondly, empowerment in this relationship should be the easiest to achieve. An NGO espousing empowerment should be able to act in those terms at least within its own span of management control. We should expect results here before anywhere else. Thirdly, the experience of empowerment in this relationship should provide a useful model of what can be done, affecting clients' expectations of other organisations. Ideally this experience should help them to be empowered in relationships with other significant people and institutions in their lives. After all, if empowerment cannot be achieved here then what sorts of confidence can clients have in their relationships with less altruistic organisations?

We can take the same argument one step backwards, to the relationships between senior and junior staff within the NGOs. We could make a second assumption that, if field staff within an NGO are empowered in relationship to their superiors, then we might expect that that they in turn will be able to be empowering in their relationships with their immediate clients. A third and more provisional assumption can also be made. That is, the state of an NGO's relationship with its donors and significant government authorities may reflect its capacity for empowerment of others. My caution here is due to the fact that NGO's are usually located in a network of relationships with other organisations, not in a simple dominating hierarchy. These statements are assumptions, which should be treated as hypotheses to be tested, not obvious truths. They could form the basis of a useful research project. More immediately, they may stimulate a discussion that might suggest how useful such a research project would be. At best, their usefulness would become immediately apparent and people would go straight ahead and put these ideas to work in a practical way.

Proximate Versus Proxy Indicators

A proxy indicator is simply a substitute indicator. What is being proposed above is something different, it is a **proximate** indicator, that is, evidence which is more immediately at hand because it is closer to us in the chain of causation between what we do and what we hope will ultimately happen in the lives of people whom we are trying to empower.

Diagram 6: **Indicators of Change**

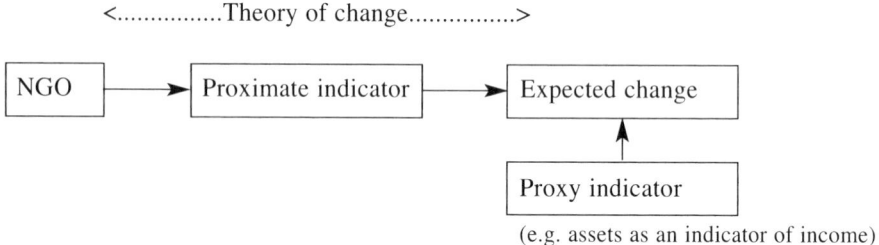

<............Theory of change............>

NGO → Proximate indicator → Expected change ← Proxy indicator

(e.g. assets as an indicator of income)

In addition to the practical arguments put forward above, a proximate indicator has an additional theoretical advantage. In order to identify a proximate indicator, as above, we have to pay some attention to theorising how our intervention might have an effect. If we find our proximate indicator shows no evidence of empowerment, then there are two possibilities. One is that we have failed, and did not manage to empower anyone. The other is that our theory of how empowerment comes about was incorrect. If we change the theory of expected cause-and-effect and come up with other proximate indicators, then we might still find some evidence of empowerment.

What to Look For?

In this section I will outline three types of indicators of empowerment, for which evidence should be close at hand. They are all qualitative indicators, and they are all based on the concept of **difference**. The base assumption is that for a person to be able to say or do something differently involves some degree of choice. Having more choice, compared to the past, implies empowerment. This view can be related to Rowlands' (1997) concept of power. Three types of difference will be considered:

- differences of opinion between individuals;
- differences between the activities undertaken by individuals;
- differences in organisational structures.

Differences of Opinion

In a healthy relationship between two individuals we might expect that both are able to express their opinions freely, including their differences, *without putting the future of that relationship at risk*. Similarly, if clients are empowered in their relationship with an NGO, we might expect them to be able to express their differences of opinion freely and openly with that NGO. The larger the NGO and the number of clients with which it is working, the more differences of opinion we might expect to find, if those clients are empowered in relationship to that NGO.

In the mid-1990s I was working with a large Bangladeshi NGO which had offices in many different parts of the country. Each of these offices was working through a number of large structures known as 'people's organisations'. There were more than 70 such organisations spread across the country. Given the number and scale of the organisations involved, it seemed inevitable that many kinds of differences of opinion would exist between that NGO and the various people's organisations with which they were working. However, when I asked individual senior staff about the existence of such differences I was told, rather surprisingly, that there were none. The same opinion was repeated again more strenuously in a large meeting between this NGO and its donors. If this reported lack of difference was really true, then the implications were very serious. Either the organisations concerned were failing to communicate their members' views or, worse, they were not even recognising their members' views. If the difference of opinion actually existed, but was not being reported by staff, this would also be disempowering of the people's organisations and their members. At the very least it would discourage any macro-level differentiation of assistance being provided to those people's organisations. This argument could be tested.

The unwillingness to disclose difference could of course be seen as primarily a reflection of that staff member's perception of his relationship with me as an outside consultant hired by one of their major donors. At the field level there may well have been many areas of disagreement of which most of the staff were all too well aware. However, if this was the case, then it suggests even more serious problems. In what should have been one of the more supportive relationships the organisation has with various organisations in its institutional environment, these staff members still felt defensive and were unable to assert the truth as they knew it without fear of repercussions. If senior staff were not empowered to do so, then to what extent should we be expecting them to be empowering their own field workers?

In other more recent settings, in the Cameroon in 1999 I found field staff of a development project ready and able to talk about the most significant differences of opinion between their team and the communities with which they were working, as represented through various committees. I also found they were willing to talk about the most significant disagreements within their team. The senior management of this project subsequently took steps to institutionalise the reporting of such differences in the team's six-monthly reports, along with a number of other changes to the project's monitoring system. I have since learned that one of the four field staff teams was unwilling to report differences of opinion within their own team. In my judgement this team was one of the less effective of the four area teams of field staff. The other area teams were willing to report on internal differences and appeared to be more capable in their work. The actions of the non-disclosing team suggested vulnerability rather than empowerment.

Differences in Behaviour

At the population level, diversity of behaviour can be seen as a gross indicator of agency (the ability to make choices), *relative* to homogeneous behaviour by the same set of people. Diversity of behaviour suggests that there is a range of possibilities which individuals can pursue. At the other extreme is standardisation of behaviour, which we often associate with limited choice, the most notable example being perhaps that of an army. An army is a highly organised structure where individuality is not encouraged, and where standardised and predictable behaviour is very important. Like the term 'NGO' or 'non-profit', diversity is defined by something that it is not a condition where there is no common constraint, which would otherwise lead to a homogeneity of response. Homogeneity of behaviour may arise from various sources of constraint. A flood may force all farmers in a large area to move their animals to the high ground. Everybody's responses are the same, when compared to what they would be doing on a normal day. At a certain time of the year all farmers may be planting the same crop. Here homogeneity of practice may reflect common constraints arising from a combination of sources: the nature of both the physical environment and of particular local economies.

Constraints on diversity can also arise within the assisting organisation. Credit programmes can impose rules on loan use, specific repayment schedules and loan terms, as well as limiting access to credit, or specify how quickly approval will be given. Ideally, the diversity of economic activities undertaken by an NGO's clients, with the assistance of NGO credit, will be greater than that which existed before or without the NGO credit. We could then theorise as to which of the NGO-imposed constraints make the biggest difference to the diversity of activities undertaken with that credit. Timing of credit availability may, for example, make a bigger difference than the absolute amount of credit available for any one loan. The removal of that constraint would then become one proximate indicator of empowerment in that setting.

What we need are ways of separating out the sources of constraint at different levels of analysis. At the more macro-level there are **constraints** arising out of the assisting organisation, versus the economic and physical environment. At the more micro-level there are the constraints arising from different requirements associated with agency services. One way is to look for *differences in diversity* across different settings. This issue will be returned to later in this section.

Differences in Organisational Structures

As Fritz Wils (above) has pointed out, 'the subjects of empowerment – the ultimate beneficiaries – can be both groups and individual'. One way of identifying the absence of empowerment in a set of organisations is to look for **homogeneity** in their structures and processes. An interesting example are the peoples' organisations of the kind that have been promoted by the large NGOs in Bangladesh. If these organisations have evolved over time in response to local needs and pressures, we should expect a fairly high degree of diversity in their structure and process. **Diversity** should increase over time, unless there are some common dominating constraints. However, if those organisations were developed primarily to meet the needs of the NGO assisting them, then we might expect more homogeneity in structure and process. Standardised structures are more efficient and noiseless channels through which to pass commands and to receive information. My impression of one large NGO in 1995 was that peoples' organisations were remarkably homogeneous, despite being scattered across the country, and in some cases being quite old. They appeared as unpaid extensions of the NGO's own organisational structure.

One candidate for proximate indicator of organisational diversity is the degree to which the control over **financial resources** is decentralised, or not. To what extent do they have control, if any, over grant funds and to what extent do they make final decisions over loan authorisations? In the past, the evidence for significant devolution of financial control has not been very impressive. In 1991 IIED sent a questionnaire out to more than 1,000 rural development organisations in fifty countries. The main conclusion of their research was that 'local community participation in problems assessment and analysis is fairly common...[but] substantially less so for the monitoring and evaluation phases and more notably, there is very limited complete financial control given to the local community in all four phases of the work' (Guijt 1991).

How to Monitor Change?
Differences in Opinions

In the Cameroon project mentioned above, we also explored the dynamic nature of differences between people. In normal life some differences of opinion are resolved, others remain a continuing concern. The resolution of significant differences of opinion in relationships between an organisation and its clients can be seen as an indication of empowerment of both parties, if both parties agree that the result is a successful resolution. Conversely, the persistence over time of unresolved differences can be seen as an indication of ineffectiveness, or lack of empowerment. In the Cameroon project one of the area teams used a simple table format (below) to document two types of *resolved* and *unresolved* differences of opinion. One was of opinions within the membership of a particular stakeholder group; the other was of differences in that group's relationship with others.

Table 11 was constructed by the members of a Natural Resources Management Committee (NRMC). This is an apex group representing a wide range of different stakeholders interested in the fate of a nearby forest area called Bimbia Bonadikombo, in southern Cameroun. They were assisted in this exercise by field staff who had already done a similar kind of analysis in respect to the functioning of their own team.

Table 11: **Team Functioning**

	Most Significant Disagreement in the Last Six Months	
	Resolved	**Unresolved**
Internal (within NRMC)	Definition of who is a stakeholder: This affects who is represented in the NRMC, and thus how their interests are addressed.	When to conduct a farm survey in northern Bimbia Bonadikombo: If neglected, people in that area may feel marginalised
External (with others)	Location of inner core boundary of the forest reserve. (northern part): (Consequences not detailed)	Low incentives paid to Management Committee members during field work: (Consequences not detailed)

Each cell was expected to contain information – in the form of a 'difference that makes a difference'. The difference of opinion that was identified as most significant is in bold. The consequences of that difference are given in italics. It is expected that this information will be collected on a six-monthly basis. At the end of a six-monthly reporting period three different forms of change are possible:

- The worst possibility will be that the contents of all the cells are the same. Unresolved issues remain unresolved. In the face of this problem, no other important issues have emerged and been resolved.

- A better result will be that the contents of half the cells remain the same and half will have changed. Either (a) The unresolved issues remain the same, but other important issues have arisen and been resolved. These will be visible in the first column. Or (b) The most important unresolved issues from the previous six months have been resolved, but other important issues that have arisen have not yet been resolved. In this case the contents of the second column would have moved to the first column, and there would be new contents in the second column.

- In the best case the contents of all cells will have changed completely. Previously unresolved issues have been resolved and new more important issues have arisen and been resolved.

These three grades of evidence could be made more substantial by providing more cases. Additional rows representing differences between other types of stakeholders could be included. The relative significance of resolved and unresolved differences in any row could in turn be weighted, by ranking rows so that the most important relationships were at the top and the least important at the bottom of the table.

Diversity of Behaviour and Organisational Structures

Some changes in diversity are self-evident. In savings and credit groups *new* economic activities may be undertaken for the first time, and easily be reported by the members themselves or others. The *range* of activities undertaken by one group compared to another may also be easy to identify in many circumstances. This aspect of diversity has been described as *'variety'*, by Stirling (1998), in his analysis of the significance of diversity within economics.

A more sophisticated assessment might look at the degree of concentration, in terms of numbers of people involved, or amount of money invested, in one category of activity versus others. Stirling has described this aspect of diversity as *'balance'*. His view is that for a particular system of given variety, the more equal the fractions (for example, of money, people), the more even is the balance, the greater the diversity. Stirling also proposes a third aspect, called *'disparity'*. This relates to the nature and degree to which the categories themselves are different from each other. It is notions of disparity which determine when a particular type of option is recognised as falling into one category and when it is judged to be two. Disparity can be seen in the proximity of different branches in a tree structure representing the evolution of species. In Diagram 7 (a) and (b) could be people and chimpanzees, whereas (c) could be insects. Human genealogies can show this type of difference (disparity) in the same way.

In the case of human activities Stirling makes the important comment that *such disparity is an intrinsically qualitative, subjective and context-dependent aspect of diversity. Notions of disparity will vary, depending on the particular frame of reference which is adopted for any given purpose* (Stirling 1998). Disparity seems much more difficult to measure, or even observe, than variety or balance. In an earlier unpublished paper, I have spelled out a tree mapping method which can be used to elicit peoples' classification of other people, places or events (Davies 1997). This method leads to a nested categorisation structure of the same kind as shown above.

Diagram 7: **Disparities in Genealogies**

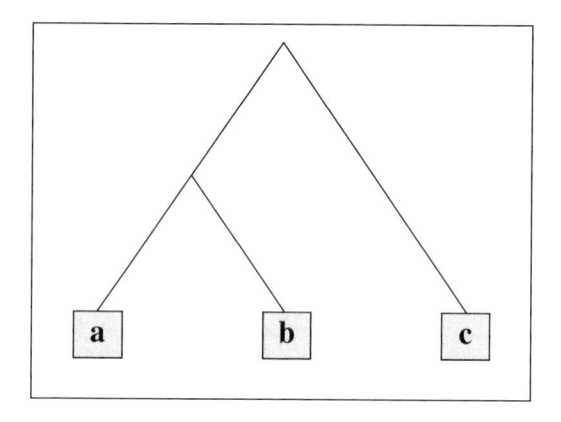

[Diagram showing a tree structure with three leaf nodes labeled a, b, and c, where a and b branch from a common node which then joins with c at the top.]

The subjectivity of this method is not necessarily a problem, if it is applied in an appropriate context. At this stage it is useful to return to the idea of proximate indicators, discussed earlier in this section. Diversity may exist to some degree in reality, but what also matters is the extent to which that diversity is *recognised* or not, especially by key actors within the assisting NGOs. If field staff, or middle managers, do not recognise important differences between their clients (in their behaviour or opinions, for example), they cannot respond differentially. Their denial of difference is effectively disempowering.

However, the ability to differentiate clients' opinions and behaviours to a great degree of detail (i.e. using many categories and sub-categories) holds out the potential to be empowering. Clients' different needs and opinions may be responded to in an appropriate manner. If differences are recognised in great detail, then we can go on to check less proximate indicators of empowerment.

The tree mapping method was designed to elicit informal and almost tacit knowledge. We can also proceed to explore whether NGO staff recognise client differences in other ways. We can consider an organisation's formal representations of its world, including its client population. We can consider progress reports and examine the types of difference that are prioritised in the form of the report structure: its headings and sub-headings, and even the structuring of paragraphs within those sub-sections. To what extent are major differences between clients the basis of this structure, or are they even visible at all? My own experience with this sort of analysis over the past few years is that clients' differences are rarely the basis of report structures, and instead the focus is on differences between the various activities the NGO is implementing. This experience reinforces my view that James' concern about organisational myopia on power issues was not misplaced, but rather that he was seriously underestimating the scale of the problem. The lack of recognition of differences between clients suggests that many organisations have serious difficulty with the most basic of empowerment tasks, which is simply *listening* to people.

Wider Issues: The Limits to Empowerment
There are clearly limits to the scale on which empowerment can take place. Some differences of opinion between individuals cannot be expressed without undermining the future of their relationship. Some differences in needs between clients cannot be responded to by an NGO since they are perceived as being outside the organisation's. At the level of larger groups and societies the extension of some forms of choice (for example, gun ownership) may diminish other forms of choice, and even threaten a larger-scale collapse of choice; for example, via civil war. In the biosphere, the diversity of ecosystems can be degraded, rather than extended, through the introduction of new species; for example, cats in the Australian bush. The relationship between individual and collective empowerment is obviously a complex one.

When we are talking about empowerment we are, by definition, not able to specify particular desirable outcomes at the level of individuals. Such an approach contradicts the very notion of choice. But we can define desirable outcomes in their collective form, at a population level. In the paragraph above, the implied ideal is a *sustainable expansion of diversity*. Such a view can even be applied as an ideal beyond the human sphere to the wider biosphere. Doing so is a salutary exercise, to say the least, since homo sapiens is believed to be responsible for the most recent 'great extinction' of species (Wilson 1992). Finally, we should note that proximate indicators may be helpful in advocacy work, where the chain of causation is often long and intermeshed with the influence of many other actors. For example, NGOs could start by looking at those who have been the immediate recipients of their advocacy communications and ask what types of change would they expect to find in that person's knowledge and attitudes if advocacy messages were beginning to have an effect. Do the people concerned know more than they have originally been told? In what areas have they developed more knowledge and what does that signify?

5.3 Grasping the Monitoring and Evaluation Framework as a Tool for Empowerment
Mark Waddington

Accountability
Accountability is a double-edged sword. In theory, it is a vital element of maintaining our integrity: that what we say we do as development practitioners is actually what we do. And with most of our funds being 'given' to us, we are all very

conscious of the need to account for them. But accountability to whom? Sure, we're accountable to our funders. Many of us are membership organisations and so we are also accountable to our members. However, our *primary stakeholders*, the *beneficiaries*, the *poor*, the people in the villages, are the people for whom most of our organisations were established to serve. The greater weight of our accountability should, therefore, be to these people. If this is truly the case, then accountability becomes a structural element of **empowerment**. We assume that our being accountable to the people we work with will enable them to achieve empowerment in their relationship with us.

But is this Really the Case?
In practice, we allow accountability to serve as an **obstacle** to empowerment. We manage information in such a way that our donors and trustees can make us accountable. This is good. But in servicing this accountability, the way we manage information is, at best, usually opaque to the people we work with. Our accountability to these people is serviced through how we choose to be accountable to them. There are few projects in which the beneficiaries are aware of the total budget, let alone how much staff are paid as part of those project costs. How would I explain the complexities of a project's budget to a village group? How would I communicate the value of my work and justify the activities I'm involved in? I can't walk into a village with my log frame, quarterly targets and annual report. Now that would be accountability. And they would be empowered. I would have to justify my salary and the costs of the whole management machinery to supporting their empowerment. So it is safer to assume that the people we work with would not fully understand. After all, we have the big picture, the wider context. We are accountable to them in the way we chose to be accountable to them. They are not actually able to make us accountable. We are trusting ourselves to be accountable to them. This is not accountability. It is benevolent paternalism. It's ironic that in seeking to stimulate empowerment, we have taken control of the process itself and actually constructed accountability as an obstacle to that purpose. We have to be responsible for changing this.

Conceptualisation
In designing the conceptual framework for our monitoring and evaluation systems, we inevitably seek to secure our information needs. And wherever we centralise the conceptualisation of M&E structures and systems – developing them in our offices – inevitably in practice they will remain extractive, informing *our* decision-making, driving *our* learning and servicing *our* notion of accountability. A centrally-conceived M&E framework is intrinsically non-experiential and so does not reinforce the capacity of people involved within it to learn. It is often cumbersome and, because it is imposed, it stifles creativity and initiative. Such frameworks do not

empower. They actually serve as an obstacle to empowerment.

The conceptual tools we use respond to our need to simplify and conceptualise development for others. There are few more infectious tools than the log frame. And we allow this to encourage our intellectualising of empowerment. All good stuff, but we are in danger of losing substance, and completely divorcing empowerment from reality. And what an amazing vocabulary it has bred around M&E. For many NGO staff, and especially for the people in the villages whose first language is not English, we are effectively excluding them from the empowerment process and ownership of the M&E framework. It becomes useless to those who are actively agitating for empowerment.

The convenience of a centralised conceptualisation of M&E frameworks, and subsequent control of the information that they maintain, locks us into orthodox monitoring and evaluation approaches. These include the extractive, non-participatory world of the questionnaire, and even rapid rural appraisal, which can pollute the potentially more empowering approaches such as participatory rural appraisal. The log frame can therefore sully processes of genuine empowerment, and constitute conceptual colonialism. Many of us accept that if *we* are to be effective in contributing to the genuine empowerment of others, then we are actually going to have to relinquish some of our own power. This is uncomfortable. In order to do this we need to challenge our inherent feeling to control. And part of this need is expressed in the centralised conceptualisation of M&E frameworks.

Prescription

Where we view **empowerment** as a **process**, empowerment will be defined and redefined in the course of that process, locally and within a context that is far greater in scope. To me, there seems to be a nonsense in setting **indicators of empowerment**. By doing so we are actually creating an M&E framework that prescribes the very process we are trying to measure, before it actually defines itself. And that we use so-called *logical* frameworks to do this is questionable. In practice, because the emphasis of our accountability is skewed towards donors, we allow ourselves to become indicator-led. Where this happens, the focus of our management loses sight of project objectives and the rationale upon which they are based – the foundation of our very legitimacy in any given intervention – and we lock ourselves into forcing change as a means of seeing the indicators we have set actually emerge.

This dilemma is amplified when empowerment is perceived as an end in itself rather than a process. The setting of indicators actually reinforces our capacity to *do* empowerment to others – because we have already prescribed what we want empowerment to be for them. This is a contradiction in terms.

The linearity that prescription fosters – objectives – activities – outputs – outcomes – does not promote effective learning and change and so challenges one of its key purposes. M&E frameworks based on such linearity all too often measure achievement rather than progress. By definition, achievement is too late. There's nothing you can do about changing it. The project cycle is complete. Because linear models of project management are highly prescriptive, M&E frameworks inevitably become extractive. In this way, we are once again measuring the empowerment we do to others. Probably the greatest irony of prescription is that it locks our M&E frameworks into identifying and measuring *success*. It does not promote balance and objectivity is lost. The only way we are able to pick up failures or problems is by assessing the level of our success in achieving prescribed indicators. Our success (or lack of it) might actually be seen as a failure by others, but since they are not prescribing success or how to measure it, let alone defining it, we are able to assess it on our terms and for our own purposes. This spits squarely in the eye of accountability. The log frame, with its prescriptive outputs and indicators located within a glorious logic, skews our M&E towards a very unbalanced focus on success.

Prescription also has other dimensions. We are continuously attempting to define our target groups: *the poor, beneficiaries, primary stakeholders or clients*. Is our obsession with slapping labels on everything an expression of an intrinsic need to define and control? Because if it is, we are setting up problems for ourselves within the empowerment process. If we accept that the people we work with are actually the agents of their own change – often driving processes of their own empowerment regardless of our intervention – then it would be logical for us to accept that they are the subjects of their own rights, not objects within *our* projects. The implications of this cut to the core of our own identity and role. In this sense, surely M&E becomes the mechanism through which people construct information and experiences, ideas and so on, around issues in their lives to reflect upon, analyse and take action. It is we who actually have to learn from this in order to improve the service we negotiate within the empowerment process. It is up to us, therefore, to ensure that our M&E frameworks are *not* centrally conceptualised or prescribe empowerment for others, but actually respond to the learning and accountability needs of the people we work with as a means of provoking a shift in power relations. And if we are transparent, our own accountability is changed from being a purpose and objective to becoming a natural function of the way we work. This might just free us up to get on with legitimately claiming our own role in the empowerment process. It's unlikely that these three areas are actually discrete dimensions; rather, they overlap, reinforcing the causes of wider problems.

Monitoring and Evaluation in the Hands of the People

Like most agencies, Village AiD has been struggling with many of the above issues. Indeed, we continue to do so. Village AiD has been running a literacy project in Lower Saloum District, the Gambia, funded by DFID. Upon undertaking the first evaluation of the work, we were faced with the usual self-made problem of minimal baseline information against which to judge prescribed indicators. And we wanted the evaluation exercise to provide a genuine opportunity for the women involved in the project to assess their progress for themselves as well as generate their own recommendations, while influencing the future management of the intervention. It was decided that rather than seek to pursue an evaluation based upon the assessment of prescribed indicators, which lack a baseline, we would actually discard the original M&E framework. We took a leap of faith in the team, with the women in the literacy groups to generate the information we would need to compile a report and capture learning relevant to Village Aid's needs, as a natural process during the course of the exercise. Terms of reference for this exercise were generated with the project team and in consultation with literacy facilitators and representatives of their groups, who were exclusively women.

Role Play

With each group we started the day with food, drumming and dancing. They were going to talk about their lives, and we were going to provoke them. They wanted to animate their stories. We really wanted to listen. We invited one of the more vocal women to take up the role of a wife who had had no exposure to literacy. Another woman was invited to play the role of her husband. The *wife* was asked to discuss her problems with her *husband*. Role play in this sense provides a safe environment - a fictional setting in which people can raise sensitive issues. During the session the nodding of heads and vocal agreement in encouraging the theme and nature of the discourse provided fuel for discussions among the wider group. Using stop(start drama techniques, the group was able to influence, qualify and challenge what was being discussed. Conflicts, inconsistencies and areas of consensus were identified. This was repeated several times, depending on the size of the group. Open discussions on the issues emerging generated a broad profile of *life before literacy*. Most of the conversation painted a picture of the women as victims and dependents; always requesting money from their husbands, complaining of lack of support, and seeking permission to leave the compound for the market, unable to take decisions for themselves.

Next a woman was invited to play the *wife*, but this time as someone who had been involved in the literacy group. This was repeated several times. A shift in the emphasis of priorities clearly emerged. The results were exciting. The women consistently demonstrated an increase in confidence to take up their own initiatives, such as petty trading. Because of the frequency with which they were cheated by traders and market sellers – a function of their inability to read weighing scales, count money – they had constructed a lack of confidence as a major obstacle to taking up their own initiatives. More fundamentally, in the scene they were able to claim mobility as a right. They acknowledged that it was convenient for them to assume that their husbands would not permit them to leave the compound and their village, nor allow them to earn money. But in so doing, they ignored their own responsibility for changing their circumstances.

Throughout the entire role play exercise, a before and after picture emerged. The baseline had been mapped out, the distance from it had been qualitatively measured, the outputs identified, and indicators such as reduced frequency of being cheated, increased mobility, increased income and so on were identified and verified. Cause–effect mechanisms were also identified, leading to the mapping out of several outcomes. Increased mobility, for instance, was seen by the women as a means of raising their awareness. One woman presented a question to her group, which they agreed generated a clear *indication* **of empowerment:**

> How many of us here had heard of family planning before we began to travel outside our communities? No hands went up.
>
> How many of us understand what it is now? Most of the hands went up.
>
> Why do you travel out of your community?
>
> Because I can. Responded one woman: I can read sign posts, bus number plates, count money, and no one can cheat me now.

The discussion that followed clearly indicated that many of the women knew how to access family planning services from a local NGO.

Finally, a critical indicator emerged from a key informant interview that I held with a market trader in Kaur who claimed that:

> Lately, the women from the Gimbala's and Genge Wollof are a lot more troublesome. Troublesomeness – perhaps a proxy indicator of empowerment?

Floor Mapping

The richness of graphics that might emerge from using this approach reflects the complexity and sophistication of people's lives. Each group mapped out its village. The themes for the mapping exercise were left open so that each group was able to construct its map according to the local context of its life. Most of the women were familiar with floor mapping through their involvement in the wider participatory rural appraisal (PRA) process that Village AiD had been facilitating. This was, therefore, a relatively easy tool to use with the literacy groups. Some agencies had evaluated their non-formal literacy work in the Gambia by using formal approaches such as exams and tests. We felt that such an approach would not enable us to explore whether or not literacy was really an element of the increasing confidence women were claiming to have and their wider empowerment – and if it was, whether they were aware of this themselves. So rather than symbolise the features through objects and pictures, the women were requested to use flash cards to write the name of the feature.

For example, where the shop was identified, a flash card was placed in the location of the shop and the local word for shop was written. The goods that the shop had on sale were listed on another flash card with their respective prices. Various combinations of goods were added and subtracted as a means of assessing numeracy. Unfortunately we did not have group-specific baseline data against which to assess progress made in terms of the number of words individuals could write and recognise, or the number of words which the group as a whole was originally able to write and recognise. However, in the subsequent discussion, we explored what the initial level of literacy was through the use of trend mapping. And we tested out with the group our assumption that the women would not have given their time over to learning, were they not actually recognising improvements in their literacy capacity for themselves.

However, the major benefit of this exercise was the information which the women generated themselves and their excitement about how they could use it. For the first time, they could see the extent of their literacy in relation to their lives in their village. They had developed their own indicators.

We can see that we are able to recognise and write 63 words on this map.
By the end of the dry season we want to increase this to 100 words.

Comparing the number of words generated by each group was a very effective means of helping us to identify which groups were doing well. Was it the facilitator and could we use that person to train and mentor other facilitators, or was it that the women were effective at organising themselves to mobilise a common fund which paid for the fuel for their lamp so that they could run night sessions? This type of practical information was much more useful to us in effectively servicing our role in the project. But we didn't know that we needed it until it presented itself to us during the evaluation!

Floor mapping generates a great deal of discussion. It became clear at an early stage that the original linear M&E framework would need to be reviewed in order to ensure that the processes catalysed during the course of the evaluation would continue. It was also clear that other issues would need to be embraced within any new framework. So with some groups we took the opportunity to feed the discussions from the floor mapping into impromptu trend mapping exercises.

Trend Mapping

In collaboration with the women, we needed a means of assessing which of the issues were actually feasible. In order to determine this we undertook trend mapping.

Symbols can be used to identify the issue being mapped, but in our case writing them down was a means of exploring literacy capacity as well. The point is to identify change – small change or big change. Actual numbers and means of verification can be identified by using complementary techniques, such as expenditure analysis or key informant interviews. Informal discussions with individual women in their households – asking them to go through their workbooks with us, and discuss their daily routines and so on – proved to be very useful. We had previously found in evaluation work in northern Ghana that informal focus group discussions generated a great deal of information and subsequent conversation that was useful to both us and the women. It's amazing what people will tell you! Although extractive, such techniques can feed information back into wider discussions at a later stage, to challenge what has been previously agreed. They can also inform follow-up work after the dust from the adventures of the time-bound evaluation has settled.

Retention

The way people store the information that they have generated, the analyses that they have made and the decisions that they have resolved upon is crucial. This is particularly so if a process M&E framework is to be successful. It is cumbersome and often counterproductive to have to keep on regenerating analyses, when it is easier to renegotiate what has been agreed over time. Village AiD has negotiated several ways of doing this with the people we work with. Where role play was used during the course of the evaluation of the literacy project in the Gambia, they were actually transcribed. The transcriptions were formulated with each group to reflect the key points of their learning. These were then printed in the relevant language. Not only did they constitute a written record of what was achieved and the action points mapped out, but they also served as a self-generated primer with a valuable input to the literacy development process itself. The graphics produced during these sessions are also a good way of recording analyses and decisions. And they provide a baseline for ongoing monitoring. Photographs of participants and their involvement in the exercises have proven to be effective prompts in recalling what has been decided upon and how decisions were reached.

In Ghana, Village AiD has recently developed evaluation story-boards with communities in developing video reports. The involvement of the people in the editing of the video is crucial to their maintaining ownership of the evaluation process. This has also proved to be a very effective means of facilitating participation, and especially of mobilising people's interest in the issues being dealt with. Our experience with this, however, is limited. In Cameroon, baseline analyses have actually been recorded in communities simply as plays. Stories and songs have also been used. And there's no reason why a local teacher, if mandated by their community, cannot be asked to record the key points in a small notebook. Ensuring that the people we work with have a clear record of what they have constructed, analysed and decided is crucial to their capacity to make us genuinely accountable to them – because they also record what it is we have agreed to do, how and by when.

Some Weaknesses

There are broadly four areas of **weakness** in the approaches presented here, and between them they breed a range of risks that need to be prevented or mitigated.

The use of recall techniques: This places us in danger of identifying only positive change. Because the scale of change has not been prescribed, any change will constitute achievement. Success can, therefore, be judged in any way we want it to be judged. This problem can be reduced, but not fully overcome, by using a variety of methods.

- First, we have found it extremely useful to recruit internal advisers who have a wider range than drawing in external experiences and providing advice on the setting of indicators. They are recruited primarily to identify and challenge negative conventions, spot where group think is occurring (especially within the project team), identify vested as well as conflicting interests and assess whether they are influencing the project.

- Second, the need to **triangulate** information and verify it from different perspectives is vital – one person's empowerment is likely to disempower another. The continuously growing tool box of participatory techniques provides us with many ways of triangulating and verifying information.

- Third, we have found **contra-indicators** useful – essentially proximate indicators used to detect and measure the emergence of risks and threats – in ensuring that we generate some balance. For example, the work being undertaken by Village AiD with its partners in Cameroon is focusing on the exclusion of a specific ethnic group, and of women within that group. We have identified an increase or decrease in the frequency of domestic violence as a proximate indicator of women's empowerment within the project. Several contingencies have been put in place to prevent this from happening. Nevertheless, these indicators are prescribed.

- Finally, the need for **contextual** information can never be underestimated. The opinions, perceptions and experiences of people not directly involved in the project are crucial in identifying potential or actual problems, teasing out failures, determining what other forces beyond the project's are acting within the chain of causation to generate the effects we are assessing. They are also useful in gaining an understanding of where value is being added. Contextual information must be a focus of the initial research and development process and must be maintained in the course of monitoring and evaluation.

Recall techniques do not easily allow us to deconstruct the rationale of a project and thereby assess its continuing legitimacy. If used in isolation, there are serious constraints on our ability to judge whether or not the project is actually assisting people to address their priority or rather what we believe to be their priority. Once again, the need for contextual information is vital. Floor mapping techniques continue to be very useful in identifying the breadth of issues people are dealing with, and matrix ranking serves as one way in which people might define where the issues a project seeks to address are located on their scale of priorities.

These approaches are heavily dependent on two **participatory frameworks**, PRA and social drama. PRA, although incredibly useful, has suffered greatly during the course of its recent scaling-up and globalisation, to the extent that the facilitation of genuine participation is often questionable at best. Furthermore, there are concerns that it brings a framework to a village and imposes a new way of viewing the world, their world, on them and so might not always be appropriate to dealing with issues related to empowerment. Social drama currently has more space for people to express themselves, construct their ideas and information, and take decisions in ways that they can at least identify with. Nevertheless, there are limitations in terms of the way the framework is structured in practice. Village AiD is currently exploring the potential of a new participatory paradigm in which it utilises local norms and values, means of communicating and decision-making. This is being piloted in northern Ghana. In the meantime, we should not underestimate sitting down with someone in their compound, or under the mango tree with a calabash of local brew, and just talking with them.

The scientific rigour is not strong. The repeatability is there, but dependence on arbitrary variables (the mood of a facilitator, the infinite diversity of group dynamics, the different priorities of individuals and so on) makes the approach open and sensitive to change. Ensuring that the evaluation team are involved in developing the terms of reference, and that at least some prior consultation of people has been undertaken in advance, assists in generating a shared understanding of purpose. Training and briefing sessions of team members also assist in maintaining some uniformity of approach. And we have found that appointing an itinerant coordinator to move between evaluation sub-teams can keep the approach within the parameters set for it. If the key purpose of monitoring and evaluation is as a means of empowerment in its own right, then it absolutely has to be locally contextualised by the people who use it. Ensuring the necessary rigour for meaningful comparative assessment is a problem for the academics.

Engaging our Information Management with Upward Learning

It is obviously crucial that we record information generated during the course of the M&E process. We need it to be accountable, we need it to inform our own decision-making, and we need it to remain empowering. Village AiD's experiences here suggest that the basic principle is simply to allow the information generated during the course of the upward learning process to build the structures through which we manage that information. Our challenge is to identify what is useful information to us now and, more difficult, what is likely to be useful information in the future.

Community and Group Profiles

At the simplest level, we have found community or group profiles useful in recording information. Standard formats can be built very quickly once the upward learning process kicks in, and new tables, sections and so on can be bolted on in time. Inevitably, there is some processing of the information - possibly summarising statistics in tables where the addition of columns builds up a picture of an issue over time, or using graphics such as bar charts and so on. Recording the raw stuff such as floor maps is particularly useful – if you play with the scales, you can overlay floor maps and produce exciting insights. But profiles need to be developed creatively in order to be able to deal with change and track process. The issue of time as a linear dimension must, therefore, serve as the backbone of the profile. What Village AiD has not achieved as yet is transferring the hard copy profiles in order to be able to create a computerised database management system.

However, we should not lose sight of the purpose of the exercise. As soon as we have information, we use it to generate knowledge, and *knowledge is power*. The wealth of knowledge we have concerning many people and their groups and communities is a privilege. It is important that the necessary policy, training and enrolment mechanisms be in place to ensure that the profiles feed back into the upward learning process, rather than take control of it and force it towards generating the information we require to verify the emergence of our expectations. One of the key benefits of maintaining community profiles is that we are generating a profile of our own perception of the people we work with. This is incredibly useful as both their perceptions of themselves and their own circumstances, as well as our perceptions of them, will inevitably change over time. The profile serves as a resource, therefore, in identifying inconsistencies and contrasting perceptions. If people know that we have a different view to them, and understand why, then it is more likely that space for influence and negotiation (another location of empowerment) rather than control and authority (a location of disempowerment) will expand.

Log Frames

This article is actually located within a wider process of review of Village AiD's management structures and systems. In practice, we have already stepped away from an orthodox means of planning. We cannot have a project log frame without a project management framework upon which to build it.

The whole framework is based on an underlying rationale. This rationale represents the baseline circumstance and identifies the key issues requiring change. It relates directly to each of the six structural elements – aims, objectives, targets, outputs, outcomes and impact. If this framework is to be meaningful in terms of empowerment, the research and development process (generating the rationale and mapping out aims, objectives and targets) must be participatory. Village AiD has learned from its own mistakes here of the problems of convincing ourselves that undertaking a comprehensive PRA exercise will enable us to develop a project intervention that empowers. We simply use PRA to extract the information to generate our own analysis, upon which we construct our project doing empowerment unto others again. The intervention (rationale, objectives, activities and budget) needs to be generated during the course of the PRA exercise with the people it will affect.

How the Framework Works

The aims of the framework refer to the key areas of the rationale which the project or intervention will seek to address at the broadest level. The objectives, while directly interpreting specific elements of the rationale, also serve to interpret the aims divided into manageable areas. The targets serve as the interface between planning and action, and when implemented generate outputs.

This framework allows for both prescribed and unprescribed outputs. The M&E loop between targets and outputs feeds directly into planning of further activities and the emergence of further outputs. Activities implemented directly from objectives as well as in the follow-up to outputs generate the outcomes – again, they can be prescribed or allowed to emerge through upward learning. Similarly, the M&E loop informs further actions (as well as the renegotiations of objectives when appropriate) and the reinforcing of existing outcomes as well as the emergence of new ones.

The impact (if this is a dimension needed to be included in the management framework) is generated with activities, which come directly from the aims, and in follow-ups to outputs and outcomes. As before, the M&E loop feeds back into further actions and the renegotiations of aims (if appropriate). It is this fluidity, which occurs naturally in practice, which drives the process. And because of the way in which it remains fundamentally linked to the rationale, the rationale itself is regularly deconstructed and assessed as a means of evaluating the continuing legitimacy of the intervention.

Process log frames have been around for many a moon. But most are cumbersome because they are unable to adjust easily to what emerges from the short end of the wedge, the reality of our work.

The first process log frame that Village AiD experimented with moved linearly by objective from targets, which were used to generate activities, through a prescriptive framework which mapped out expected outputs and outcomes, in turn assessed through participatory evaluation techniques. It looped further actions back to renegotiating existing targets, setting new ones and directly into planning activities. The feedback loops were not immediately obvious in practice, such that over time it crept back towards linearity. It was also prescriptive. So we desegregated it and exposed it to upward learning. This sounds terribly reductionist, but what worked about fragmenting the framework into three components (targets, outputs, outcomes) was that the process loops became more obvious. And reporting became easier because the causation of discrepancies, emerging outputs and emerging outcomes could be identified and reviewed more clearly.

This desegregated process log frame is presented at the end of this. It runs through quarterly and annual cycles, which feed into each other.

- For each objective, annual targets are set at the beginning of a year.
- Activities are planned for the first quarter.
- A budget is then generated for that quarter and activities are undertaken.
- The actual activities achieved are reviewed and discrepancies identified (a column can be inserted to specifically record these discrepancies).
- A review of expenditure is recorded.
- Progress against annual targets is reviewed.
- Further actions are identified. The further actions are used to renegotiate existing targets (where relevant) or add new ones. The further actions also, where appropriate, feed directly into the planned activities column under the relevant targets. Together with the actual activities achieved they serve to produce outputs.
- Annual reviews assess the achievement of annual targets and identify emerging outputs, their associated indicators and means of verifying them through upward learning mechanisms – which are being used throughout the ongoing process of project management.
- The further actions, developed subsequent to the identification of emerging outputs, are used to renegotiate existing targets (where relevant) or add new ones. And where appropriate, they feed directly into the planned activities column under the relevant targets. Together with the actual activities achieved and the emerging further actions (from targets and outputs) they combine to produce outcomes.

- Annual reviews identify emerging outcomes, their associated indicators and means of verifying them through upward learning mechanisms – which are being used throughout the ongoing process of project management. Annual expenditure is then reported against the year's budget which has been cumulatively constructed.
- Targets are then generated for the subsequent year and embrace the further actions which flow out of all three tables.
- A detailed picture of achievement is built up over time, but achievement does not lead the development of the work to a prescribed location; this is driven by the process which emerges from assessing progress which, in this case, defines itself.

The log frame easily adjusts to changes (and accommodates process simply) because new targets and activities are bolted onto columns as new rows, and because outputs and outcomes are not prescribed, they are also added in as new rows within their relevant columns.

Since the log frame has been desegregated, it can be constructed through worksheets within a spreadsheet programme.

There are, however, two further points worth noting:

- How can we budget for something we do not know we are going to do? Target setting allows us to construct detailed short-term budgets. In the meantime, there are other ways in which projects and programmes can be constructed with a focus on core activities and so affect the way in which we budget projects. These respond directly to the key dimensions of the rationale – thereby cutting out the need to re-interpret what needs to be **done** (not achieved!), which is a means by which NGOs (often unwittingly) take control of the empowerment process. And let's face it, many of us have significant amounts of unrestricted funds. Are we actually prepared to put this where our mouth is, or will we continue to allocate them to what we think they needs to be spent on – and in so doing secure our own agenda. This would mean relinquishing some of our power?

- This log frame can, unfortunately, be effectively used as a prescriptive and process management tool. Define your objectives and, for each objective simply map out your targets as before. Instead of emerging outputs, outcomes and impact (if you want it), simply re-title your columns – expected outputs, outcomes and so on and prescribe away with your indicators. Of course, you could have your cake and eat it. Each table can be split horizontally into two sections – the top section mapping out expected outputs or outcomes, the bottom section mapping out unexpected outputs and outcomes (which use upward learning mechanisms for qualification through locally generated, process-driven indicators).

Both of these points lead us towards the issue of planning.

As the development sector scrambles towards empowerment and gradually relinquishes its emphasis on provision of material needs, the locus of accountability will shift from people in communities/groups through NGOs to funders, to a paradigm built on a web of mutual accountability between all three groups of stakeholders. This shift will require a different approach to management. With a focus on empowerment we have changed the terrain we want to work in. We're off-roading now, so we need '4-wheel drive' management. We cannot continue to manage in the way we used to manage if we are serious about empowerment. This could be something we consider for the next workshop.

Perhaps we need to challenge ourselves. It is so convenient for us to claim that our need to be accountable to our funders will not provide us with the space to step out of orthodox and often inappropriate management paradigms. How can we be accountable without objectives, prescribed outputs and indicators? Possibly the question we need to ask is, how can we involve ourselves in genuine processes of empowerment by dictating what empowerment will be for others through the prescription of objectives, outputs and indicators? Just because some of us are unable to see how we can be accountable without *managing by objectives* does not mean that other possibilities do not exist. They clearly do. The corporate sector has demonstrated this. We should not be captives of the limitations we impose on our own imagination. Nor should we avoid responsibility for change by constructing perceived obstacles which we blame on others.

Funders are actually very flexible. A recent proposal submitted to and funded by the National Lottery Charities Board by Village AiD had not a single aim or objective laid out in the form. We have had no vehement request (and we have proposed major budgetary re-allocations) turned down by any funder in the 11 year history of the organisation. Every proposal maps out the rationale and clearly outlines how we intend to manage work through process frameworks. The funders have the information they need to make their decisions and we report back to them clearly and transparently. The same funders are often more genuinely concerned about what they are calling the *primary* stakeholders than NGOs are. We need more effective lobbying and advocacy systems within our own institutions to continue driving the shift towards stimulating true empowerment – a core issue which the funders are clearly buying into.

5.4 Participatory Programme Learning for Women's Empowerment in Micro-finance Programmes: Negotiating Complexity, Conflict and Change
Linda Mayoux

Introduction

Micro-finance programmes for women are currently promoted not only as a strategy for poverty alleviation but also for women's empowerment (Results 1997). The linking of micro-finance with women's empowerment is neither new, nor is it a Northern imposition. Building on the work of SEWA in India and other organisations in the South, the problem of women's access to credit was given particular emphasis at the First International Women's Conference in Mexico in 1975. Access to credit was seen as vital to women's ability to earn an income, in turn seen as central to their wider status and autonomy (Mayoux 1995). At the same time a number of academic studies have questioned the supposed automatic benefits of programmes for women (Ebdon 1995; Goetz and Sengupta 1996), adding to other critiques of prevailing models of micro-finance as a tool for poverty alleviation (Hulme and Moseley 1996; Johnson and Rogaly 1997). These concerns, together with increasing emphasis on gender policy within NGOs and donor agencies, have led to pressure for gender impact studies and evaluations of micro-finance programmes. This information is crucial to ensuring that the potential contributions of micro-finance to women's empowerment are realised in practice, and potential disbenefits to women participants and vulnerable non-participants are minimised.

However, conventional quantitative and qualitative approaches to impact assessment are costly and rarely integrated into practice. This section proposes a participatory approach for integrating women's empowerment concern into ongoing programme learning, itself a contribution to empowerment. The section first discusses some of the problems faced by policy-relevant research on **women's empowerment**. It then outlines principles, methods and elements of a participatory programme learning approach and proposes a framework for analysing the interrelationships between different aspects of empowerment and policy. Finally, it examines some continuing methodological and institutional challenges faced that will need to be addressed.

Gender Impact Assessment and Women's Empowerment: Some Tricky Issues

There has been no systematic comparative study of contextual and programme factors affecting the contribution of micro-finance to different dimensions of empowerment. The most detailed studies of women's empowerment have been done in Bangladesh. These have been very important in challenging current complacency about automatic benefits of targeting women in micro-finance programmes.

Nevertheless methodologies and analyses have been continually contested on the grounds of **identification, measurement** and **weighting of indicators** and choice of samples and control groups, as discussed in detail by the author elsewhere. Other studies have analysed financial data and economic impacts, provided information on 'well-being' impacts for women and children, women's control of loans, income and resources and wider social impacts. These studies have, however, either been limited in the questions asked in statistical analysis or very short consultancies with small samples of women (Mayoux 1998). The Bangladesh studies and others have drawn policy implications but different studies have drawn different, though not necessarily mutually exclusive, conclusions about the same programmes.

The complexity of inter-linkages between different dimensions of gender subordination and its all-encompassing nature further exacerbate inherent problems faced by conventional quantitative and qualitative approaches to impact assessment of micro-finance programmes. The continuing debates highlight the fact that programme evaluation cannot be an 'exact science' where definitive conclusions can be proved about unambiguous impacts on empowerment of particular policies which are valid for all time in all contexts for all women, even within the same programme. Firstly, 'empowerment' is a highly contested concept. In the view of the author, it is convenient shorthand to highlight:

- the inter-linked nature of different dimensions of gender subordination and hence the processes of challenging this subordination;
- the centrality of underlying power relations in influencing women's aspirations and strategies and constraining their ability to achieve these;
- the importance of looking at positive action for change by women themselves rather than simply examining gender impacts of existing agency interventions.

However, the identification of 'key' criteria and measurable indicators by which empowerment can be assessed is inevitably an attempt to select particular partial aspects of a complex and interconnected reality. Different approaches to microfinance have focused on very different aspects and made different assumptions about inter-linkages, all of which need to be questioned in the light of existing evidence.

- Women's access to or control of income cannot be inferred from financial statistics on women's take up of financial services, repayment levels or enterprise performance.

- Women's wellbeing cannot be inferred from impact on household income or even increased income from women's economic activities.

- Women's increased income earning may not lead to either changes in gender roles or wider social, political or legal empowerment. Women themselves may prioritise income earning over either control over income or wider social, political or legal empowerment.

Gender Impact Assessment and Empowerment

Analytical Questions

What is Empowerment? Complexity, Relevance and Reliability?
- What type of empowerment? Problem of criteria; in view of inter-linkages and trade-offs between many different dimensions of empowerment, is it possible to identify some as in any way more 'key' than others?
- How can it be identified? Problem of measurable or observable indicators; even if criteria can be established, how can they be assessed in any particular context?
- How much empowerment? Problem of product versus process; within any particular context how much change in dimensions of an ongoing process qualifies as change?

Whose Empowerment? Difference, Conflict and Representation?
- Who should be represented? Problem of sampling; in view of the different situations of women and their differing priorities and experiences, how should different categories of women be identified and who should be included in the sample population?
- Whose interests should be prioritised? Problem of aggregation; empowerment may not be a win(win process and there may not be one 'correct view' but multiple interpretations of a process depending on particular perspectives and interests. So how should benefits and disbenefits to different people be compared or statistically aggregated?

How can empowerment be supported? Policy relevance and implementing change?
- How far are changes identified as due to micro-finance? Problems of attribution since credit and savings are often combined with other resources, or disappear into a household cash pool; so how can uses and effects be assessed? Even where usage of savings and credit is identified, these are rarely the sole factor in bringing about change - so how can degree of contribution be evaluated?
- Which particular programme policies have contributed? Problem of inter-linked effects; different policies within programmes are typically dependent

on other programme features for effectiveness or may be contradicted by them. How can the particular mix of policies contributing to empowerment be identified?
- What are the implications for policy in the future? Problem of inferring potential for change from current impacts; emerging trends or isolated innovation may be more useful for increasing future contribution to empowerment than statistically prevalent impacts.

- What are the implications for replication elsewhere? Both analysis and potential for change may be highly context-specific and dependent on particular organisational and institutional structures.

Methodological Questions
- Do people know? Interviewees may not remember or even know the responses to questions, even about income levels and changes.
- Do they want to tell you? Interviewees may not have the time or interest to respond.
- Whom do they want to tell? Responses may vary considerably depending on relationship with the interviewer.
- How should what they say be interpreted? In view of the above, responses may only be partial and may change over time

Ethical Questions
- Impact assessment in whose interests? How can the research process itself benefit those involved?
- Research versus practice? How can the research process maximise contribution to programme development?

Programmes also typically have both negative and positive impacts on individual women's lives. There are frequently trade-offs, for example between different uses of time and resources. Women may gain control over small amounts of their own earned income but men may decrease contributions to the household income pool and women's workload may significantly increase (Mayoux 1998).

Particularly contentious is the delicate balance and in some cases inherent tension between women's own (generally diverse) aims and aspirations and externally devised criteria established a priori from underlying theories of development, poverty or feminist analysis. Women's own aspirations and strategies are a central (and for some the only) element in any definition of empowerment as well as an important factor in explaining programme outcomes and must therefore be included in any analysis. At the same time, as amply demonstrated in the feminist literature, women's aspirations, knowledge and strategies for empowerment must be seen in the context of gender subordination which limits women's knowledge of macro-level factors and ability to challenge views of gender subordination as 'natural' rather than amenable to change. For example, women may see use of credit for dowry payments as a crucial investment in their daughter's future and source of status for themselves. However, dowry payment may fail to avert ill-treatment of brides and, where loans are used for this purpose on a wide scale within an area, the overall effect may be to create an upward spiral of dowry inflation. Where women choose to invest in their husband's enterprises, indirect benefits may not materialise for the women concerned and the wider effect may be to reinforce gender subordination and stereotypes. Women may become extremely vulnerable in ways unforeseen by them if dependent on male incomes for debt repayment. There are dangers therefore that relying solely on women's own criteria, indicators and accounts may omit important dimensions of analysis. Reliance on local analyses alone may also limit the possibilities for cross-contextual comparison.

Secondly women are not a **homogeneous group** as assumed in many impact studies. Programme impacts typically differ between women. It may not therefore be possible to identify one set of criteria and indicators that are equally relevant for all women. Better-off women may be able to use very different enterprise strategies aimed at maximising profits, but very poor women may be more concerned to decrease vulnerability to crises. For some women individual control of their own income may be crucial to benefiting from micro-finance. For other women, in different types of household or ethnic groups, it may be more important to strengthen the marital bond and joint negotiation over use of household resources, including their share of male income. Women may even have conflicting interests. Mothers or mothers-in-law may wish to increase their incomes and use the unpaid labour of daughters or daughters-in-law. Richer women may want to increase their market advantage over poorer women. In many cases there will be no one 'definitive correct version' of impact, but a range of competing perspectives, each relevant in its own way to particular stakeholders.

A further set of problems is posed in attempts to link changes in empowerment indicators identified with particular policies and draw conclusions for programme change. Quantitative economic impact assessment of micro-finance programmes as a whole face well-documented problems of tracing the usage of credit and savings and distinguishing programme impacts from contextual factors. These problems are compounded in any attempt to identify the impact of particular programme features, as these may well be inextricably interlinked. Loan amounts, timing and repayment schedules and patterns of savings may be crucial to women's ability to control income and investment within the household. However, similar conditions of credit delivery, groups of formally similar structures or similar training programmes may have very different impacts, depending on whether they are being implemented within a programme framework emphasising empowerment or emphasising financial sustainability. Wider programme aims also influence the types of skills emphasised in recruitment policy, incentive structures, and choice of allocation of time and resources, which affect implementation by programme staff (Mayoux 1998). Convincing conclusions cannot be reached by comparative statistical analysis because of wide variation in programme models and diversity within models in inclusion of gender-relevant policies. Moreover, assessment of current impact of particular programmes does not necessarily indicate the most appropriate strategies for change in the future or possibilities for replication elsewhere.

In addition to these analytical problems there are well-documented methodological problems in the research process itself. Respondents frequently do not recall the particular information required and may only be able to give a partial picture. This is particularly the case with very detailed information about incomes, livelihoods, decision-making or other dimensions of empowerment unless locally important indicators and events have been established beforehand. People may also be unwilling to divulge information because of lack of time or in anticipation of the consequences. They may misrepresent impacts on incomes, depending on how they think this will affect their access to credit. Women may be particularly vulnerable to violent repercussions within households and communities and unwilling to reveal to public scrutiny their strategies for pursuing their interests. They may understate or overstate changes in their lives depending on their relationship with the interviewer (particularly their gender) and what they think the interviewer wants to hear. There are problems on the one hand with long detailed questionnaires, which women may have neither the time nor the interest to answer, and on the other with shorter open-ended questions which often get only vague general answers. Responses are therefore frequently difficult to interpret, particularly when dealing with patterns of decision-making or power inequalities.

Finally, in some programmes there are now signs of *'assessment fatigue'*. In addition to the consequences for data reliability this raises some ethical questions. It is obviously unreasonable to expect all research to benefit all those involved and research may very usefully document 'best practice' or expose 'bad practice' even if researchers cannot themselves be directly involved in implementing change. Nevertheless there are important ethical questions to be asked – as an integral part of research design – about ways in which the research process itself can maximise positive contributions to empowerment of participants, and direct contribution to programme development within given time, resource and skills constraints. These questions need to be asked as an integral part of research design.

A Participatory Learning Approach: Frameworks and Methodologies for Examining Empowerment

What follows are proposals for a new participatory learning approach which would fully integrate empowerment concerns into a process of participatory programme learning. This would address, though not necessarily definitively resolve, the issues under discussion. The approach would be based on underlying principles and combine a number of elements and methodologies that are distinct from most current approaches to gender impact assessment

Firstly, it would focus on examining women's own priorities and strategies as the starting-point rather than criteria and indicators decided a priori. This would, however, be done in the context of a commitment to addressing the underlying power inequalities that constrain women's aspirations and ability to fulfil them rather than focusing solely on economic impact or well-being. Secondly, it would include a concern to minimise adverse impact on poorer and disadvantaged women and other vulnerable groups, even if these are not direct programme participants. Thirdly, research and practice would be integrated through the establishment of structures to link participatory information exchange to decision-making.

The participatory learning process would consist of a number of elements interlinked in a reflexive learning loop. The approach would use a combination of methodologies now commonly referred to under the umbrellas of 'Participatory Learning and Action' (PLA) and 'Soft Systems Analysis' (SSA). It would build on and integrate existing but currently dispersed programme experience.

A Participatory Learning Approach: Principles, Elements and Continuing Challenges

Principles:
- Focus on women's own aspirations and strategies for change and prioritisation of their interests.
- Commitment to equity and the challenging of power inequalities in all programme activities.
- Integration of research and practice for empowerment through establishment of structures for linking participatory learning to decision-making

Combined Methodologies:
- PLA and SSA visual techniques for use in groups, and individual questionnaires.
- Group discussions and workshops with different stakeholders, both separately and combined.
- Quantitative analysis of statistical survey data generated by MIS.
- In-depth quantitative and qualitative research by independent outsiders, carefully targeted through reference to information generated through the programme.

> *Elements of the Participatory Learning Loop:*
> - Participatory identification of priority empowerment criteria and measurable or observable indicators by using multi-dimensional, multi-stakeholder framework for analysis and PLA techniques in group workshops.
> - Integration of indicators into existing programme management information systems by including questions or PLA visual elements in questionnaires canvassed for participants on entry into the programme, loan applications and exit, and added to other information routinely collected by programme staff.
> - Support for information exchange between women themselves through existing and new networks. This might also develop special PLA/soft systems visual techniques to aid discussion, collation and representation of information.
> - Participatory analysis of information generated to assess policy implications, ways forward and issues on which in-depth independent research is needed through using SSA and PLA methods in group discussions and workshops with different stakeholders, both separately and combined.
> - Participatory identification of ways in which the findings would be integrated into practice by using SSA and PLA methods in group discussions and workshops with different stakeholders, both separately and combined.
> - Restarting the loop through reconsideration of further empowerment criteria and indicators.
> - Participatory methodologies for gender analysis, gender awareness and feminist mobilisation.
> - Integration of poverty impact assessment by programme staff into routine programme management.
> - Visual methodologies for research and information exchange by illiterate women.
> - Integration of participatory research into participatory management structures.

The process would start by explicitly prioritising criteria for assessing empowerment using a comprehensive framework. In one matrix this would combine:

- *different dimensions of empowerment:* economic empowerment, contribution to well-being and social, political and legal empowerment;

- *different domains of empowerment:* individual, household, community, market, national level;

- *an underlying analysis of power relations* distinguishing between: power within, power to, power over and power with.

This enables different criteria to be categorised relative to each other as part of a complex interlinked whole. It includes – but goes beyond – frameworks proposed elsewhere (Longwe 1991; Moser 1994; and Chen 1997). It also allows for an empirically-based investigation of connections between women's diverse individual and collective strategies at different levels, rather than imposing a preconceived hierarchy starting with material concerns. For some women, freedom from violence or control over their own income and fertility and/or the support of other women may be crucial preconditions before they can even begin to think about health, nutrition or increasing incomes.

PLA ranking exercises in group workshops might initially generate new criteria to be added but would then prioritise a limited number of these to be combined into a single framework for that particular programme. Alternatively, if consensus is difficult to reach, a series of separate matrices could be agreed for different groups: for example, women from different backgrounds, NGO staff and maybe also men. The framework would therefore be treated as a guide to aspects for analysis and some of the questions to be asked, rather than a definitive checklist of criteria. It would also serve as a point of reference to the questions that were not being asked but have been identified by feminist analysis as important aspects of the empowerment process. This may be crucial in signalling to women and programme staff that such issues as control over income and violence are open for discussion, even if they choose not to include them. In this case these issues might be addressed at further points in the reflexive loop or through in-depth independent research.

Depending on the particular criteria identified, there are a range of well-tested PLA visual techniques which could usefully be used or adapted to establish locally relevant measurable or observable **indicators**. For example, gender(sensitive wealth ranking could be used to identify indicators of increased income. Decision-making matrices could form the basis of indicators of control in the household. Mapping could also establish indicators for mobility. Role plays or 'balloon exercises' could be used to establish more sensitive indicators for changes in power relations. By introducing an element of the hypothetical and theatrical, these exercises allow people to express views and act out scenarios which are generally suppressed and concealed from outsiders without exposing people to retaliation. Although they cannot be taken at face value as 'hard data', they are potentially extremely useful in exploring the range of potential impacts and interlinkages, and particularly exposing some of the most contentious issues.

Table 12: **A Framework for Analysing Women's Empowerment**

Type of Power Relation	Economic Empowerment	Well-being Benefits	Cultural/Legal and Political Empowerment
Power Within: • increased awareness and desire for change for individual woman	• women's positive evaluation of their economic contribution • desire for equal economic opportunities • desire for equal rights to resources in the household and community	• women's confidence and happiness • women's desire for equal well-being • desire to take decisions about self and others • desire to take control over own fertility	• assertiveness and sense of autonomy • recognition of need to challenge gender subordination including cultural 'tradition', legal discrimination and political exclusion • desire to engage in cultural, legal and political processes
Power To: • increased individual capacity for change • increased opportunities for access	• access to micro-finance services • access to income • access to productive assets and household property • access to markets • reduction in burden of unpaid domestic work including childcare	• skills including literacy • health and nutrition status • awareness of and access to reproductive health services • availability of public welfare services	• mobility and access to the world outside the home • knowledge of cultural, legal and political processes • removal of formal barriers to access to cultural, legal and political processes
Power Over: • changes in underlying resource and power • constraints at household, community and macro-level	• control over loans and savings use and income therefrom • control over income from other household productive activities	• control over parameters of household consumption and other valued areas of household decision-making including fertility decisions	• individual action to challenge and change cultural perceptions of women's capacities and rights at household and community levels

Type of Power Relation	Economic Empowerment	Well-being Benefits	Cultural/Legal and Political Empowerment
• **individual power/action to challenge these constraints**	• control over productive assets and household property • control over household labour allocation • individual action to challenge discrimination in access to resources and markets	• individual action to defend self against violence in the household and community	• individual engagement with and taking positions of authority within cultural, legal and political processes
<u>Power With:</u> • **or increased solidarity/joint action with other women to challenge underlying resource and power constraints at household, community and macro-level**	• acting as role model for other women, particularly in lucrative and non-traditional occupations • provision of wage employment for other women at good wages • joint action to challenge discrimination in women's access to resources (including land rights), markets and gender discrimination in macro-economic context	• higher valuation and increased expenditure on girl children and other female family members • joint action for increased public welfare provision for women	• increase in networks for support in times of crisis • joint action to defend other women against abuse in the household and community • participation in movements to challenge cultural, challenge cultural, gender subordination at the community and macro-level

Once the criteria and indicators have been established, these could firstly be integrated into existing Management Information Systems (MIS). The particular nature of MIS varies between programmes, with some programmes having very limited information, others comprehensive computerised information on financial performance and others special impact and evaluation procedures. Relevant information could be relatively easily and cheaply collected through rewording of loan application forms, data collected for loan monitoring and programme exit forms. This would enable statistical information for individuals to be collected on an ongoing basis and directly available for policy formation. There is now an increasing experience of integrating poverty impact assessment into programme monitoring. In most programmes involved in the pilot study, however, there was very limited gender analysis of financial data and empowerment issues had not been included in impact and procedures. It is also likely that women themselves would be interested in collecting and exchanging information on aspects of empowerment they themselves have identified as important. In many programmes women's groups already exchange information on production and marketing. PRADAN in India is collecting longitudinal data on livelihoods from women's own visual diaries (PRADAN 1996). In Zambuko in Zimbabwe credit and savings groups have themselves spontaneously formed a focus of discussion about gender issues such as 'how to manage your husband and mother-in-law' as well as exchanging information about marketing and increasing incomes (Charrington, personal communication 1998). Some micro-finance programmes with more explicit empowerment objectives have increased women's access to formal political institutions, such as panchayats in India (Fernandez 1993). A range of PLA and SSA techniques could be adapted or developed to facilitate this process through existing networks, group meetings or developing new networks. It is also possible to integrate 'guess-timates' into diagrams to get an idea of the representativeness or consensus arrived at in the different group activities.

Analysis of empowerment would be linked to policy in combination with a second framework of questions, to assess the interlinkages between changes in different dimensions of empowerment, different contextual opportunities and constraints, and specific programme policies. This would, firstly, place programme contributions within the context of what is feasible in view of contextual constraints at the individual, household and macro-levels. Secondly it would not assume that positive changes are due only to programme interventions, but also to women's existing strategies and the actions of men and other agencies. Thirdly, it would distinguish between planned outcomes of strategic policies for empowerment, unplanned assumed or hoped-for positive outcomes and unplanned, unintended negative outcomes. These would, however, need to be assessed on the basis of participatory discussions rather than guessed in advance on the basis of stereotypes.

> **Framework for Examining Relationships between Empowerment, Context and Policy**
>
> **Contextual constraints:** operating on different dimensions of empowerment at the individual, household and macro-levels
>
> **Contextual opportunities:** for different dimensions of empowerment at the individual, household and macro-levels
>
> **Positive contributions of strategically planned gender policies**
>
> **Other assumed or hoped-for positive impacts**
>
> **Unintended negative impacts**

This process would need to start by modelling the complex interrelationships between different dimensions of empowerment and different, but frequently interlinked, dimensions of programme policy. PLA and SSA institutional mapping and diagramming techniques could be adapted for this purpose and used in workshops with different stakeholders. These diagrams could inform the ways in which empowerment indicators are integrated into different parts of the MIS and also form the basis for development of information exchange within participant groups. They would form the basis for rigorous analysis based on detailed investigation of interlinkages between empowerment and policy within programmes. Importantly, the whole process would form a loop with different elements feeding into each other in an ongoing process of learning. For example information generated through MIS or group learning might lead to changes in criteria and indicators as programmes succeed in addressing some problems and new ones arise. These would then lead to new questions about policy.

Negotiating Complexity, Conflict and Change: Continuing Challenges
It is not assumed that a participatory learning process will be easy, or necessarily cheap in the short term. Many of the methodologies suggested here will need to be adapted and developed to address a number of inherent tensions and problems.

Firstly, local-level power relations and inequalities influence whose views are expressed as well as who participates. When well done and documented, participatory methods are a means of rapidly collecting a range of information. This can be achieved by pooling the knowledge of participants, filling in gaps or clarifying differences between knowledge and views of different individuals and groups (Chambers 1994). However, existing practice has often treated visual products uncritically, and failed to include the poorest. They have consequently ended up with a shopping list of unrealisable and unprioritised demands. The process requires careful facilitation to ensure that sensitive issues are addressed. It also requires attention to timing, location, and ways in which issues are discussed to ensure these are appropriate for the particular participants involved. Furthermore, it requires open and informed dialogue between participants and programmes about opportunities and constraints for change. There is a need for careful and systematic documentation of the research process: who is participating, interrelationships between them and how particular visual products and diagrams evolved and why. Participants will also need ongoing access to information to enable them to participate meaningfully.

Continuing Methodological and Institutional Challenges

Methodological Challenges
- What questions are to be asked? Facilitating public discussion of sensitive and non-stereotypical views.
- Who is to participate and how?: What timing, location, facilitators and issues are appropriate for the particular participants involved? How should different stakeholder groups be identified? How and when should they be separate or engaged in dialogue?
- Avoiding heightened expectations and shopping lists: What sorts of knowledge do people need in order for them to be enabled to make informed policy decisions?
- Understanding and documenting process: What sorts of contextual knowledge is needed prior to starting the process? Are there any general guidelines for documentation of the research process?

Institutional Challenges
- What information should be shared, how and by whom? Should all information be shared by all stakeholders? What institutional mechanisms are needed? Should some information be confined to certain stakeholders?

- How should information inform practice and who should decide? What structures exist for stakeholder representation and role in decision-making? What structures exist for supporting vulnerable participants and mediating conflicts of interest between participants and programmes?

- How can the costs of setting up the participatory process be met and by whom? How far can costs be met from resources of participants and/or programmes? What changes are needed in donor practices and priorities?

There are also a number of institutional challenges that will affect the ways in which **information** is generated and how it is fed into practice. There are practical questions about how information can be shared, e.g. where it should be collated, in what form and how access is arranged. There are also questions of confidentiality and sensitivity of much of the data. For the participatory process to work, programmes themselves must be seen as partial stakeholders rather than neutral investigators and will need to be as open to scrutiny as they expect programme participants to be (Goyder et al. 1998). There are also questions about appropriate structures for representation in decision-making and how potential conflicts of interest can be dealt with. In some programmes there are already federated structures for representation. In others allowing programme participants to have any say in decision-making will require a profound change in both structure and organisational culture.

Finally there will be **costs** involved in initiating the process of adapting methods to the needs of the participants concerned, to the context and to the skills, resources and structures of the programme. Developing the skills and networks of women's groups will also need initial, and possibly ongoing, support. Participatory techniques may need to be preceded by consultation of secondary source material and in many programmes outside facilitators with experience of gender analysis would be needed. Periodic external monitoring might also be needed to avoid the process becoming dominated by vested interests. Importantly, the approach is not a substitute for in-depth feminist analysis but a useful complement to it. There are therefore questions about how these costs might be met. Participatory learning is part of the discourse of neo-liberal orthodoxy with its stress on market relevance (Otero and Rhyne 1994) though largely ignored in the current donor preoccupation with financial self-sustainability. Supporting such a process would require more dialogue and discussion between gender advocates and micro-finance/economics divisions in donor agencies. It would require a change of emphasis in their own micro-finance guidelines and evaluation procedures to include questions on empowerment and participation, which are prominent in rhetoric but absent in practice. Nevertheless, despite potential problems, participatory organisational learning is an essential part of ensuring responsiveness to need and adaptability to changing circumstances. If micro-finance programmes and their donors are accessing funds for development, on the basis of contribution to poverty alleviation and empowerment, then impact assessment needs to be as integral a part of MIS and programme accountability as financial statistics. Firstly, the quantitative and qualitative information obtained through programme-level MIS and participant groups on an ongoing basis would be directly and immediately available to inform policy decisions. The methodologies developed and familiarity of participants and staff with them would decrease the need for costly outsider research and enable it to be more cost effectively targeted. Secondly, the process itself would be a contribution to empowerment. Programme staff would be given a more representative and reliable exposure to the priorities and problems of programme participants. It would develop networks and a forum for discussion between women themselves on issues relevant to their interests and integrated into programme decision-making. This would decrease the need for separate gender awareness training for staff, which has often had little impact. It would also decrease the need for 'expert' training for participants and increase women's commitment and ownership of the programme. This would in turn increase repayment and decrease drop-out rates. Although there would be some costs, the approach would be an important contribution to long-term programme sustainability and wider institutional development.

CHAPTER 6
Concluding Discussion
Peter Oakley

The discussions and contributions of the Fourth International Workshop confirmed that the concept of empowerment is well and truly embedded in development discourse. Indeed, over the past decade the literature on empowerment has become quite prodigious. Inevitably, however, this literature has blended with, or become an extension of, the even greater body of literature on 'participation'. For example, on the World Bank continuum of the stages of participation, 'empowerment' is shown as the ultimate objective (World Bank 1996). Indeed there is much confusion in the use of the two terms, with significant support for the World Bank view. What cannot be questioned, however, is the remarkable way that the concept has captured the development debate and become the focus of so many development initiatives. In some respects this is yet another example – of which there have been many over the past three decades – of the 'development community' homing in on a 'new' perspective or approach as part of the endless search for the holy grail! The evidence for this is the quite random use of the concept in a wide range of activities. Few major policy statements concerning development are made these days without reference to 'empowerment' – in one form or another – as a primary objective. In this respect some would argue that the concept has become debased and so generalised in its use that the core of its message has largely been lost. Empowerment is not just another benign input into development practice!

Rahman (above) sets the correct tone when he links empowerment to a long radical tradition – born of Freirian analysis – that sees people as the subjects of their own 'development' and empowerment as having deep spiritual and ethical dimensions. Alas, in today's world of project cycles and log frames, such inner dimensions fall by the wayside. The very term 'empowerment' would imply that some external force or facilitator could **empower** supposedly powerless groups. Empowerment has become the latest strategic objective of planned social change, but the project remains the basic instrument. Hence the innumerable reports and project-based documents that describe actions that are intended to 'empower' local people. Taylor (above) rightly points to this misapprehension on the part of those whose mission is to empower. On the contrary, empowerment is a process by which *'people accumulate more power'* (Moore 2000). We should not seek to 'develop' people, but we may **intervene** in already existing processes of development in order to support a particular group or organisation. In this respect 'power' will already be a key dimension of this ongoing process and our intervention must become part of this. Yet the tendency to conceptualise development as an act of 'external delivery' is ingrained in our psyche and, while there are many encouraging examples built around the 'yahoo word' of 'participatory' development (White 1996), even NGOs are now beginning to feel the pinch of promoting such approaches in an era of results and upward accountability (Mebrahtu 2001).

In terms of updating our understanding of the M&E of empowerment, the sections by Wils (Chapter 2) and Taylor, Davies, Waddington and Mayoux – all Chapter 5 – are pertinent contributions to current inquiries. Of these contributions, Taylor's is a refreshing polemic on the whole empowerment 'movement' and he wisely fears the inevitable reductionist approach that will reduce the concept to the quick-fix mentality of much development work. For Taylor, the centrality of power should never be forgotten and should lie at the heart of any M&E of empowerment that is essentially concerned with measuring shifts in **power relations**. However, Davies suggests that we should 'begin at home', in the sense of examining the 'power relationship' between, for example, NGOs and the groups they supposedly seek to empower. Davies's argument forcefully supports previous criticism of development agencies that promoted participation, but rarely practised it within their own organisations. Davies has already pioneered thinking on the M&E of qualitative processes through his work in Bangladesh in the early 1990s. His use of the notion of **differences** of opinion, in behaviour and in organisational structure, is an intriguing contribution to the notion of measuring change. Both Waddington's and Mayoux's sections are based more on the practice and, in particular, offer us glimpses into the use of indicators to measure empowerment. Waddington poses the question whether 'indicators' are indeed the means to measure such concepts – an issue raised at the Third International Workshop in 1996. To counterbalance this challenge, Mayoux's contribution is particularly strong on the issue of indicators of women's empowerment and on the structuring generally of a process of empowerment. Collectively these contributions represent most of the key issues relating to the M&E of empowerment and individually they offer us a distinctive aspect of our current search for effective means of understanding the change brought about by the process.

As a tool of analysis, the concept of empowerment is relevant at all levels of political and social interaction. At one level it can be equated with citizen participation in processes to which they may previously have had restricted access. The recent waves of initiatives to 'strengthen civil society' – especially in the sense of greater democratic involvement – are illustrative of this dimension (Carothers 1999). However, there is a healthy scepticism about whether we can equate 'empowerment' simply with access to the ballot box (Cornwall and Gaventa 2001). Much of this approach is built around the concept of Deliberative and Inclusive Processes (DIP) that seek to give a voice to the historically excluded. Such macro-frameworks are a broad canvas and 'empowerment' is based upon a number of highly visible and quantifiable key actions that indicate that, in some sense, formal power has been bestowed and exercised. These macro-frameworks are the backdrop against which development agencies that support deliberate and focused development interventions have to pitch their own initiatives to 'empower' the powerless. In this respect we have seen in the institutional presentations above (Chapter 3) how three such agencies – DFID, SIDA and ActionAid – have set out their objectives in terms of empowerment. This is the major challenge facing development agencies seeking to promote empowerment – how to **operationalise** the concept so that it becomes a meaningful and intelligible process that can be followed and understood.

In terms of **operationalisation**, the evidence from the workshop confirms that this still has some way to go before we could confidently say that 'empowerment' lies at the core of social development project interventions and that mechanisms and instruments are in place that will help us to understand its progress. On the basis of the discussions and the evidence presented at the Fourth Workshop, we could **summarise** the situation under the following issues:

The Challenge of Operationalisation

Empowerment appears to have been largely included as a **key objective** of the development strategies and programmes of development agencies across the board. Certainly it has forcefully entered the formal publications and discourse of development agencies. Cox and Healey (1999) provide evidence of its mainstreaming in terms of European bilateral agencies while Oakley and Clayton (1999) include many references to NGO promotion of empowerment in their resource book. However, all of this is familiar territory in the sense that development agencies usually pick up trends and new 'ideas' quite quickly and, particularly at the bilateral level, insert them in their strategy documents. The rub is to operationalise them in terms of concrete development activities that can be seen to have an impact on the locus and distribution of power within a particular context. Given the intensely subjective nature of empowerment, such activities would need to be specific, visible and participatory. In this respect the operationalisation of empowerment is still mainly in its infancy and at the level of rhetoric. While this is largely the case, at the workshop we were presented with several examples (of which there will be hundreds more) of its operationalisation: RELMA (Abaru 2000), FODEP (Rubvuta

2000), YWCA-Zambia (Chileshe 2000), Pact Peru (Bucheli 2000) and ActionAid (2000). Some might argue that 'participation' – and in particular the massive expansion of PRA techniques – have 'empowered' previously powerless groups. But the evidence is sketchy. The critical issue is that of power and the body of literature and documentation currently available largely fails to get down to the operational level.

Promoting Empowerment in the Project Context

The discussions at the Fourth Workshop – and, in particular, the meetings of the home groups – confirmed the **variety of ways** in which development agencies are currently seeking to promote empowerment. This is a positive sign that the concept *is* beginning to filter into development practice and not merely staying at the level of strategic intent. In terms of the range of purposes of empowerment as outlined in Chapter 2 above, the workshop suggested that the three main activities around which empowerment is being promoted as an operational concept are:

- *Empowerment as participation:* the linking of empowerment to an ongoing process of participation, and as its ultimate objective, is the strongest characteristic of current practice. The completion of a process of participation should result in the empowerment of local groups and communities. This is empowerment in a political sense and one that results in the more active participation of previously excluded groups in such areas as the design, management and evaluation of development projects.

- *Empowerment as Capacity-Building:* many of the Northern development agencies that attended the workshop work in 'partnership' with similar agencies in the South. Also in the South many Southern development agencies work in partnership with community-based or other civil society organisations. In this relationship empowerment is seen as the process whereby partner organisations are strengthened and, as a result, have more power in terms of the multiple challenges and tasks that they confront.

- *Empowerment through Economic Improvement:* the link between power and resources is a major driving force behind many of the efforts of both Southern and Northern development agencies to promote the empowerment of the powerless. These efforts have been greatly enhanced by the recent explosion in micro-credit activities targeted at the poor. The link is convincing and many development agencies are pursuing it. Furthermore, in terms of M&E, the quantifiable activities of micro-credit programmes offer the prospect of tangible evidence of economic empowerment, always bearing in mind the distortions that can occur in such programmes.

While current practice is also influenced by empowerment in the sense of, for example, 'self-awareness' and 'democratisation', the above three areas represent its more tangible manifestation. There is evidence to conclude that most development agencies – apart from those that overtly work within a 'democratisation' process – link their promotion of participation to concrete and tangible actions, while recognising the potential for spin-off in terms of these broader processes. Added to these is the considerable attention that is being given to the empowerment of **women**. The recent DAC Guidelines (2000) on Gender Evaluation are illustrative of this increasing focus on women's groups in terms of empowerment. This is confirmed in the several regional reports, while Mayoux' section (above) is illustrative of the substantial literature that is now available on efforts to promote the empowerment of women. The focus of these efforts falls largely within the Women in Development (WID) approach to targeting development initiatives at women and tends to take less of a gender perspective to understanding women's empowerment in terms of changes in gender relations and roles.

Asking the Key Questions

Fundamental to the M&E of qualitative processes is the formulation of the key questions that will help us to structure the monitoring and also to identify appropriate indicators. However, it would appear that this important element in the process is rarely undertaken and most projects move directly from objectives to indicators. The usefulness of the formulation of the key questions is that it helps us to understand what could be the main outcomes of a process of empowerment within a specific context. The key questions help to break open a qualitative process that may not be readily intelligible and to give it some concrete meaning in terms of real activities. It is also useful in the crucial phase of the identification of appropriate indicators in a way that links them to visible actions or behaviour and makes their monitoring more feasible. Finally, asking the key questions can be a challenging exercise. It can oblige the project team *not* merely to formulate a number of quantitative indicators but to get to grips with the possible outcomes of a process of empowerment and determine *what* will need to be monitored if its consequences are to be understood.

A key assumption in the formulation of these key questions is that a quantitative and qualitative **contextual analysis** has been undertaken prior to project implementation. This contextual analysis would give us the 'before' and 'after' situation in terms of 'power' and its location, use and distribution within the project context that would allow us ultimately to evaluate the project intervention. This contextual analysis would also look at the differential use of power in terms of gender relations. Another assumption that we make is that 'empowerment' is an **explicit objective** of the development intervention and that the intervention is undertaken in a manner that promotes active local participation. This is an important assumption since there are many instances of development interventions that supposedly promote empowerment but that, under more detailed examination, reveal little substantial evidence that it is indeed a fundamental purpose. The term 'empowerment' is often quite liberally scattered through a project text but with little supporting evidence to suggest that it has been explicitly promoted.

If we take the five broad operational understandings of empowerment as outlined in Chapter 1 above, we could formulate the following set of **key questions** for each one:

Empowerment as Participation
- What have been the changes in terms of the nature of the participation of the target group or community?
- How far has the participation of the target group moved from being 'passive' to being 'active'?
- What have been the immediate effects of the more active participation of the target population?
- What could be the possible longer-term consequences – both negative and positive – of the active participation of the target group?

Empowerment as Capacity-Building
- In what ways has the capacity of the individual/group/organisation been enhanced as a result of the project intervention?
- What have been the immediate effects of this enhancement?
- How far has the capacity-building of the target group affected its relations with other bodies within the immediate and wider context?
- What could be the ultimate and long-term impact of the capacity-building initiative?

Empowerment as Democratisation
- In what ways has the project intervention helped participants to exercise their democratic/citizen's rights?
- What links have been established between project level participation by the target group and more active participation in broader political processes?
- What have been the main challenges and problems that the process of democratisation has faced?
- In what ways has the target group's empowerment affected or altered policy decision-making processes, mainly at the immediate administrative level or perhaps higher?

Empowerment as Economic Improvement
- In quantitative terms, in what ways has the development intervention improved

the economic resource base of the target group?
- As a result of the above, what other concrete changes have occurred in the lives of the target group?
- In what ways has improved economic security allowed the target group to pursue other development activities or interests?
- How far has the target group's economic empowerment been sustained and altered its social and political status?

Empowerment and the Individual
- What have been the immediate changes noted in participants as a result of their involvement in the project?
- What have been the consequences – both positive and negative – of these changes?
- In what ways have participants used the changes as a means of improving the basis of their livelihoods?
- How far have these changes been sustained?

The above are **illustrative** of the kinds of questions that we could formulate in order to begin to structure an understanding of how a process of empowerment might develop and what could be the outcomes that we would need to monitor. The questions, therefore, essentially help us to identify those possible changes – based on a contextual understanding – that could occur as a result of the intervention. Understandably the questions are, to some extent, generic in that they are examining the same process but from different perspectives. But certainly the exercise of formulating the key questions can be critical in the early stages of the project since it can help to build an initial picture of how the process of empowerment might evolve. Given the largely intangible nature of empowerment, such a picture can be useful in helping both participants and project staff to focus on the process and not reduce its monitoring to a few general observations.

Identifying Appropriate Indicators

In terms of the M&E of empowerment, the workshop produced both written and verbal evidence that quite considerable progress has been made – particularly by the NGOs – to identify **indicators** that could help to structure the monitoring of the process. We have already seen in Chapter 2 above examples of the kinds of indicators that development agencies are using to monitor empowerment. These were supplemented during the workshop by a number of examples of indicators of empowerment (Mayoux above; Chileshe 2000; Hadjipateras 2000; Paudyal 2000). In each of these sets of indicators we see a strong influence of the M&E of 'participation' forming the basis of the monitoring of empowerment. Furthermore, there is also a strong influence of the personal or inner dimensions of empowerment, akin to the conscientisation process developed by Freire (1972). For example, Paudyal (2000) identifies indicators of the empowerment of poor rural women in Nepal 'before and after' a process of participation:

Table 13: **Indicators of Empowerment**

Indicators of Change	Before Participation	Current Status
Work division	Women are limited to the household	Women's access has been increased
Attitude towards girls	Few girls go to school	Number of girls going to school increased
Access to household property	Less access	Access increased as a result of saving and credit programme
Control over resources	Men control resources	Increasing women's control
Participation	Passive and hesitant	More active and articulate
Organisation	Less collective voice	Group collectives and bargaining power increased
Self-confidence	Less self-confident in articulating and making decisions	More self-confident in each of these areas
Social status	Low self-esteem	Less gap observed between women and men
Work pattern	Mainly reproductive work	More productive work

Table 13 above offers good set of indicators that could be constructed for a process of empowerment. The key question now is: How could they be **operationalised**? Indeed this is one of the major challenges that 'qualitative' M&E faces. Since the early 1990s, when the M&E of qualitative processes such as empowerment first began to engage both practitioners and academics' attention, the operationalisation of the selected indicators has always seemed a barrier that few development agencies could break down. Indeed there was almost a common sense of relief once relevant indicators had been identified. This relief was quickly shaken once it was realised that indicators are not much use if they are not operationalised in the series of actions to collect data and information that would show whether a particular change or expected outcome had been achieved. For example, in Table 13 how would one monitor changes in 'self-confidence' or 'social status' and what instruments would be used to do so? This whole area of the operationalisation of qualitative indicators has not progressed much in the past four to five years and, in general terms, most development agencies that promote empowerment and wish to understand the effect or impact of this work have not made any substantial breakthrough.

Laverack's (2001) recent review of community empowerment initiatives would tend to confirm this conclusion. There is now quite widespread recognition of the importance of both qualitative as well as quantitative approaches to M&E and an increasing knowledge and skills base for this work. However, there are still precious few substantial examples of development agencies that have managed to 'move beyond the indicators' and shown conclusively how to effectively monitor and draw reliable conclusions from a process such as empowerment. The reasons for this state of affairs are many and some can be generalised. The acknowledged demands of a log frame form of presentation and monitoring, the current fashion for 'results', the lack of relevant skills particularly at the Northern agency level and the continuing time-bound nature of most development interventions, all contribute to the weakness in this area. In the current jargon, in terms of the development agencies professed support for empowerment, they need to 'walk the talk' and not merely express commitment but also set up the methods and instruments to monitor this support. The operationalisation of the M&E of empowerment includes:

Definition >> Strategy >> Method of Implementation >> Determining the Key Questions >> Identification of Indicators for Monitoring >> Setting Up the Means of Data/Information Collection and Storage >> Interpretation >> Analysis

---

This is a demanding process that goes far beyond the more controlled set of activities designed to monitor activities and output. In the period prior to the workshop we called for examples of such a process in practice. We received few. The participants of the workshop came from several of the main development agencies in the North and could be regarded as illustrative of their current involvement with empowerment. In this respect we could conclude that the evidence suggests that few Northern development agencies have yet moved beyond the identification of indicators, and many probably not even to this stage. Institutionally the evidence is not dissimilar from that of Mebrahtu (2001) concerning Northern NGOs and their attempts to M&E 'participation'.

> **Key Elements in the M&E of Empowerment**
> - an integrative, systemic, relational understanding of the world;
> - an understanding of development as an innate natural process that results in shifts in the relationships between the elements of the system;
> - the ability to undertake participatory developmental assessments which locate the subjects on their own path of development and identify and describe the nature and quality of existing formative relationships;
> - identification of those relationships that most need to change in order to allow the developmental process to progress;
> - creation of an image of the preferred relationships with observable indicators of successful achievement;
> - the measurement of change that involves using the indicators as a means of identifying whether the change has occurred; and the ability to describe the changes in a narrative form.
>
> (Taylor, Chapter 5 above)

Future Actions to Strengthen the M&E of Empowerment

At the end of the workshop we tried to pull together suggestions for the kinds of action that development agencies could undertake as a means of developing their capacity to monitor empowerment. Inevitably we concluded with a variety of actions ranging from the macro- to the micro-levels. Furthermore most of the proposed actions were more focused on the concept itself and on the internal debates that will need to take place with development agencies as a precursor to mainstreaming commitment to the process. In the light of the evidence that few development agencies appear to have moved far forward in the operationalisation of empowerment as a development objective – indeed only ActionAid produced tangible evidence in this respect – inevitably possible actions relating to its M&E appeared a distant concern. With this in mind, we can summarise the five principal suggestions for action put forward by the workshop.

1. As a first step the majority of development agencies still need to agree their own **operational definition** of empowerment. Many agencies have certainly taken up the term and identified themselves with the aims of empowerment. But the evidence suggests that few of the agencies have moved beyond familiarity

with and declarations of support for the process into actually formulating an operational definition within the context of their work. Understandably, until this is done, it is premature to talk of monitoring the process. Furthermore there is need for clarity and recognition that empowerment is a distinctive process. In the literature – and the practice – confusion has arisen in the past decade with the widespread use of such methods as PRA and PME. Empowerment is not the same as either of these two methods – it is a goal, not a method. A process of empowerment may use PRA or PME methods to achieve its aims, but it should not be confused with them.

2. Before intervening to promote empowerment, there is a critical need to under take a **contextual analysis** that, among others, focuses on the issue of power within the project context. Power is a dominant feature and dynamic of all socio-political contexts and the environments within which development projects are undertaken will be no exception. External intervention to deliberately seek to 'influence and alter' the locus and distribution of power within a particular context will expect to have an impact on the existing situation. If a contextual analysis is not undertaken to explain the existing situation, it will be impossible to assess any changes that the intervention may have had on existing patterns of power and its use.

3. If empowerment is seen as a fundamental operational goal of development agencies, then there is a need for them to recognise and to tackle the **organisational and administrative constraints** that stop them from adequately monitoring and evaluating the process. In this respect the issue concerns the current strait-jacket of M&E practice into which most development agencies have fallen over the past decade. There are many reasons for this situation but this is not the place to review them. Suffice it to say that the current state of affairs is lamentable and, in terms of the M & E of the subtle qualitative processes of development, most development agencies at this moment are severely constrained in terms of what they can do. For as long as upward accountability, results and financial probity rule the roost, development agencies will be vocal in their support for empowerment. However, they will be powerless to promtoe effectively and completely unable to assess what this support may have achieved.

4. Following on from the above, there is an urgent need for development agencies not necessarily to have the capacity to M&E empowerment, but at least to develop their own **human resource skills** in areas other than report writing! While the major bilateral agencies will have evaluation departments and the larger NGOs may have one or more evaluation officers, most development agencies have few – if any – staff with basic knowledge and skills in M&E. When

this situation is then placed against the widespread commitment to promote empowerment, then disfunction is all too apparent. It is a remarkable state of affairs with which the major donors appear to be at ease since it does not challenge their demands for output and results. Furthermore, there is little evidence that the recipient development agencies are in a position to do much about it.

5. At a minimum, development agencies should be able at least to structure their **operationalisation** of empowerment in a manner outlined above and try and structure their support to the process on this basis. At present most agencies are essentially paralysed in terms of knowing how to operationalise the process within their project work, with the result that it largely disappears under the concrete activities and results. Development agencies need to **structure** their operationalisation of the process and use this as the basis for supporting the process and beginning to see where it is going and what it might be leading to.

Concluding Comments

On the basis of the discussions held and the presentations made at the Fourth Workshop it would be decidedly premature to assume that 'empowerment' is being vigorously promoted by development agencies and that there is a clear understanding of the effect and impact of this work. Indeed all of the evidence would suggest the contrary! The workshop brought together some of the main 'exponents' of empowerment and it certainly generated much debate, but it was not entirely successful in substantially moving matters forward. Participants recognised that 'power' lies at the heart of most developing (and developed) contexts in which competition and confrontation between different socio-economic groups are a permanent dynamic. In such situations to intervene to deliberately promote the empowerment of a particular group will have consequences that few will be able to predict adequately. Overall, workshop participants recognised the crucial role of 'power' in determining and negotiating relations between different competing groups – and the importance of seeking to help powerless groups achieve some degree of power or influence – but concluded that our ability to monitor and evaluate changes brought about by these efforts is still inadequate. Current M&E systems are geared to measuring improvements in terms of the physical environment, services and production. Empowerment is to do with **change**, and few development agencies are currently able to 'measure' social change as a result of project interventions. While it is recognised that the only people who can authentically assess changes in power relations are those whose livelihoods are directly affected. However, current M&E systems simply do not allow for such a shift in focus apart from informal consultation. There are, of course, some exceptions to this situation – ActionAid, for example – but most development agencies fervently promote empowerment but are unable to adequately evaluate its impact structurally.

Overall Conclusions of the Fourth International Workshop

1. We have come a long way since the First Workshop towards recognising social development in terms of social change, equity and transformation. We must ensure that empowerment as a concept is not diluted but retains the importance of transforming power relations in favour of excluded groups.

2. The M&E of empowerment can be both an empowering and a disempowering process in itself. It is critical to ensure that it is undertaken in a participatory and transparent manner and also one that promotes two(way accountability. Furthermore many methods and approaches are insufficiently aware of the need to desegregate by gender, socio(economic group, ethnic grouping and so on, and to distinguish the differences in power status of different groups.

3. There is no need for us to apologise continually for the use of qualitative methods. The challenge is how to get a mix between client and agency(based methods of M&E and also between qualitative and quantitative methods. We need to make pluralism work within the M&E of empowerment.

4. An important first step of any M&E system is to get the overall conceptual and operational framework in place before starting activities. Such a framework will help us to clarify many of the critical aspects of empowerment: power and women, power and different groups. Once the framework is in place, we can develop the appropriate methods and instruments.

5. There is a clear and urgent need for development agencies to develop the skills and knowledge necessary for the M&E of empowerment. M&E activities are often the poor relations of development work and it is abundantly clear that most development agencies are in no position to understand the possible outcome and impact of a process that they actively promote.

Brian Pratt, Executive Director, INTRAC, on the Fourth International Workshop

The above five statements aptly summarise the main conclusions that emerged from the Fourth Workshop. Power lies at the heart of **poverty** and yet few development agencies place empowerment at the *heart* of their work. Instead they pursue the same broadly sectoral improvement approach that has characterised development co-operation for the past 30 years but argue that, in this approach, they will also 'empower' local people and, in particular, women. Empowerment has, in many ways, become an assumed outcome of development interventions – largely because the intervention is based on a 'participatory' approach – but we would have to search hard and long for any evidence that this is the case. Undoubtedly sectoral programmes to make resources available to poorer groups, for example, may well result in some of the beneficiaries gaining more 'power'. Also capacity-building programmes might strengthen a community organisation and thus 'empower' its members. But unless development agencies are able to verify – over a period of time – that this 'empowerment' is actually taking place, it is all supposition. Given the supposed seriousness of the intent and the volume of resources still pouring into development projects expected to empower the powerless, our knowledge and understanding of the process as an operational concept is still rather scanty.

In this situation the Fourth Workshop has been apposite in terms of recognising the knowledge and practice that already exist and making it available to a wider audience. At the same time it has taken stock of the situation and suggested a number of key actions. The case for 'empowerment' has been made, and the recognition of power as central to any understanding of poverty widely accepted. What is needed now is a concerted effort by the major actors to concede some space that would encourage more effective actions by the key stakeholders to understand the changes that a process of empowerment could bring about and whether they are sustainable.

List of Conference Participants

Name	Organisation	Country
Millie Abaru	RELMA	Kenya
Munif Abu-Rish	JOHUD	Jordan
Jerry Adams	INTRAC	England
Farid Ahmed	Oxfam	Bangladesh
Jemal Ahmed	ActionAid	Ethiopia
Rabia Ahmed	ActionAid	Pakistan
Judith Bakirya	STRONGO	Uganda
Tamsyn Barton	ITDG	England
Gweneth Berge	NCA	Norway
Floris Blankenberg	SNV	Netherlands
Therese Borrman	SIDA	Sweden
Harold Brown	Oxfam	England
Brenda Bucheli	PACT	Peru
Charles Chabala	SCC	Zambia
Subrata Chakrabarty	CARE	Bangladesh
Modesta Chileshe	YWCA	Zambia
Admos Chimhowu	IDPM	England
Ivy Chipofya-Mshali	PSP	Malawi
Wiseman Chirwa	CSR	Malawi
Andy Clayton	INTRAC	England
Gary Craig	Univ. Humberside	England
Howard Dalzell	Concern	Ireland
Ros David	ActionAid	England
Rick Davies	CDS	Wales
Mirtha Ditren Perdomo	World Vision	Dominican Republic
Yvonne Es	Novib	Netherlands
Connell Foley	Concern	Ireland
Chris Friend	Sight Savers	England
Ricardo Furman	CARE	Peru

List of Conference Participants

Anne Garbutt	**INTRAC**	England
Maria Cristina Garcia	**CINDE**	Colombia
Janice Giffen	**INTRAC**	England
Fionnuala Gilsenan	**Trocaire**	Ireland
Jack Goddard	**INTRAC Trustee**	England
Maria-Jose Gonzalez	**Oxfam Fair Trade**	England
Liz Goold	**INTRAC**	England
Elsebeth Gravgaaed	**DCA**	Denmark
Ann Grunnet	**SID**	Denmark
Rosemary Gumba	**Univ. Reading**	England
Angelah Hadjipateras	**ACORD**	England
Girmay Haile	**UNICEF**	Eritrea
Caroline Hartnell	**Alliance**	England
Simon Heap	**INTRAC**	England
Lone Hogel	**DCA**	Denmark
Ngongang Iere	**IDPM**	England
Kate Ijeh	**Univ. Uppsala**	Sweden
Bill Jackson	**INTRAC Trustee**	England
Gulmira Jamanova	**CASDIN**	Kazakstan
Iqbal Jatoi	**ActionAid**	Pakistan
Helene Jeansson	**SCC**	Sweden
Steven Kaindaneh	**ActionAid**	Sierra Leone
Musimbi Kanyoro	**YWCA**	Switzerland
Anne Karanji	**ISS**	Netherlands
Colin Kirk	**DfID**	UK
Susanne Krysiak	**DCA**	Denmark
Gracy Kutty Middey	**Oxfam**	Ghana
Betty Kwagala	**NUDIPU**	Uganda
Carolyn Lawrence	**INTRAC**	England
Ylva Lindstrom	**SIDA**	Sweden
Brenda Lipson	**INTRAC**	England
Ronald Lucardie	**Cordaid**	Netherlands
M Malwatte	**PHSWT**	Sri Lanka

Oscar Marleyn	**South Research**	Belgium
Linda Mayoux	**Open University**	UK
Esther Mebrahtu	**IDS**	England
Ali Mokhtar	**CDS**	Egypt
Ilja Mottier	**DECS**	Netherlands
Grace Mukasa	**Redd Barna**	Uganda
Lukas Muntingh	**NICRO**	South Africa
Alex Muyebe	**JCTR**	Zambia
Margaret Mwaura	**CORAT**	Kenya
Amjad Nazeer	**SAP**	Pakistan
Jan Neggers	**NOVIB**	Netherlands
Thanh Nguyen	**Univ. Uppsala**	Sweden
Sering Falu Njie	**ActionAid**	Gambia
Peter Oakley	**INTRAC**	England
Anne Offermans	**CORDAID**	Netherlands
Charles Owusu	**ActionAid**	England
Raj Patel	**Opportunity International**	India
Fenella Porter	**Open University**	England
Brian Pratt	**INTRAC**	England
Anisur Rahman	**Independent**	Bangladesh
Wafa' Abdel Rahman	**ISS**	Netherlands
Bimala Rai Poudyal	**ActionAid**	Nepal
Jo Rowlands	**VSO**	England
Jim Rugh	**CARE**	USA
Elijah Ruvuta	**FDP**	Zambia
Ambika Sahay	**Univ East Anglia**	England
Asiya Sasykbaeva	**Centre Interbilim**	Kyrgykstan
Emily Sikazwe	**Women for Change**	Zambia
Soraya Solomon	**NICRO**	South Africa
Ulla Strobech	**MS**	Denmark
James Taylor	**CDRA**	South Africa
Jon Taylor	**INTRAC**	England

List of Conference Participants

Tom Thomas	**ActionAid**	India
Janet Townsend	**Univ. Durham**	England
Marjan Van Es	**HIVOS**	Netherlands
Ineke Van Halsema	**Dutch Co-financing Programme**	Netherlands
Mark Waddington	**Village Aid**	England
Hettie Walters	**GDTC**	Netherlands
Aubrey Webson	**Hilton Perkins Programme**	USA
Karen Westley	**CARE**	England
Frits Wils	**ISS**	Netherlands

Bibliography

Abaru, M. (2000) 'Empowerment: RELMA's Experience', paper presented at the Fourth International Workshop. Oxford: INTRAC.

ActionAid (1999) *Fighting Poverty Together. ActionAid's Strategy 1999–2003*. London: ActionAid.

ActionAid (2000) *Participation, Literacy and Empowerment*. London: ActionAid.

Bergdall, T. (1997) 'Grassroots Empowerment in Ethiopian Villages', in J. Burbridge (ed.) *Beyond Prince and Merchant: Citizen Participation and the Rise of Civil Society*. New York: Pact Publications.

Bhasin (1984) *The Empowerment of Women*. Rome: FAO.

Biekart, K. (1999) *The Politics of Civil Society Building: European Private Agencies and Democratic Transitions in Central America*. Utrecht: IB&TI.

Bucheli, B. (2000) 'Organisational Capacity Assessment', paper presented at the Fourth International Workshop. Oxford: INTRAC.

Carmen, R. (1996) *Autonomous Development: Humanising the Landscape. An Excursion into Radical Thinking and Practice*. London: Zed Books.

Carothers, T. (1999) *Aiding Democracy Abroad: the Learning Curve*. Washington DC: Carnegie.

Casley, D. and Kumar, K. (1987) *Project Monitoring and Evaluation in Agriculture*. Washington DC: World Bank.

Chabal, P. (1994) *Power in Africa. An Essay in Political Interpretation*. London: Macmillan Press.

Chambers, R. (1983) *Rural Development: Putting the Last First*. London: Longman.

Chambers, R. (1994) *Paradigm Shifts and the Participatory Research and Development*. IDS Working Paper.

Cheater, A. (ed.) (1999) *The Anthropology of Power: Empowerment and Disempowerment in Changing Structures*. London: Routledge.

Chen, M. A. (1997) *A Guide for Assessing the Impact of Microenterprise Services at the Individual Level*. Washington: AIMS, MSI.

Chileshe, M. (2000) 'YWCA Council of Zambia', paper presented at the Fourth International Workshop. Oxford: INTRAC.

Clarke, J. (1991) *Democratising Development: The Role of Voluntary Organisations*. London: Earthscan.

Cleaver, F. (1999) 'Paradoxes of Participation: Questioning Participatory Approaches to Development', *Journal of International Development*, 11: 597-612.

Cornwall, A., and Gaventa, J. (2001) 'Bridging the Gap: Citizenship, Participation and Accountability', in *PLA Notes*, London: IIED.

Cox, A., and Healey, J. (1999) *Promises to the Poor: The Record of European*

Development Agencies. London: Macmillan Press.

Craig, G., and Mayo, M. (eds.) (1995) *Community Participation and Empowerment: The Human Face of Structural Adjustment or Tools for Democratic Transformation?*, in *Community Empowerment: A Reader in Participation and Development.* London: Zed Books.

DAC (2000) *Guidelines on Gender Evaluation.* Paris:OECD.

DanChurchAid (1998) *Participatory Development in Practice.* Copenhagen: DanChurchAid.

Davies, R. (1995) *An Evolutionary Approach to Facilitating Organisational Learning: An Experiment by the Christian Commission for Development in Bangladesh.* Swansea: CDS, Swansea University.

Davies, R. J. (1997) 'Tree Maps: A Tool for Structuring, Exploring and Summarising Qualitative Information'. Unpublished paper.

DFID (1997) 'White Paper on International Development'. London: DFID.

DFID (1999) 'Departmental Report'. London: DFID.

DFID (2000) 'White Paper on International Development'. London: DFID.

Diakonia (1999) 'Evaluating Qualitative Objectives of Development'. Stockholm: unpublished internal manuscript.

Dichter, H. (1992) *Demystifying Popular Participation.* Washington DC: World Bank.

Eade, D. (1997) *Capacity-Building. An Approach to People-Centred Development.* Oxford: Oxfam.

Ebdon, R. (1995) 'NGO Expansion and the Fight to Reach the Poor: Gender Implications of NGO Scaling-up in Bangladesh', *IDS Bulletin,* 26/3, July.

Fernandez, A. (1993) *Credit for Rain-Fed Farmers.* Bangalore: MYRADA.

Fetterman, D. (1999) *Empowerment Evaluation.* San Francisco: Sage.

Fowler, A. (1997) *Striking a Balance. A Guide to Enhancing the Effectiveness of NGOs in International Development.* London: Earthscan.

Franco, F. et al (1993) *Empowerment Through Entitlement.* The Hague: Cebemo/DGIS.

Freire, P. (1974) *Pedagogy of the Oppressed.* Hammondsworth: Penguin.

Friedmann, J. (1992) *Empowerment: The Politics of Alternative Development.* Oxford: Blackwell.

Galjart, B. (1987) 'Participatory Development Projects: The History of a Research Project and a Summary of Results', *Netherlands Review of Development Studies,* No.1.

Galjart, B., and Buijs, D. (eds.) (1982) *Participation of the Poor in Development.* University of Leiden.

Goetz, A. M., and Sengupta, R. (1996) 'Who Takes The Credit? Gender, Power and Control over Loan Use in Rural Credit Programmes in Bangladesh', *World Development,* January.

Gosling, L and Edwards, M. (1995) 'A Practical Guide to Assessment, Monitoring, Review and Evaluation Toolkits', *Development Manual 5*. London: Save the Children Fund.

Goyder, H., Davies, R., and Williamson, W. (1998) 'Participatory Impact Assessment: A Report on a DFID-Funded Research Project on Methods and Indicators for Measuring the Impact of Poverty Reduction'. London: ActionAid.

Guijt, I. (1991) *Perspectives on Participation: Views From Africa, An Inventory of Rural Development Institutions and Their Uses of Participatory Methods*. London: IIED.

Hadjipateras, A. (2000) 'Impact Flow Chart for Women', paper presented at the Fourth International Workshop. Oxford: INTRAC.

Herrera, R., and Hansen, F. (1999) *Thematic Study of Capacity-Building Within the Context of Partnership*. Copenhagen: DANIDA.

Hulme, D., and Mosley, P. (eds.) (1996) *Finance Against Poverty*. London: Routledge.

Jackson, C. (1995) 'Sustainable Development at the Sharp End: Field Worker Experience in a Participatory Project'. Norwich School of Development Studies, UEA.

James, R. (2001) *Power and Partnership. Experiences of NGO Capacity-Building*. INTRAC NGO Management Policy Series No. 12. Oxford: INTRAC.

James, W. (1999) 'Empowering Ambiguities,' in A. Cheater (ed.) *The Anthropology of Power: Empowerment and Disempowerment in Changing Societies*. London: Routledge.

Jellema, A. (1998) 'Women's Empowerment through REFLECT,' in *Gender and Women's Rights*. London: ActionAid.

Johnson, S., and Rogaly, B. (1997) *Financial Services and Poverty Reduction*. Oxford: Oxfam and ActionAid.

Kaare, B., and Nielsen, H. (1999) *Assessing the Impact of the Kibondo Development Project*. Coppenhagen: DANIDA.

Kabeer, N. (1998) 'Money Can't Buy Me Love?', in Re-evaluating Gender, Credit and Empowerment in Rural Bangladesh. Brighton: IDS discussion paper.

Kaplan, A. (1996) *Development Practitioner's Handbook*. London: Pluto Press.

Kapra, F. (1997) *The Web of Life: A New Understanding of Living Systems*. Doubleday.

Khadka, R. (1999) 'Claiming the Land: Grassroots Advocacy in Nepal', in *IA Exchanges*, August. ActionAid.

Korten, D.c. (1990) *Getting to the 21st Century: Voluntary Action and the Global Agenda*. Connecticut: Kumarian Press.

Laverack, G. (2001) 'An Identification and Interpretation of the Organisational Aspects of Community Empowerment', *Community Development Journal*, 36/2:134–145.

BIBLIOGRAPHY

Long, N. (1977) *Introduction to the Sociology of Rural Development*. London: Tavistock.

Longwe, S. H. (1991) 'Gender Awareness: the Missing Element in the Third World Development Project', in T. Wallace and C. March (eds.) *Changing Perceptions: Writings on Gender and Development*. Oxford: Oxfam.

Marsden, D., and Oakley, P. (1990) *Evaluating Social Development*. Oxford: Oxfam.

Marsden, D., Oakley, P. and Pratt, B. (1994) *Measuring the Process*. Oxford: INTRAC.

Mayoux, L. (1995) 'From Vicious to Virtuous Circles? Gender and Micro-Enterprise Development'. UNRISD Occasional Paper No. 3, Geneva.

Mayoux, L. (1998) 'Women's Empowerment and Micro-finance programmes: Approaches, Evidence, SCs and Ways Forward.' Discussion Paper No. 41. Milton Keynes: The Open University.

Mebrahtu, E. (2001) 'Monitoring and Evaluating Participation: INGO Experiences in Ethiopia'. Unpublished Ph.D. thesis, University of Sussex.

Moore, M. (2000) *Putting Politics into Poverty Reduction: The World Development Report on Empowerment*. London: ODI.

Moser, C. (1991) *Gender Planning and Development*. London: Routledge.

Moser, C. (1994) *Gender Planning and Development: Theory, Practice and Training*. London: Routledge.

Oakley, P. (1999) *The Danish NGO Impact Study: Overview Report*. Copenhagen: DANIDA.

Oakley, P., and Clayton, A. (1999) *The Monitoring and Evaluation of Empowerment: A Resource Document*. Oxford: INTRAC.

Oakley, P., and Winder, D. (1981) 'The Concept and Practice of Rural Social Development', Manchester Papers on Development. No. 1, University of Manchester.

Oakley, P., Pratt, B., and Clayton, A. (1998) *Outcomes and Impact: Evaluating Change in Social Development*. Oxford: INTRAC.

Ocampo, A. (1996) 'The Empowering Dimension of Social Evaluation'. unpublished MSc dissertation, University of Wales.

Otero, M. and Rhyne, E. (eds.) (1994) *The New World of Microenterprise Finance: Building Healthy Financial Institutions for the Poor*. London: IT Publications.

Oxfam (1995) *The Oxfam Handbook of Development and Relief*. Oxford: OXFAM.

Paudayl, B. R. (2000) 'Institutionalisation and Monitoring of Empowerment Process in Action Aid Nepal', paper presented at the Fourth International Workshop. Oxford: INTRAC.

Pearce, A., and Stiefel, M. (1979) *Inquiry into Participation*. Geneva: UNRISD.

PRADAN (1996) *Kal-album User Manual:* South India: PRADAN.

Rahman, M. A. (1984) *Participatory Organisation of the Rural Poor*. Geneva: ILO.

Rahman, M. A. (1993) *People's Self-Development*. London: Zed Books.

RESULTS (1997) 'The Micro-credit Summit February 2-4, 1997 Declaration and Plan of Action'. Washington DC: RESULTS.

Riddell, R, et al. (1997) *Searching for Impact and Methods. NGO Evaluation Synthesis Study: A Report Prepared for the OECD/DAC Expert Group on Evaluation*. Oxford: OECD.

Roberts, G. (1974) *Poverty is Powerlessness*. London: Hutchinson.

Roche, C. (1999) *Impact Assessment for Development Agencies – Learning to Value Change*. Oxford: OXFAM.

Rowlands, J. (1997) *Questioning Empowerment: Working with Women in Honduras*. Oxford: Oxfam.

Rubvuta, E. (2000) 'Monitoring and Evaluation of Empowerment Programmes: Experience of FODEP', paper presented at the Fourth International Workshop. Oxford: INTRAC.

Sahley, C. (1995) *Strengthening the Capacity of NGOs: Cases of Small Enterprise Development Agencies in Africa*. NGO Management and Policy Series No. 4. Oxford: INTRAC.

Schneider, H. (1999) 'Participatory Governance for Poverty Reduction' *Journal for International Development*, 11:521–34.

Sebstad, J., and Chen, G. (1996) *Overview of Studies of Micro-enterprise Credit*. Washington DC: AIMS.

Shetty, S. (1991) 'The Assessment of "Empowerment" in Development Projects – An Enquiry'. London School of Economics, unpublished MSc paper.

Shetty, S. (1994) Development Project in Assessing Empowerment. New Delhi: PRIA.

SIDA (2000) *Discussing Women's Empowerment – Theory and Practice*. Stockholm: SIDA.

Smith, S. (1999) *Measuring Women's Empowerment in India*. Oxford: Oxfam.

Stiefel, M., and Wolfe, M. (1994) *Voice for the Excluded: Popular Participation in Development, Utopia or Necessity?* London: Zed Books.

Stirling, A. (1998) 'On the Economics and Analysis of Diversity. Science Policy Research Unit'. Electronic Working Papers Series, No. 28. Brighton: University of Sussex.

Strachan, P., with Peters, C. (1997) *Empowering Communities: A Casebook from West Sudan*. Oxford: Oxfam.

Tandon, R. (1987) *Participatory Training for Rural Development*. New Delhi: PRIA.

Tilakaratna, S. (1984) *Grassroots Self-reliance in Sri Lanka: Organizations of the Poor*. Geneva: ILO.

UN (1995) World Summit for Social Development: Copenhagen. *Declaration and Programme of Action*. New York: UN.

UNDP (1998) *Integrating Human Rights with Sustainable Development: A Policy Document*. New York: UNDP.

Valdez, J., and Bamberger, M. (1994) *Monitoring and Evaluating Social Programmes in Developing Countries*. Washington DC: World Bank.

Van Eyken, W. (1991) *The Concept and Process of Empowerment*. The Hague: Bernard van Leer Foundation.

Werbner, R. (1999) 'The Reach of the Post-Colonial State: Development and Empowerment' in A. Cheater (ed.) *The Anthropology of Power: Empowerment and Disempowerment in Changing Structures*. London: Routledge.

Westendorff, D. and Ghai, D. (1993) *Monitoring Social Progress in the 1990s*. Geneva: UNRISD.

White, S. (1996) 'Depoliticising Development: The Uses and Abuses of Participation' in D. Eade (ed.) Development, NGOs, and Civil Society. Oxford: Oxfam:142-156.

Whitemore, E. (1998) 'The Role of Empowerment in the Evaluation of a Mexican Farmer's Co-operative', in Jackson, E. T. and Kassam, Y. (eds.) *Knowledge Shared. Participatory Evaluation in Development Co-operation*. Connecticut: Kumarian Press.

Whiteside, M. (1999) *Empowering the Landless: Case Studies in Land Distribution and Tenure Security for the Poor*. London: Christian Aid.

Wils, F. (1991) *NGO Evaluation: Notes on its Dynamics and Organisation*. The Hague: ICCO.

Wils, F., and Archarya, (1997) *Promoting Self-reliance of the Rural Poor in India*. Programme Evaluation ICCO. The Hague.

Wils, F., and Helmsing, B. (1998) 'Community Participation, Community Management and Government Enablement in Theory and Practice'. Regional Variations and General Conclusions. Nairobi: UNCHS/CDP.

Wilson, E. O. (1993) *The Diversity of Life*. London: The Penguin Press.

Wolfe, M. (1996) *Elusive Development*. London: Zed Books.

World Bank (1996) *Participation and the World Bank: Successes, Constraints and Responses*. Washington DC.

World Bank (1998) *Participation Handbook*. Washington DC.